4.75

K

NO G.O.D.s IN THE CLASSROOM: INQUIRY AND SECONDARY SOCIAL STUDIES

JOHN T. MALLAN
RICHARD HERSH

University of Toledo

1972

W. B. SAUNDERS COMPANY

PHILADELPHIA • LONDON • TORONTO

W. B. Saunders Company: West Washington Square
Philadelphia, Pa.   19105

12 Dyott Street
London, WC1A   1DB

833 Oxford Street
Toronto 18, Ontario

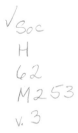

No G.O.D.s In the Classroom:
Inquiry and Secondary Social Studies

ISBN 0-7216-6005-3

Print No.:   9   8   7   6   5   4   3   2   1

The following books are titles in the
Controversies in Education Series, Editorial Board
THE UNIVERSITY OF MASSACHUSETTS SCHOOL OF EDUCATION

Cooper—DIFFERENTIATED STAFFING

Hicks and Hunka—THE TEACHER AND THE COMPUTER

Lacey—SEEING WITH FEELING Film in the Classroom

Gentry, Jones, Peelle, Phillips,
Woodbury and Woodbury—URBAN EDUCATION: The Hope Factor

Mallan and Hersh—NO G.O.D.s IN THE CLASSROOM: Inquiry into
        Inquiry

Mallan and Hersh—NO G.O.D.s IN THE CLASSROOM: Inquiry and
        Elementary Social Studies

Mallan and Hersh—NO G.O.D.s IN THE CLASSROOM: Inquiry and
        Secondary Social Studies

" If God had intended for us TO THINK, He wouldn't have given us ideas..."

OPEN LETTER TO THE READER

When one looks at a book, he may ask, "What's it about?" and let it go at that.

Or, one might look at a book and ask, "What will this book *do* for me?" and then assess the book in terms of criteria related to specific functions.

No G.O.D.s in the Classroom: Inquiry and Secondary Social Studies is *about* social studies teaching at the secondary level. The G.O.D. stands for Givers Of Directions — directions aimed at manipulating students, materials, and school experiences toward predetermined "set" ways of behaving and toward predetermined "set" answers or conclusions. For example, "Turn to chapter three in your text, answer the first four questions at the end of the chapter, and be sure you can give *the* reason why the United States entered the First World War." In this case the student follows directions (and is rewarded for such) in the use of certain materials, in the questions he must answer, and in the predetermined conclusion he must reach. The qualifying "No" in front of the "G.O.D.s" strongly suggests that this type of teacher — student activity should *not* take place in the classroom: that there are other ways of teaching and learning.

Inquiry and Secondary Social Studies attempts to indicate another qualification to the idea of G.O.D.s in the Classroom. Inquiry is another way of teaching and learning. Inquiry teaching is *not* an alternative to teaching content but rather a way of *using* content. Inquiry is done *with* content: with facts, concepts, and experiences.

What's the book about? Using inquiry to teach secondary social studies. This still doesn't say very much. There are countless other books available that can be generally described in the same broad manner.

What will this book do for you? This is a different kind of question. We can't play the G.O.D. role and guarantee that the book will do anything for you. Knowing that no student encounters any new experience or data without some pre-existing frame of reference which interacts with the new and which works at creating meaning out of the transactions, we make a transfer to the reader and thus find it untenable to pretend a G.O.D. stance.

We can only state what we designed the book to *help* you do. Our intentions are honorable—but, as with all forms of teaching, the measure of achievement is *not* the teacher's intentions but rather what the student is able to *do* as a result of an experience. A response to the second question must make it clear that a book is a *transaction* between the reader and the author—a limited transaction because, unlike classroom situations, there is no opportunity for mutual feed-back and mutual modifications. A book is one of several means used to help one function more effectively as a teacher. In a sense, it is only a vehicle. What a vehicle will or will not transport depends upon how it is used. This puts you in the driver's seat.

What kind of a vehicle is *No G.O.D.s in the Classroom: Inquiry and Secondary Social Studies?* What was it designed to do?

It is primarily designed to help prospective secondary school social studies teachers *to be able to select and manipulate content within an inquiry framework.* It takes into account the de facto situational factors encountered when teaching—for example, realistic situations in which a teacher finds that he is required to cover prescribed material or is asked to teach an area in which he has minimal background. This happens. It also takes into account how one can *relate* academic coursework with professional education courses—how learning about content can be related to learning how to teach the use of the content.

As a vehicle, the book is designed to help you:

1. Recognize and use the larger social context when selecting and using social studies content.
2. Select and manipulate content in ways that facilitate inquiry processes on the part of students.
3. Recognize the countless sources of materials and be able to transform content materials into teaching vehicles.
4. Use content in a variety of different ways and thus use content for a number of different, yet related, purposes.
5. Develop your own system for selecting and determining potential uses of content *prior* to getting into your own classroom.
6. Use inquiry processes in planning the use of content: in other words, use inquiry *with* content in ways designed to promote further inquiry.
7. Identify and use a "concept" framework for working on

content with a view toward: your own objectives, student objectives, student questions, student activities, and teaching strategies allowing you to relate methods with content.

8. Recognize different alternatives available when in different situations calling for the use of "subject matter"—in situations in which you feel comfortable about your own academic preparation and also in situations that find you ready and willing but without the necessary academic preparation.

It is a substantial task to design a vehicle to help prospective teachers do the above. We have tried. The attempt necessitated bringing a specific focus to *one* aspect of teaching: the use of content. It does not presume to address the other aspects in any sophisticated way. If one is interested in how the other aspects relate in the teaching of social studies, we suggest reading *No G.O.D.s in the Classroom: Inquiry into Inquiry*, W. B. Saunders Company, Philadelphia, 1972. You will notice that in the present volume, which brings a focus to content, we have tried to provide a number of specific and detailed examples of content use—examples of how actual classroom planning took into account various kinds of content. The examples can be used to initiate a content "bank" for prospective teachers. However, the examples are *not* included as "models" in any pure and idealized sense. They beg to be modified, changed, deleted, reorganized, added to, and questioned, as one starts his *own* "system" for planning the use of content.

And, just as a student brings his own frame of reference, so do the authors. We assume that you find excitement, interest, and motivation in the content included in the area of social studies. If not, one questions whether or not a person should make a career of teaching the use of content in the social studies. We also assume what differentiates formal schooling from the larger education prompted by living is that formal schooling involves, at least, a reflective approach to experience: that inquiry is reflective, creative, and exciting—for *both* the teacher and the student.

One final word about content. It is often said that people just aren't interested in the content fundamental to social studies. This explains why studies show that youngsters don't like social studies. This is interesting. Books on history and the social sciences are in demand *outside* the school situations. And, on a recent "talk show" a historian used the radio audience to help explore the ten most important dates in American history and the ten most important persons in American history. The reaction to this specific program was far greater than that evidenced by other programs conducted by the show—including discussions of topless go-go girls and UFO's. This might lead one to wonder whether people don't like the content of the social studies *or* whether they don't like the way we usually teach or use the content.

We hope you have fun with the material. Remember, at this point we have tried to provide a viable vehicle for the use of content. The use of the vehicle is up to you—the eternal hope involved in teaching is that the student goes beyond the teacher: this hope leads to *No G.O.D.s in the Classroom.*

JOHN MALLAN
RICHARD HERSH

INTRODUCTION

We offer a different kind of introduction.

Usually, introductions inform the reader of a general background for the writing of the book, an over-view of what the book will attempt to do, and sometimes they provide a public expression of appreciation to those who directly and indirectly contributed to the book. To be perfectly honest, the background is not too important. You can get an over-view by reading the table of contents and by thumbing through the material. And, the nature of learning being what it is, it would take a volume four times this size to thank people for the help given to the authors. The test of any book or any learning experience is what people *do* as a result of the experience—not what they verbalize. We are concerned that students become competent social studies teachers. It's that simple.

So, our introduction is simply a copy of what a secondary school student did in class. It's authentic. (Check the spelling!) It was done by a youngster in a "slow learner" social studies class. It was not done as a required assignment. It is one of a number of such efforts done by the student—one of a number of papers the student handed in to the wastepaper basket at the end of a class session.

It raises the key issues.

Read it and think.

It serves as our introduction.

"WHAT'S THAT?"

"IT'S A BOOK. IT'S ALL ABOUT A GOVERNMENT
RUN BY WISE MEN WHO KNOW ALL THE RIGHT
ANSWERS SO TO KEEP THE PEOPLE THINKING THE
RIGHT THINGS THE WISE MEN FORM A
COMITTEE OF THOUGHT POLICE AN' START TO
STAMP OUT ALL WRONG BELIEVERS."

"AREN'T THEY SUPRESSING OTHER BELIEFS AND
ALSO SUPRESSING FREEDOM OF THOUGHT?"

"OH NO - THEY SUPRESS THEM VERY DEMOCRATICLY."

"IT'S AMAZING WHAT THEY'RE DOING WITH
DEMOCRACY THESE DAYS."

"HOW DO THESE THOUGHT POLICE OPERATE?"

"THEY JUST COME UP BEHIND YOU AND SAY ...."
       "YOU'RE WRONG!"

"HEY! WHAT'S THE TITLE OF THE BOOK?"

"1970"

CONTENTS

NO
G.O.D.s

IN THE CLASSROOM

**INQUIRY AND
SECONDARY SOCIAL STUDIES**

SITE OF THE
DEPARTMENT OF
PHILOSOPHY
BUILDING
ENDOWED 1931
BY
CYRUS J. BENDINCT
BURNT DOWN 1970
BY
CYRUS J. BENDINCT III

By Kenneth Mahood. Copyright 1971, Saturday Review, Inc.

1

THE "OLD" WITH THE "NEW"

There was a dachshund once, so long
He hadn't any notion
How long it took to notify
His tail of his emotion:
And so it happened, while his eyes
Were filled with woe and sadness,
His little tail went wagging on
Because of previous gladness.

SMITH, T. V.

To be sure, T.V. Smith found a different context for his little poem about his dog—but one must confess reading it and thinking immediately of the present state of social science education in the United States. In general terms, those of us in social science education are saddened by what we see and yet in most educational attempts our sad tale is consumed in a wagging gladness. To say that this is inconsistent is putting it mildly.

The problem of informing our tail of our present emotion is difficult and complex.

A few centuries ago Francis Bacon felt that scholars were placing too much emphasis on fixed ideas and admonished them to see the need for "minds washed clear of prejudices and preconceptions" when he said that "We are not to imagine or to suppose, but to discover, what nature does or may be made to do."

Descartes went further and recommended "the methodic doubt of everything. . . and to start again with thyself asking questions and looking for explanations that can be proved."

Others joined in this view and noted that the search for truth was not mere jargon or a superficial phrase—it was actually *an experience in living.*

Thus began our journey of disseminating information. But even the first steps in the search—in collecting and disseminating

3

knowledge—were not welcomed by all. For example, in 1613 a scholar was bemoaning the fact that:

one of the diseases of this age is the multiplicity of books; they doth so overcharge the world that it is not able to digest the abundance of idle matter that is every day hatched and brought forth into the world.

To be sure, when one discovers or derives new information to be added on the cumulative stockpile, the complexity of the human experience grows more intense. We can sympathize with the scholars of the 17th century. We also may take a look at ourselves in the 20th century.

Professor Derek Price of Yale made a study of the accumulated knowledge and concluded that the amount of scientific knowledge doubles every ten years. At the present time there are over 600,000 learned (and some not so learned) papers presented each year. There are over 30,000 current scientific journals. Since the middle of the 17th century over 10,000,000 science papers have been written by over 3,000,000 authors; and of the 3,000,000 authors, *over 90 per cent are living today.*

Lest we think that the term "science" is restricted to certain subjects and not a descriptive term for a way of knowing, one need only glance at *Science*, the publication of the American Association for the Advancement of Science, or at *Scientific American* to note that knowledge about human behavior—the social sciences if we will—is definitely included. The ramification of new information finds no inherent boundaries.

Whitehead once wrote that the greatest invention of the 19th century was the *method* of invention; this certainly knows no boundaries. So, our eyes look out upon an increasing tempo of change. And, whether we like it or not, we have to act in such a world.

One reason the public school has hesitated to address the social sciences may stem from a misunderstanding of the heart of the scientific revolution: we accept and expect the products but, in human affairs, we expect too much from the method of scientific inquiry. While the method can give only probable assurance, we ask for certainty. While the method recognizes the human being as fallible, we ask for infallibility.

"What do you guarantee?" one high school principal asked. The response "nothing" shocked him. Telling him that the Universe was so complex that even the widest-ranging vision was at best partial and tentative was heresy of the highest order. Frankly, it appears to be a vicious circle: we don't teach the method, yet not to grasp the method. . . keeps us from teaching the method.

With all the findings related to learning theory and the information available in the social sciences, with all our distress over the knowledge explosion, population explosion, nuclear explosion, we cling to a safe and pastoral traditional program. Educating children in the 20th century to live most of their lives in the 21st century, we continue to pass on the 18th century tool chest. Walter Lippman said it: "Men are choked with the debris of dead notions in which they are unable to believe and unwilling to disbelieve."

HISTORY AND THE USE OF HISTORY

What is this traditional program? It is pretty much history and geography—that is, history and geography as they appeared to be in the 18th and 19th centuries.

Betty Bridgman,[1] writing in the *Christian Science Monitor*, contends that *the way we study* history has a tendency to put us on the side of kings and priests and asks that we move from what Chesterfield called a "confused heap of facts," past pitfalls of fallacy, into a functional realization that history is partial in the sense of never using *all* the information (even if we had it), and partial in the sense of taking sides.

She is not intent upon destroying history in the schools. She only asks that we heed Alan Griffin's thought as it appears in *The World Book:* "Everyone knows what history is until he begins to think about it. After that, nobody knows." She implies that we should not ask history and historians to be more and to do more that what they can. To foist unrealistic expectations upon "history" can lead to cynicism among teachers and unfounded rejection of history by the "now generation."

Few would argue that one role of the public school is to equip the young with knowledge, the best available, in order to help guide their behavior and to assist in making intelligent decisions in their private and public worlds. If we accept what some historians tell us about the functions of history, we would have to evaluate social studies programs and social studies teaching in terms of whether or not they examine social issues and develop critical thinking, *and commitment to democratic values.* The criteria would apply to the old as well as to any suggested new alternatives. Too often both the educator and the public forget

---

[1]Betty Bridgman, "History Never Happened," *Christian Science Monitor,* Jan. 1965, p. 213.

such things when new programs and different teaching styles are offered. What is sauce for the gosling is sauce for the goose.

LEARNING FROM HISTORY?

With these criteria in mind, let's take a look at some of the major ideas or concepts of history — if you will, the hypotheses which assert relationships among data. There is an underlying assumption that knowledge can somehow *transfer* from one situation to another and therefore provide some guide to behavior. To claim that a study of history can aid the citizen in intelligent decision making assumes that there are certain processes developed in a study of history and that content of history is applicable and appropriate in terms of situations to be faced.

Most are aware that man depends upon different levels of ideas or concepts. To help make sense of the constant barrage of data, we screen our sense data and place what we select into categories. The categories take the form of concepts. The concepts assist us in understanding our world and thus influence our actions and reactions to the world around us. Ideas have consequences. The need to generalize about past experience is not questioned. Rather, the need is so great, we must pay close attention to the meaningfulness and utility of the concepts history has to offer.

Raymond H. Muessig and Vincent R. Rogers, in their "Suggested Methods for Teachers" in Henry Steele Commager's *The Nature and the Study of History,* identified some "compelling ideas" from the study of history which could be of use for social studies teaching and social studies programs.[2]

Some of the ideas:

1. Continuous and unrelenting change has been a universal condition of human society.

2. History offers no immutable laws, givens, or inevitables upon which to base decisions. History allows man to choose among rational alternatives concerning the time in which he lives.

3. Historical events should be examined in light of standards, values, attitudes, and beliefs which were dominant in a certain period of time and for a given people.

4. Events cannot be explained through simple one-to-

---

[2]Henry Steele Commager, *The Nature and the Study of History* (Charles E. Merrill Social Science Seminar Series), Charles E. Merrill, Columbus, Ohio, 1965.

one causal terms, through simple cause-effect relationships.

5. The record of the past is fragmentary, selective, and biased. Historical facts vary with individuals studying such facts and each generation tends to re-create and rewrite history in terms of its own perspective, needs, and aspirations.

The above listing raises several questions. With the exception possibly of number three, are any of the ideas found solely within the province of history, or does history confirm interdisciplinary concepts derived from a number of disciplines addressing a scientific study of man? Are the ideas or concepts similar to those found in other disciplines? (For example, a child's initial orientation to political authority stems from a personalized view of government—a feeling for and toward leaders and what leaders do.)[3] Do such ideas act as guides or targets for the history areas of social studies programs? (Or, do we still find students being asked to place the presidents in chronological order or to give the four causes of the Civil War?)

It should be obvious that a study of history has a decided part to play in social studies teaching. That part has to do with how one *uses* history. The problem of the *use* of history rests not with history and historians but with educators who must determine the *educational* use. In the last fifty years—and especially the last twenty—historians have found it necessary to turn to the social and natural sciences for both concepts and tools with which to work in order to use historical data.

New Tools, Old Ways

For example, in the Preface to *The Historian and the World of the Twentieth Century*, some of the issues making current historical scholarship different from that of the 1920's and 1930's are discussed.[4] Scientific discovery, technological development, transformation in political life and political processes, reorganization of economic activity, and new kinds of moral preoccupations have led historians to seek entirely new kinds of facts to answer "wholly new kinds of questions." Such a context poses new questions which help guide historical research. The historian rec-

---

[3]David Easton and Jack Dennis, "The Child's Image of Government," *The Annals* of the American Academy of Political and Social Science, Sept., 1965.
[4]*The Historian and the World of the Twentieth Century*, Daedalus, Spring, 1971.

ognizes that specialization and focus do not exempt the effort to integrate and relate findings. As areas such as urban history come on the scene, there is need to use the insights of the social and behavioral sciences and there is need for a type of history that also emphasizes "confusion, ignorance, chance, and sheer stupidity," "the felt texture of events," to go along with the non-participant, documented, descriptive history.

Different tools and instruments are emerging. For example, Western historians have depended a great deal on written texts, but there is also a need for analysis of oral traditions. This calls for some familiarity with linguistic, literary, and anthropological techniques and concepts. Computers have enabled the historian to handle more complex data but this added tool makes the creative and reflective organization of materials even more demanding.

It is logical to assume that all this ferment would have some implications for social studies programs and for the selection, correlation, and teaching of content. But tradition is strong. Complacency is comfortable and comforting.

In the 12th century there was a school in Paris under the leadership of an educator named Hugo who was more or less the James Conant of his period. He is credited with putting out the first school text in history. The utility of his history was that of interpreting the scriptures and that of training the memory. To Hugo all history revolved around knowing the people who performed the deeds, knowing the places where the deeds were done, and knowing the ages in which they were accomplished. The mind "rejoiced in brevity" and all events must be first summarized and then committed to memory. What was so committed had to be recapitulated frequently or else forgotten. His text had over seventy pages of names, dates, and places. We might say that Hugo was the daddy of the three "R's": Rote, Regurgitation, and Rigidity.

In an *Introduction to the Study of History* (for the use of schools), published in 1847, the author suggests that the student memorize the larger type and have that which was committed to memory reviewed many times in order that he maintain the outline for life. The history text starts with The Creation, which took place exactly 4004 years B.C., and then moves from Adam and Eve's transgression through the murder of Abel, the flood, up through 1845. Hugo's conventional wisdom had breathing room over a 600-year period.

What are the traditional offerings at the 5th grade, 8th grade, and 11th grade in the American Public School? Too often they are sizzling platters of dates and nuts, committed to memory, regurgitated periodically on local or national examinations. To be sure, we copy tables of contents, calling them Courses of Study. Out of necessity, we have chopped up the time spans in order to better accomplish what Hugo had in mind. But the times are changing and we have begun to ask questions about "new" social studies curricula.

GOALS FOR STUDENTS

When one reviews the current literature he cannot help but note a pervasive awareness of a major social frame of reference. This is not surprising, as the multitude of recent changes place the public school in the matrix of all transition. This awkward placement is compounded in complexity when we realize that the traditional nature of the school has been conservative — conservative in the sense that public education justified its expensive role in the economy by implying that it was socializing the young in terms of those values which the major society considered important enough to be preserved. The transition which we are experiencing has challenged some of the traditional values and hence has challenged the role of the public school.

It would seem that we are at the point of asking the school, the administrator, the teacher, and perhaps the student to identify respective frames of reference. We are asking those involved in public education to question why they are doing what they are doing. For example, to ask a teacher in the social studies why he is teaching about the Colonies and have him answer "A student *has* to know this," is to beg the question. Why does a student have to learn about the fertile crescent, the Renaissance, the date 1066? If the learning of such material is a means to an end and not an end in itself, is it asking too much to identify the end in view? And is it asking too much to note alternative approaches which might better, more effectively, arrive at the "end" which is now cognitive? Whatever thinking is, it is not easy and sometimes not at all reassuring. Yet, do we abolish the problem by the refusal to recognize it? To what extent are we rational and to what extent are we rationalizing? It is rather disconcerting to recognize that the social studies teacher is no less immune from the ostrich posture so readily recognized among his colleagues. Are we in fact saying to the students that when one studies the interaction of man and his social and physical environments the first thing to do is to deny the existence of major problems because we are not able to cope with them?

PROGRAM AIMS

The fundamental aim of a social studies program involves having a student assess what he is, who he is, what he knows, and the types of evidence he accepts for knowing; to assess what it means to be a social being and to so recognize that a world interaction necessitates identifying what other people think they are, who they are, what they know, and the evidence the other fellow accepts for knowing.

It is to assess sources of values, and the difficulties and promises in communication.

It is to understand types of decision making, and the implications of compromise.

It is to be able to dissect problems and structure alternatives for resolving these problems.

It is to recognize that answers are often situational and that to rationally appraise the situation is to consult our oracle.

It is to identify the relationship between means and ends which justifies the rights of a minority and of individuals.

It is to struggle with a meaning of the relationship between individual and social freedom.

It is to ask questions.

It is to study all forms of social living—political, economic, and social in order to better know one's self.

And it is to be aware that all the above is meaningless, unless one acts, one lives, according to his ideas of what living implies.

But, we are told that the teachers are not qualified to pursue such a program. This is true if we maintain that the teacher stands as the sage, offering the answers which he himself has been given. It is not true if the teacher is perceived (and evaluated) in terms of his also being a student, actively looking, guiding, and asking in a terrain which he has scouted to a greater degree than have his students.

STUDENT GOALS

1. A willingness to search for data upon which to derive viewpoints and generalizations.

2. An ability to differentiate between different types of evidence which may lend reliability to data.

3. An ability to dissect complex social situations, note the

types of information needed and interacting relationships, and to identify the cognitive meaning which he brings to the complexity of a situation.

4. A willingness to suspend judgment and yet a willingness to act with a recognition that he will seldom have all the possible available information and that his "solution" is only probable and open to change and correction.

5. A willingness to evaluate others' opinions, values, and attitudes.

6. An intellectual humility in the sense that his search is not pursued to prove himself correct but to offer his opinion and justification to the public test.

7. The ability to recognize and live according to the ethics implied in social interaction.

8. An active attitude and behavior based on a recognition that as a social being, his behavior is functionally related to the rest of mankind.

9. A willingness to accept the responsibility for all areas of his behavior.

10. A willingness to defend (and justify the defense) the rights of minorities and individuals under due process even though their use of the rights may threaten some of his beliefs.

11. An ability to recognize the sources of law and the need for law and order, and yet be willing to use the open process of change to bring about desired changes in the forms of social interaction.

12. A willingness to act in the knowledge that the individual's importance is not measured in terms of numbers but rather in terms of effective participation. Effective participation involves the use of persuasion and sanctioned processes in order to reach a position which lends power to his attitudes and opinions.

13. A willingness to share the responsibility for what his societies do as long as he is allowed an opportunity to partake in decision making.

14. A recognition that all living is a process of change and that all ideas must necessarily be allowed to compete in an open marketplace of ideas.

15. A willingness to present his convictions for public evaluation and yet accept the characteristics of integrity, fortitude, courage, and perseverance as ethical components in making his assumptions, logic, alternatives, and perceived consequences open to public analysis.

16. An ability and willingness to explain why he behaves as he does, why he believes as he does, and the perceived relationship between the two.

17. An empathy for people and peoples differing in behavior and viewpoints from those he embraces, recognizing the multitude of factors involved in their approach to satisfying basic and secondary needs.

18. A willingness to act with firmness when any attempt is made to limit the structural process of change and correction. With equal firmness he will deny any attempt which limits any area of possible change and correction.

In summary, we should aim at having a human being so educated as to act in the realization that pluralism recognizes no "one" answer to social problems other than the process of resolving immediate problematic situations. Having no one set answer denies any one group from dictating answers but rather encourages all people to contribute and to recognize that compromise is part of participation. The human is social in that he interacts with others according to the process and is willing to accept responsibility for social planning and for the consequences of this planning.

CRITERIA FOR TEACHING THE USE OF SOCIAL STUDIES

Any rationale addressing social studies program change and teaching will have to come face-to-face with the following criteria.

1. **Rationality:** There must be some overt and logical connection between the "ends" that are held and the "means" selected to achieve the desired ends. To say "I am teaching the Colonial Period because students have to know it" will no longer suffice.

2. **New Knowledge:** Information and concepts from the social and behavioral sciences will emerge as tools. There will be less emphasis on history for the sake of history and a greater emphasis on the *use* of history in conjunction *with* the findings of the social and behavioral sciences.

3. **Inquiry and Discovery:** Teaching methods will move from "telling" prescribed normative answers to engaging in *discovering* relationships through inquiry.

4. **Integration of Knowledge:** There will be an increase in using concepts in multidisciplinary and interdisciplinary content areas.

5. **Greater Amount of Data:** Ideas, concepts, and themes do not exist in a void. They are learned by using data. To move into conceptual teaching is to court the use of more, not less, factual material.

6. **Use of Individual Teacher Styles and Strengths:** Each teacher brings *himself*—his style, his academic proficiency, his interests. Greater teacher flexibility will evolve and with it greater teacher accountability.

7. **Emphasis on the Transfer of Concepts and Skills:** Information for the sake of information will no longer suffice. Teaching and learning will focus on the *use* of what is learned, on *transfer* of learnings to other data and to new situations. Learning becomes a process of developing and using "tools."

8. **Selection and Use of Materials as Vehicles:** There must be selection and use of materials (data banks, fact sheets, case studies, maps) as vehicles or means to concept development.

9. **Change Processes:** There will be no lessening of emphasis upon structure but rather a view of structure that allows stability while being flexible enough to allow for ongoing modification: reforming concepts, materials, student (and teacher) needs.

If the above criteria are valid, it raises some of the basic issues in teacher preparation for the use of social studies. If, as Fochet urges, we bring the embers and not the ashes from the past, the foundation of the effort rests with the individual teacher having a clear formulation of his own convictions and his own basic reasons for teaching the use of social studies.

TEACHING THE *USE* OF SOCIAL STUDIES

What constitutes the social studies? As has been noted, "social studies" appears to mean such things as history, geography, and government. And the major objective, in many cases, is related to the teaching of good citizenship. In other words, a number of people view social studies education as a means rather than an end in itself. And, we have noted the view that teaching the social studies necessitates identifying the basic facts and "body of content" which a student should learn.

The teacher's dilemma is encountered when one assesses the difference between teaching the social studies (commonly viewed as history, geography, and government) and teaching the *use* of the social studies. In the former, the teaching approach can be anchored to subject matter. In teaching the *use* of the social studies, the teaching approach can be based upon putting the academic disciplines *to work:* to use the social studies as a *means; to inquire with content.*

Most people, when they think of science, think of people who are studying the things which nature has provided. Most of us use what these people find. We ride in cars and airplanes, we use the telephones, we use medicine and medical treatments, we use synthetic clothes, we use elevators. Almost everything we use has been made possible because of the people who study nature and who have found different ways of using what nature provides.

But there is another part of our surroundings which were *not* made by nature. These are the surroundings (environment) which man has made for himself. These surroundings are quite important, too.

The first environment is called the "natural" environment. The second environment is called the "social" environment. The social environment is concerned with how a human being, how each of us, acts with other human beings and with the part of his surroundings which men make.

Man uses many of the discoveries of the natural scientists to make things: the cars, the airplanes, the telephones, the space ships, are all man-made. Man looked at nature, studied it, and found ways to combine what he found and to make things which human beings can use. Man's *social* environment includes these things, but also includes a study of how man gets his ideas, a study of his languages, his laws, his work, his way of living, his government, and how and why he gets into conflict with his fellow men.

It is hard to divide man's total environment into two parts. We do this because it helps man to study. Man has to ask questions which he can answer through inquiry processes.

HOW THE SOCIAL SCIENTIST MIGHT APPROACH HIS WORK

WHY ARE SOME PEOPLE POOR?

Some might answer this question by quickly saying that people who are poor find themselves poor because they are lazy or not too smart. These persons may tell you that it is only natural that some people are poor.

If we stopped with this type of answer to the question, there would be no need to continue looking for evidence. There would be no need to observe, to collect information, to look for patterns, and to interpret.

The social scientist would not accept the answer that *all* poor people are poor because they are either lazy or not too smart. He uses inquiry. He might observe a specific family—family "X". The family is poor. He collects information which shows that the father was always a good worker. If so, how come he does not have a job? He collects information and finds out that the local factory has shut down and that the kind of work which the father did is no longer needed. He collects information and finds out that the father is fairly smart.

The social scientist asks himself: "Is this family poor because the father is lazy?" What other reasons might there be?

By looking at a *specific* family and by looking at the facts, he starts to doubt if *all* poor families are poor because they are lazy. So, he thinks that the first answer he was told may not be correct.

The social scientist's task is to look at many poor families, collect information, and try to see if there are patterns. He probably will not conclude that *all* poor families are lazy. And, he probably will conclude that *some* of the poor families he studies are lazy.

WHY CAN'T MAN LIVE IN PEACE WITH HIS FELLOW HUMAN BEINGS?

Some people would say that man will *always* have war because "it is just the way man is!" They say that he is born with the desire to fight.

The social scientist is not content with this answer. "What way *is* man?" he asks himself and others. "Can we study him in order to help us find out?" If the social scientist just accepted the idea that all men are born with the urge to fight, then there would not be much that he could do to prevent war. Most of us say that we want peace among men. How about it?

Through observation, the social scientist sees certain individuals and certain groups which do not fight. He looks to history and finds out that there are a few countries which have not had wars for a long time.

The social scientist asks himself: "What is it about the people who do not have wars that can help us in preventing war?" He does not accept the first answer. He starts studying in a scientific way.

How Do People Change?

Some persons would say that all you have to do is educate people. They say that if you provide people with information, they will act on it.

The social scientist does not just accept this answer. He wants to test it.

In Rochester, New York, some social scientists found out how many students smoked. They gave information to the students showing that smoking was bad. The students learned a lot about how bad smoking cigarettes was for them. After getting some new information, the students were able to tell their teachers what the new information said.

But the students who smoked before they learned the new information still continued to smoke.

The social scientists said that maybe just telling people would not be enough to change them. They said that just absorbing information was not enough. "How," they asked, "can people take new information and *use* it?" They did not know the answer. But they did know that the first answer was not correct.

The social scientist uses *inquiry* in areas of social concern or interests.

HUMAN USES OF THE SOCIAL SCIENCES

The article in this section is by Robert Redfield. Professor Redfield addresses "The Social Uses of Social Science" and sug-

gests that there is social utility found in social science: a *practical*
utility in terms of using social inquiry to guide decision making
and in helping to clarify values. Redfield saw a need to bring
greater understanding to the nature of social science, to its role as
a means to wisdom as a proving ground of values. ". . . social science is not only a box of tools. It is also a light. The social scientist
is not only a sort of plumber to the circulatory and other ills of
society; he is also, at his best, a source of understanding and enrichment. . . showing men the order and pattern of their own
lives. . . ." His appeal for understanding is not unlike that expressed by William Bevan in *Science* some twenty four years later.[5]
Bevan sees the need to relate the scientific community with the
larger community and shows anxiety over the development of
"esoteric elitism" which further separates the communities,
anxiety over the persistence, by some, that science is value-free,
and anxiety over the apprehension that lay people fear not being
able to control what they do not understand.

Both Redfield and Bevan seem to raise the issue of having science understood as having a unitary nature with implications for
application to a wide range of problems.

Redfield's article is preceded by a number of *Focus Ideas*.
Focus Ideas are not meant to be learned in the sense of swallowing
idea capsules. Rather, they are presented as jumping off positions,
as hypotheses, as ideas to be tested and then modified, qualified,
deleted, enlarged, as experience dictates. The Focus Ideas may be
partially tested with information appearing in the article and further
tested by using other sources of experience.

Redfield's article is followed by a number of *Focus Issues*
raised. You may want to test the Focus Ideas and address some of
the Focus Issues. If teaching is somehow an attempt to make students able to *use* social studies, then perhaps some of the ideas and
issues may help in establishing some broad perimeters for social
studies teaching.

FOCUS IDEAS

Social science, as an institution, serves functions and goals
and the social uses of social science can be reviewed much

---

[5]William Bevan, "The General Scientific Association! A Bridge to Society at
Large," *Science*, April 23, 1971.

as the functions and goals of medicine, the fine arts, or the press.

Teaching is an example of the social uses of social science.

Social science is a group of disciplines providing descriptions of human nature, human activity, and human institutions. The disciplines are characterized by being scientific (stressing What Is and not What Ought to Be), and exercising objectivity in the systematic formulation of knowledge.

Social science is more illuminating than are descriptions stemming from common sense.

Social science can be applied to societal purposes and can lead to effective practical action. Just as physics and biology lead to practical applications in engineering and medicine, social science leads to understanding man in society—to practical applications in social action.

The functions of social science have grown considerably since World War I.

Social science is supported by society because it can be used in the service of mankind. It can help in prediction and this, in turn, helps in planning and implementing action.

As society turns to conscious decisions about the management of human affairs, social science may help, just as biology provides guidance for decisions regarding health and hygiene.

Social science use is not exhausted when used in practical application. A further use rests in the testing and development of social values.

Social science may not be allowed by society to study social problems because many problems are protected from rational examination because of tradition, sentiment, and inviolable attitudes.

The subject matter of social science is not morally indifferent. It is morally significant. The social scientist has convictions, prejudices, sentiments, and judgments and must understand that this becomes part of what he studies.

The freedom of the mind to inquire, propose, test, and create is a test of a country's values.

THE SOCIAL USES OF SOCIAL SCIENCE*

ROBERT REDFIELD

The subject of my remarks today might be expressed as a question for which three different forms of words suggest themselves: What beneficial functions may social science hope to perform in our society? What is the task of social science? Why have a social science?

Institutions are good, not only for what they are, but also by reason of what we strive to make them. I think, then, not only of what social science is, but also of what it might be. I think of social science as one of many institutions that contribute toward the making of the life we want and that could do it better than they do. I would review the functions and the goals of social science as I would review the functions and the goals of medicine, the fine arts, or the press.

The social uses of medicine are to reduce human suffering and to prolong life; this is well understood, and it is clear that to great degree medicine performs these functions. The social uses of the press are to tell people, truthfully and comprehensively, what happens around them, to provide forums for public discussion, and to reflect and clarify the ideals of our society. It is more or less well known that this is what our press is expected to do, whether or not it does it as well as it should. But the social uses of social science are not, I think, so generally recognized. People do not know, at once, why there should be social science or even what social science is. Therefore there is a special duty, in the case of social science, upon you and me who have thought more about that subject, to make clear its nature and its usefulness.

In our own company today it will not be necessary for me to say much about the nature of social science. It is a group of disciplines that provide descriptions of human nature, human activity, and human institutions. These disciplines are scientific, first in that they are concerned with telling us What Is, not What Ought to Be; and second, in that they exercise objectivity, pursue special knowledge, and move toward systematic formulation of this knowledge. So they strive for descriptions that are more illuminating, valid, and comprehensive than are the corresponding descriptions of common sense.

You will readily understand that I have in mind the social sciences that one meets in the catalogues of graduate schools and in the membership of the Social Science Research Council. Just which of them are to be included in any roster of the social sciences does not concern us here; the existing division of labor as among the special social sciences is not wholly

*Reprinted by permission. From *University of Colorado Bulletin*, Vol. XLVII, May 24, 1947.

defensible and may not endure. I am not thinking of ethics, which is the criticism and organization of principles of right conduct. I am not thinking of the social arts and professions, such as law or social-service administration, which are ways of acting on people to get certain results. I am thinking of the application of the scientific spirit toward the description and explanation of man in society. I am asking how its application there serves the common good.

A further limitation of my subject is required. History is not in my mind today. The social uses of history have a special and important character which I shall not discuss. History, being a content of preserved and considered experience, has those social uses which memory and tradition have. From History, as from memory, we expect "a knowledge of our own identities," "orientation in our environment, a knowledge of its usual uniformities, including. . . some knowledge of the characters with whom we must deal, their strengths and weaknesses, and what they are likely to do under given circumstances." Further, ". . . we all hope to draw from past experience help in choosing successfully between the alternatives offered by present events." These social uses of history have been recently summarized by Garrett Mattingly,* from whom I quote these phrases. Today I am thinking of that social science which is analytical rather than historical, which seeks to understand a social problem or which describes the general characteristics of some class of social phenomena. How does such social science serve the common good?

The familiar answer is that social science tells us how to do what we want to do. The reply is that the understanding that social science gives can be applied to the purposes of society. The descriptions of social science lead to more effective practical action than would be possible without social science. Social science is, from this point of view, like physics or biology. Just as those sciences reach understanding and explanation of the physical and the organic worlds which lead to practical applications in engineering and in medicine, so social science reaches understanding of man in society which leads to practical applications in social action.

Surely it is true that social science does this. It does tell us how to do what we want to do. It tells us some things that common sense does not tell us or does not tell us nearly so well about how to select people to pilot airplanes or to perform other special tasks, how to predict the consequences of a given tax policy, or how quickly to discover fluctuations in the opinions of over a hundred million people on current issues. The competence of social science to guide useful social action has grown greatly in a few years. The contributions of social science to the national effort at the time of

*"A Sample Discipline—The Teaching of History," address delivered February 20, 1947, at the Princeton University Bicentennial Conference.)

World War I were almost limited to certain studies in prices, to the work of historians in war information, and to developments in mental testing. The contributions of social science in connection with World War II were so numerous and varied that a mere list of them would fill many pages. In the army and in the navy, and in scores of civilian agencies, social scientists were employed for the reason that their efforts as social scientists were recognized as helping to win the war or the peace. This direct service to the community, through the application of their special knowledge, continues in the efforts of social scientists after the war. Of the many fields of research which have already found practical justification I mention three: the understanding of problems of morale and of human relations in industry; the prediction of human behavior in regard to the stability of marriage, criminal recidivism, and certain other kinds of behavior where dependable prediction is useful; and the analysis and control of communication made to mass audiences through print, radio, or screen. Social science had indeed so well established its usefulness in certain fields that specialized technicians are recognized in those fields — professional appliers of social-science knowledge. I mention clinical psychiatrists and city planners.

The question I asked appears at once to be answered. Why have a social science? Have it because it is useful. Have a social science because it gets things done that society wants done. According to this answer social science has the same nature and the same justification that physics and chemistry have. It is supported by society as physics and chemistry are supported by society: because what is learned can be directly applied to the service of mankind. Society less and less can take care of itself; more and more it is true that conscious decisions are required in the management of human affairs, and social science provides guidance in the making of these decisions, just as biological science provides guidance for decisions as to health and hygiene. This is the simple answer that is often made.

I will state my own position at once. I think that this is a true answer but that it is far from a complete answer. I think social science is notably different from physics and chemistry, and that its social uses are not exhausted when one has recognized the practical applications of social science. I think that social science has other important social uses in the testing and in the development of social values.

What has social science to do with the proving and making of values?

What is its role in regard not merely to the valuation of a means to reach an end sought, but also to the more ultimate values of society?

The plainest values with which social science is concerned are those necessary to science: objectivity, honesty, accuracy, and humility before the facts. To the preservation and cultivation of these the social sciences are devoted. In the course of carrying out research the social scientist shares with the physicist and the biologist the effort to maintain and extend the common morality of the scientific mind. It is, moreover, a morality quite consistent with the morality which the citizen who is not a scientist may embrace. Honesty, accuracy, humility before the facts, and faith in the power of truth to prevail in Milton's free encounter are virtues in their own right. Science is one of the institutions that contribute to the cultivation of these virtues.

In the work of cultivation of these values the position of social science is critical because it is by no means sure that even our free and liberal society will allow the extension of the scientific spirit in the study of social problems. Many people do not understand that it is useful to society to extend it there. While the usefulness of physics and biology is generally acknowledged, the scientific study of many social problems is popularly regarded as either futile or dangerous. This is because many of the subjects studied by the social sciences are protected from rational examination, for the general population, by tradition, sentiment, and inviolable attitude.

In short, the subject matter of social science is not morally indifferent. It is morally significant. The social scientist himself, and his neighbors and fellow citizens, are also concerned with that subject matter. They have convictions, prejudices, sentiments, and judgments about the tariff, party politics, relation between the sexes, and race relations. All of these things the social scientist studies, and what he has to say about them in the course of his trying to improve our understanding of them encounters these convictions, prejudices, sentiments, and judgments. They are all "tender" subjects. People feel a sense of distress if their convictions or assumptions on these matters are challenged or controverted. Often they are distressed at the mere looking at these subjects objectively. Some social scientists study such subjects as the relations between husband and wife or the attitudes people have toward racial or religious minorities or the profit motive in economic activity. It makes some people uncomfortable to hear that these subjects are being studied with critical impersonality. The social scientist is then resented or distrusted. If, furthermore, his descriptions or conclusions appear inconsistent with the more sacred values of the community, a cry may go up that the social scientist be restrained or that his publication be suppressed or that he lose his job.

Therefore social science is the test case of the vitality of those ideals I have mentioned which are common to all science and which play so large a part in the freedom of the modern mind. The scientists as a whole understand this. In discussions which are now going on as to the drafting of a bill for a national science foundation, it appears that almost all the scientists, natural scientists as well as social scientists, think that if government money is to be provided for the support of science, social science should be included. On the other hand,

with similar unanimity the scientists understand that Congress-
men are much less likely to provide such support for social
science than for natural science. The scientists see that
science is one way of looking at the world around us, a way
applicable to men and society as it is applicable to molecules
and cells. They feel this common morality of the scientific
mind and respect the usefulness of social science in not only
making useful social inventions but also in developing this
morality throughout society. But they also know that people
who are not scientists do not see it that way and imagine social
science to be political propaganda or doctrine, or speculative
futility. These scientists perhaps realize what I believe to be
true: that that freedom of the mind to inquire, propose, test,
and create which is so central and precious a part of the more
ultimate values of our manner of life may, in a military or
reactionary trend of events, be first tested and won or lost in
our country in the freedom of social science.

In effect, social science is a new instrument, not only for
the getting of certain specific things done in the management
of society, but for the clarification and development of our
more ultimate values. The social uses of social science are not
exhausted when we have said that social science can improve
the efficiency of industrial production or test the aptitudes of
young people for one kind of occupation rather than another.
Social science is one of the ways to form our convictions as to
the good life. This it does not as preaching does it, by telling
us what the good is and what our duty is. It does not do it as
ethics does it, by examining central questions as to the nature
of conduct and by criticizing and formulating systematic rules
of conduct. It does it by remaining science. It does it by making
clear to us where our choices lead us and what means must be
employed to reach what ends. It does it by extending our
understanding of where our ideals are in conflict with our
practices and where our ideas are in conflict with each other.
And it does this through those intensive studies of particular
societies and particular men which are not ordinarily carried
on in ethics and which are outside the powers and the responsibilities of the preacher.

An example may make this clear. Recently a study of the
Negro in the United States was made by Gunnar Myrdal, a
Swedish social scientist. The resulting work is not a sermon,
nor is it an analysis of the principles of conduct. It is a description of the Negro in American business, government, and
social life. It is also a description of the white man in his
positions toward the Negro in American life. Myrdal's book
does not tell us didactically what we ought to do. The propositions that make up the books are Is-propositions not Ought-
propositions. Nevertheless the book can hardly be read carefully by anyone without some effect upon the reader's system
of values, his conceptions of duty, justice, and the good life.
The effect is enhanced, in this particular case of social-
science research, because the author and his collaborators

took for their problem the relation of the Negro's place in our society to the ideals of freedom, liberty, and democracy which are genuinely held in our nation. They were interested in finding out what effect, on the white man especially, results from the presence of practices and institutions inconsistent with these ideals. The book does not argue for any norm of conduct. It just tells about norms in relation to customs and institutions. But any American reader at all thoughtful finds himself understanding better than he did the choices that are open to him: less democracy, liberty, and equality, and race relations as they are; or more democracy, liberty, and equality, and a change in race relations. Or, as a third possibility, he learns something of the effects on his state of mind if the inconsistency persists. And this increased understanding is a leaven in those workings of the spirit which lead to the remaking of our system of ideals.

I think it is self-delusion for a social scientist to say that what he does has no concern with social values. I think that people are right when they express their feelings that social science does something to the values they hold with regard to such particular institutions as restrictive covenants or the tariff. For one thing social science tests those special values, by showing what they cost. It hears the people say, We want freedom. Social science listens, studies our society, and replies, Very well, if you want freedom, this is what you will pay in one kind of freedom for enjoying so much of another. To every partisan the social scientist appears an enemy. The social scientist addresses himself to the question, How much security from idleness and want is compatible with developed capitalism? and equally to the question, How much political and civil freedom is compatible with socialism? To partisans on both sides he appears unsympathetic and dangerous.

For social science, along with other science, philosophy, and the general spirit of intellectual liberty, is asserting the more general and comprehensive values of our society against the more limited and special interests and values. It hears society say, We believe in the right of the human mind to examine freely, to criticize openly, to reach conclusions from tested evidence. Very well, replies social science, if this is your desire then you must endure the pain of the examination and the testing of the particular customs and institutions which you hold dear. Social science says to all of us: Except where your special interests are involved, you recognize that mankind have passed the period in which they took their ethical convictions from their grandfathers without doubt and reflection. Now we have to think, investigate, and consider about both the means and the ends of life. Social science is that science, which in other fields you so readily admire, directed to human nature and the ways of living of man in society. By your own more general convictions you have authorized and validated its development.

It follows that the successful functioning of social science is peculiarly dependent upon education. The realization of the social uses of social science depends closely upon the dissemination of the findings of social science and of the understanding of the very nature of social science among all the people. So a responsibility falls upon you and me, who have thought something of the matter, to make social science known to all. It is for us to make it clear to our fellow citizens what social science is, and why its development is so needed today.

Social science does not need to be sold to the people. It needs only to be explained. There never was a time when social science was more needed than it is today. The extreme peril in which we live arises from the small political and social wisdom we have in the face of our immensely dangerous material strength. We should have more control over the physical world, yes, surely; but it is far more necessary that we learn to control the relations among men. We know now that we can destroy one another and the fruits of civilization, and we are far from sure that we can prevent ourselves from doing so. If social science could effect an improvement of our chances of preventing it of no more than 1 per cent, a great expenditure in social science would be justified.

In explaining social science it needs to be said that social science is not only a box of tools. It is also a light. The social scientist is not only a sort of plumber to the circulatory and other ills of society; he is also, at his best, a source of understanding and enrichment. It should be pointed out that the test of good social science is not only: Will it work? There is another test: Does it make sense? For social science also justifies itself to the extent to which it makes life comprehensible and significant. That social science, also, has worth which, though it solves no problem of unemployment or of selection of competent administrators, shows men the order and the pattern of their own lives. Good social science provides categories in terms of which we come to understand ourselves. Our buying and selling, our praying, our hopes, prejudices, and fears, as well as the institutions which embody all these, turn out — under the light of sound social science — to have form, perspective, rule. Shown the general, we are liberated from the tyranny of the particular. I am not merely I; I am an instance of a natural law.

To say this is not to say that social science should be speculative or philosophical. The significant generalization may first appear in a flash of insight. Or illuminating generalizations may be built up out of many detailed observations. Out of the innumerable painstaking studies of particular facts, in biology, anthropology, and sociology, emerges now a broad conception of society, inclusive of ants, apes, and men, and the notion that the mechanisms of evolution operate through not merely individuals but the social groups themselves. This but illustrates the fact that comprehensive general understanding of society is often the work of many men over much time.

So we will praise social science both as a practical servant of mankind, useful as biology and physics are made useful, and also as a handmaiden of the spirit. It has on the other side some of the social uses of the humanities. It makes a knowledge which helps to define the world of human relations in which we live, which makes clear to ourselves our place in a social cosmos. Social science is not essentially a series of inventions to be applied. The inventions come, and they are useful. But primarily social science is a chain of understandings to be communicated.

And we will make it clear that in this work of increasing understanding, there is a moral commitment and a moral purpose. Social science is objective in that it cultivates deliberate consideration of alternative explanations, demands proof, and submits to the conviction which facts compel. But it is not indifferent. It will not tolerate cynicism. It expects responsibility from its followers, responsibility to use special knowledge for the common good and to act on convictions reached by reason and through special knowledge. It demands that the values that are implied in the conduct of its work be declared. It commits itself to the use of man's rational nature and the methods of modern empirical investigation to the service of society. The service is one not only to the strength of the social body. It is also a contribution to its soul. Social science is a proving ground of values. It is a means to wisdom. Let us, who are social scientists, so conduct our work as to make it yield more of the wisdom the world so sorely needs. Let all of us, who know something of social science, explain that this is its purpose, its highest ideal.

FOCUS ISSUES:

We are told that whenever there is an attempt to examine value systems and value practices, there is some pain—that every partisan who wants *his* way views social science as an enemy. By remaining "science," how might social science help clarify and develop values? If social science is not speculative nor philosophical yet is concerned with values, just what *does* it offer? What is the difference between saying "You *ought* to want this" and "If you want this (and it is clear what you want) then you should do 'a', 'b', and 'c' "?

If not "science," what does man use to study himself and his behavior? *Specifically,* how do the two (or more) ways of studying and knowing differ?

What reasons might one give for including history in the social sciences? What reasons might be given for *not* including history? Is it possible to justify the view that the greater the use of social science, the greater the use of history? In order to predict, what assumptions are made? How might the uses of history and social science complement one another in teaching?

What is the difference between saying: this will happen, this possibly will happen, and this probably will happen? Redfield compares the social sciences with the physical and biological sciences. In what ways does the comparison hold up and in what ways does social science differ from the physical and biological sciences?

What *specific* taboo areas seem to appear in American society —areas that people resist examining and re-examining in a scientific way? Are there any findings from the social and behavioral sciences that might help explain such resistance? Do the social sciences work with the cognitive factors in affective behavior?

In terms of planning and implementing teaching the use of social studies, what are the implications of the issues raised for: (1) content; (2) inquiry; (3) values and attitudes; and (4) change strategies to be used by people concerned with the human use of human knowledge?

We are suggesting that the above raises questions concerning the validity of teaching social studies in the traditional rote manner. The human use of human knowledge implies that one is able to *use* knowledge. Inquiry is the process that allows us to make use of such knowledge.

INQUIRY?

Teachers are expected to do a number of instructional and non-instructional tasks. Our concern is primarily with the *in-structional* aspects of what a teacher is expected to do. In an over-simplified way, a teacher is expected to do four related instructional activities: identify the purposes of the instructional effort; plan for how the instruction is to take place; implement the plans; and evaluate whether or not—or to what extent—the purposes were achieved.

Both the methods a teacher uses *and* the content selected for use (one has to select because it is impossible to teach everything about anything) imply the goals, objectives, and purposes of instructional activity. Education is an intentional intervention in another human's life, done on purpose and with purpose. Planning is difficult unless one has some purpose or end in view. Methods are means, *planned* ways with which one works on data and/or experience in order to accomplish the purposes. Methods don't exist in a void and must necessarily relate to the selected content being used.

Basically, there are two general "methods" which a teacher can use although the two operate on a continuum and are seldom, if ever, completely divorced one from the other. The first general method is when a teacher has decided the purposes, processes the data and experiences he believes are related to the purposes, and then imparts the "products" of his labor to the students. His method of teaching, therefore, is a *means* directed at having students get the product which comes from the teacher's having worked on data and experience.

The second general method is when purposes have been decided, and the teacher shares with the students the processing of data and experience and the evaluating of products (teacher's and students') which come from working on data and experience.

In both general areas "inquiry" has been used. In the first, it was used to some extent by the teacher. In the second, it was used to some extent by the teacher and his students.

In both general areas the inquiry involved the use of data. The difference between the two general methods rests not with whether or not inquiry has been used but rather with who uses the inquiry. The difference does not rest on one method's using data and on the other's paying little concern to data. Rather, *both* are based on data. The difference is encountered when one assesses who uses the data.

THE METHOD

We are suggesting that inquiry is not *a* method. It is *the* method of processing experience. The question is simply one of who uses the method — the teacher, the students, or both? Inquiry is "the application of purpose to data in order to develop useful knowledge."[6] In this sense, inquiry is a relatively natural human

---

[6]Barry K. Beyer, "Using Inquiry in the Social Studies — Guidelines for Teaching." Monography Cooperative Center for Social Science Education, Ohio University, 1968, p. 6.

way of learning to engage and use the environment. It is human in the sense that it involves purpose, processing direct and indirect experience, and seeks some form of application in solving problems.

How does this relatively natural human activity take place? The following examples may help to clarify activity that we "just do" — activity that is commonplace, taken for granted, natural — in that we don't think about the processes in which we are engaged.

Suppose you are taking a course in social studies education. You have been given the title of the text to be used in the course. You wonder whether or not you should buy it or whether you might, on occasion, take it out from the library. A friend comments that the prof makes specific assignments from the text. You go to the bookstore, look in the aisle marked "Education," find the section carrying social studies material, locate the books under the course number and check the title. You notice that some books are new and some are used — the latter being reduced in price. You weigh the difference in price and contemplate if the used copy will suffice in terms of extent of previous use, extent to which the text will be used, and whether or not there may be use made of the text even after the course is completed. Will the money saved be worth it?

When you stop to think about it, the processes involved become quite obvious. There were a number of purposes involved. You gathered data, accepted cues, formed hypotheses, weighed alternatives, raised some questions, got additional data, and eventually made a decision. The processes did *not* follow a nice, neat sequential flow. And, you didn't just "buy a book" but rather you went through a number of *related* activities — activities that seem quite habitual, quite natural.

The professor could have arranged to have all the new texts brought to class for on-the-spot purchase. How might this have changed the processes you followed?

Suppose that the professor in your social studies course said that he didn't care what specific texts you bought for the course just as long as you purchased two — one dealing with social studies methods and a second dealing with social studies resources. You have something you are going to do. But it is not specific. You wonder what alternatives you have. You wonder about relative costs — and whether or not you might buy one and the person next to you the second. But how's the prof planning to use them. He's new to the faculty. But he must have determined some range of alternatives in order to have the bookstore order a variety of books. The titles may suggest his focus of interest. How does one determine the best or the best at the lowest price? Someone comments that those who get to the store first will have a wider range of choice; but you have a prearranged appointment after class. The appointment will hold so you go to the bookstore and end up in a mathematics section. Your eye picks up titles on the way to the social studies section and between trigonometry and plane geometry titles you observe a book with the title *Social Inquiry*. You thumb through the volume. It seems to deal with social studies methods and content. Why is it in the middle of the mathematics texts? Would the one volume suffice? You carry it with you to the social studies section. Most of your classmates apparently got there first. Very few alternatives are left. Should you pick up two of the remaining texts or should you purchase the single volume? Better call the professor in order to make sure. The phone is past the cashier. You put the single volume in with the English texts.

Again, you have gone through a number of related activities: questions, data, sub-problems, decisions, more data which might extend the possible alternatives, new immediate problems — always with some purpose, some data, some intent to apply.

Whenever you want to do something, resolve an issue, answer a question, make a decision, you are involved in inquiry. Another way of putting it is that you are involved in the processes of conceptualizing experience in a meaningful way — a way that allows you to *use* your experience.

The intended application or purpose of inquiry may be something of great importance or some small item of immediate interest; deciding to get married or whether or not to go to a particular movie. Regardless of which category we are addressing, the processes are essentially the same. And data is used.

The fact that our own functioning with experience seems so natural may minimize the importance our inquiry or conceptualizing processes appear to have. If, however, these processes are a prelude to application, and application or use of knowledge has consequences for ourselves and others, concern with how effectively and efficiently we conceptualize and concern with the products of the conceptualizing — concepts — would seem to be a vital issue in education.

Education methods are *planned* ways to effectively work on data or experience. The educational Method is Inquiry. When applied to social studies education, we find Inquiry using the data located in the social science disciplines and in the social studies disciplines of history and the humanities. Social science education allows a unique opportunity to use the data and findings of the disciplines to better understand the related activities involved in the Inquiry process. It is unique in that the content helps one to better understand the processes; the processes are some of the data and findings at work. Perhaps this is what John Goodlad meant when he wrote: "The study of education is nothing more than a study of man from still another perspective . . . the nature of knowledge and knowing, the individual and groups, learning and teaching..." resulting in no sharp differentiation between the study of education and the study of behavior.[7]

INQUIRY AND TEACHING OF INQUIRY

There is a substantial difference between inquiry and the *teaching of* inquiry. Because inquiry is "natural" it does not necessarily follow that the processes used to work on data and experience are effective or efficiently managed. For example, a youngster who enters the portals of kindergarten is able to inquire and, in fact, does! He has problems and/or things he wants to do. He gathers data, tests it, and applies it. In short, he conceptualizes the way things are and the way he can operate on his environment. To be sure, his levels of conceptualizing and his conceptualizations may not be too sophisticated. They may not be relatively effective or efficient. He comes to school to become more effective and more efficient at inquiring—to refine his *own* Method. To simply give this youngster products of inquiry done by others would deny him the opportunity to become better able to process his own life experience. It would short-circuit continued learning and growth. To simply let students experience without reflecting upon purposes, without manipulating experience and data, and without learning about the dimensions involved in the use of knowledge, denies students the opportunity to become mature, reasonable, and rational human beings. It too, short-circuits continued learning and growth.

To teach inquiry is to plan and implement ways by which a student becomes increasingly more effective and efficient in identifying purposes, in conceptualizing, and in putting his concepts to work. This sometimes is interpreted as meaning that a teacher structures a mechanical and step-by-step approach to inquiring and thus provides a student with a "set" sequence to what one does when in the process of conceptualizing or inquiring. For example, one finds almost a scientific model of the phases involved:

1. A person assesses the specific purpose or purposes involved, refines and clarifies the purposes, and makes such purposes manageable guides for the next phases of inquiry.
2. One then formulates a hypothesis or hypotheses which may satisfy the purposes that have been identified.

---

[7]John I. Goodlad, "How Do We Learn?" *Saturday Review*, June 21, 1969.

3. Data is now collected and classified in an attempt to test the hypotheses.
4. Using the data, one generalizes and forms concepts.
5. The concepts are then applied to satisfying the purposes which initiated the inquiry. If satisfied, the interacting inquiry processes are concluded in terms of the specific purposes. If not satisfying, some form of inquiry is then continued.

The above are considered to be major phases or categories which subsume the inquiring activities. But, phases do *not* imply sequential steps. The pitfall in making the leap from phase to stage is not unlike assuming that the form of *reporting* research, done by researchers, equals the flow of inquiry—how the problem was actually solved.

DEDUCING INDUCTION

For centuries education has been viewed as primarily a *deductive* process. The teacher formed the major concepts, followed his own inquiry, and then passed on the products of his activity to the students. Moving from the already determined end, the teacher would provide data which supported the conclusion of *his* efforts. Naturally not all teachers were equally sophisticated about inquiring and sometimes they acted as simply "middle-men" for passing on the products of inquiry having been done by other scholars. The primary point, however, was that the major concepts were literally "givens" as far as the students were concerned.

The last few decades have witnessed a swing away from the purely deductive approach to teacher planning and implementation. In the zest to challenge the deductive approach, the pendulum swung to the extreme of purely *inductive* approach—one which found the teacher and the students working with discrete bits of data, conceptualizing the relationships among the data into concepts, and then, in some way, finding "transfer" or application.

In the deductive approach, the main concept is given and one moves to find supportive data. In the inductive approach, one starts with the data and constructs the concept.

The use of the inductive approach, in its "pure" form, theoretically was believed to be justified in terms of the scientific method. The youngster would discover for himself the relationships among data which he would put into a stated concept. The inductive approach implied the steps or stages one followed in inquiry. The processes of interacting activities involved emerged as being viewed in a linear, sequential pattern. In other words, there was a move from phase to stage—a move which denied what people actually *do* in the process of inquiring.

It would be relatively easier for teachers to plan and to implement if the processes of inquiring were discrete stages and if the stages followed in sequential order. Unfortunately, it is not this easy. The activities involved in inquiry (in the processes involved in a person's conceptualizing) are complex and dynamic, constantly interacting with and modifying one another, and are not neatly compartmentalized.

An awareness of the above raises some issues regarding whether or not inquiry appears in any pure form—whether or not deductive approaches or inductive approaches warrant being separated and practiced at the exclusion of the other. When one thinks about what he is doing in the act of inquiring, he recognizes that he is using both inductive *and* deductive activities depending upon the time, situation, data available, or nature of the problem being addressed. Even within the *phases* of inquiring, one moves back and forth between deduction and induction. This is significant when planning inquiry experiences for students.

Having a student discover relationships among data and state the relationships in conceptual form, seems to imply that the activity is primarily inductive: a student works with data, relates data, and discovers the concept which is somehow to be applied. In reality, it is not this clean.

For example, a student may have a concept and deductively find data to support the concept and to reinforce its retention. He comes across a piece of data or an experience which challenges the concept. Some other data are encountered and these also do not support the retention of the concept in its existing form. At this point the student may begin to move inductively. He may relate the new data to one or more concepts which force his modification of the original "given" and thus lend to the need to test the newly formed relationships. That this is done naturally may be seen in the following example:

LIVING WITH QUICK DECISIONS

One is driving down a city thoroughfare. There are two lanes of traffic moving in each direction. The inside lanes move more slowly, what with buses periodically stopping at various corners. The driver stays in the fast-moving lane. He wants to continue driving straight through, neither desiring to turn left nor right at any intersection.

Looking ahead, the driver observes a signal light which is registered as being red. A red light means that he will have to stop. The driver wants to maintain his driving with the least amount of delays.

The car directly in front has its left-turn signal flashing. When the light turns green, the front car won't be able to turn until all the traffic from the other direction has moved through the light. How much traffic is moving the opposite way? The driver observes a number of vehicles already stopped at the light—enough to suggest that if he stays behind the car turning left he might be forced to stop not for one light but perhaps even for a second. What are the alternatives? The driver appraises the slower-moving inside lane. In this situation it may be slower in one sense but definitely faster for him.

He notices that the bus on the inside lane just made the light and is proceeding to a more distant intersection. The driver checks the rear-view mirror to see the number of cars behind him, and in the inside lane. If he changes to the inside lane, can he possibly get through the next green light? He looks again in the mirror and judges the speed and flow of the cars behind him. He starts to make his move to the right lane when he notices that the number of cars in the right lane, stopped for the red light he is approaching, is longer than he thought—long enough to cause some doubt. He notices a car in the right lane attempting to move into his own lane. He notices some flashing car lights blinking "caution". A car must be stalled or in trouble in the inside lane.

He slows and lets the car into his lane assuming that the car would not make a left turn and assuming that the driver left his original lane because of the stalled car.

The driver decides to stay in his lane and risk that although the car now two cars in front will be delayed, the delay would not be as long as it would if he were stuck behind the car in trouble in the right-hand lane. The decision is reinforced by the fact that the broken lines allowing lane change are now solid indicating, that at this place, he must stay in his original lane.

The driver slows down hoping for the change in the light before he has to come to a complete stop. Perhaps after he passes the stalled car he can swing over to the right lane and make the green light—at least he would know that no one would be coming up from behind on the right lane. Perhaps this is what the vehicle immediately in front of him plans to do—this might pose problems.

Most of us have done this type of inquiring. We do it so fast and so naturally that it seems to be done in a thoughtless way. Not at all. The processes were thoughtful. They may have been thoughtless if the driver just decided to make the change in lanes without getting any data and without testing the hypotheses he was forming in the situation.

Check back to what the driver did in evolving his plans for action. And note that his planning for action did not have consequences until he made a decision and took action—in this case, decided to remain in his original lane of traffic. What was the driver's immediate purpose? How many different hypotheses were formed? At what different points was he gathering and using data? Did the data force any revisions and modifications? Was there a neat pattern to his inquiring activity or did the driver constantly find his conceptualizing necessitated moving in and out of the different phases as he formed and re- formed concepts? Was his process of inquiry *strictly* inductive? *Strictly* deductive? Or did he mesh inductive and deductive thinking?

THE CHICKEN OR THE EGG

What does the mini-case study of twenty seconds of a driver's life suggest to the teacher? It suggests the importance of purpose in determining the processes to be used in selecting, relating, weighing, and using data. And it suggests that the products or concepts developed have consequences when applied in the arena of action. (One might ponder what role the emotional factors might play if, for example, the driver were trying to make the hospital in time for his wife to deliver a first-born child?) It further suggests, that if we could capture a slowed-down version of human functioning much as we can do in photographing a speeded-up version of the growth and blooming of a flower, we might find definite implications for teacher planning and implementation.

We are familiar with the "which comes first, the chicken or the egg" game. This sometimes is found involved in assessing teaching methods. Some people insist that a student must have the "facts first" *before* he can even pretend to get a product or to develop concepts. This type of insistence makes several assumptions: (1) the processes involved in inquiring are sequential; (2) there is one definite and set product or concept to be derived— that, in a sense, purposes do not change as one works on experience; (3) the relevant data, having its predetermined criteria, is also predetermined; and (4) the major thrust of inquiring is primarily that of deductive approach in which a teacher determines the purpose, concepts, and data, and that these are presented as "givens" within which a student is to function.

On the other hand, some will argue that everyone comes to any new problem or situation with a mind full of concepts which are to be used ("transfer") and tested. The argument runs that the existing concepts influence even the formulation of purposes, the screening of new data and experience, and the organization and relationships among the new data and between newly formulated concepts and those previously held. It is held that a person has concepts *before* the raw facts are entertained and used, that the concepts and purposes may be modified by the use of data, that the criteria emerges, and that the main thrust of inquiring is neither deductive nor inductive but rather *both* working in association in facilitating inquiring.

The teacher's role in planning and implementing instructional experiences is not a simplistic "either-or" condition. The "facts vs. concept" teaching skirmish encountered by social studies teachers is a dichotomous position which tends to ignore the *relationship* between the chicken and the egg. Which comes first is rather moot. Separate and disjointed, neither exists.

What you may realize at this point is that inquiry is a complex process. Perhaps this is why most teachers avoid it like the plague. No longer can the teacher rely upon memory as the only mental process required of the student. No longer can the teacher rely upon simply teaching facts or chronology. No longer can the teacher rely upon the book as the only source of data. No longer can the teacher rely upon the lecture as the only means of presenting data. No longer is coverage of content sufficient!

Teachers must now ask questions about what concepts he will teach. Teachers must understand and develop relationships between concepts and factual data, using more than the text or chronological ordering of the world. Content is not to be seen as static, added to only because it is a new year of history but because content is simply a way of organizing data. Planning strategies now must involve deciding not only what data will be used but how to get students using data to formulate and test concepts.

We are in the process of passing from the old to the new. In such a transition we are not throwing out the past but using it in different ways. The following case study concerning the concepts of Peace-War-Protest illustrates the above.

PEACE – WAR – PROTEST

FOCUS IDEAS

1. When people wage war, the casualties go beyond those who die or who are wounded.

2. Some people claim that war is found in the nature of man. Others claim that war is learned and thus can be unlearned.

3. People may be opposed to war for completely different reasons. It is difficult to know the reasons behind what a person or group of people do.

4. The reason why a nation goes to war is usually a combination of many factors.

5. All parties involved in any war have always claimed that their actions were "right" and justifiable.

6. Peace movements have encountered the issue of whether or not it is ever justified to use violence and physical resistance to accomplish their objectives.

7. It is possible to predict what a whole population thinks by studying one small and representative part of the whole.

8. Common sense may just be a personal conviction without support of evidence.

9. An individual person or a group of people may have an idea that is believed to be good and sound. But to act upon the idea, they must take into account what other people believe.

10. If what one thinks and what one does are not consistent, the value of one's ideas may be judged by the person's actions and not by his ideas.

STUDENT MATERIAL[8]

War! Human beings fighting human beings in some organized and planned way. Some say that war has been around as long as people. Some say that war is "natural" and that nation fighting nation grew out of the same reasons that an individual will fight

---

[8]*Idea sources:*
James R. Shirley, "War Protest in Wartime," *New Republic*, May 6, 1967.
Alice Felt Tyler, *Freedom's Ferment*, Harper Torchback.
Philip Converse and Howard Suchman, "Silent Majorities" and the Vietnam War, *Scientific American*, June, 1970.
U.S. Department of Defense, *The History of U.S. Decision Making Process on Vietnam Policy* (as reported in New York Times).

another individual—to protect an idea or thing or to get something that is wanted. Others say that war is *not* something that man has deep within him. They say that man *learns* reasons for fighting and that if something can be learned, it can also be unlearned. No matter what one thinks causes war, most people agree that they do not like or want war.

The casualties of war are people. Usually casualties are listed as those who have died, been killed, or physically wounded. Seldom do people think of other kinds of casualties. What about attitudes of people, the cost of war not only in money but in constructive things people could have instead—schools, hospitals, clean environment, jobs, research, improved cities, health, and a lot of other things?

The United States has been involved in wars. As a matter of fact thirteen percent of the American population today are "veterans" of some war!

And there have been those Americans who have died, been killed or been wounded in wars.

Total U.S. Casualties°

REVOLUTIONARY WAR (1775–1783)...................... 10,600
WAR OF 1812 (1812–1815)....................................... 6,800
MEXICAN WAR (1846–1848) 18,000
CIVIL WAR (1861–1865) (North and South) 808,000
SPANISH-AMERICAN WAR (1898) 4,100
WORLD WAR I (1917–1918) 320,500
WORLD WAR II (1941–1946) 1,076,200
KOREAN WAR (1950–1953)..................................... 157,500

°Estimates. For example, the Confederacy did not issue figures so these are estimates.

Of course, there is one war that is not included because it is still going on. According to estimates of casualties:

VIETNAM (1961——) (estimate) 165,000

If one thinks of casualties as those killed and wounded and those who died by disease or accident, over 3,000,000 Americans have been casualties of war since Revolutionary times. And approximately one-fifth, or 20 per cent, of American history has involved war.

The American story probably is not very different from that of other countries. Concern over war is obvious. Besides the statistics, a person meets war through motion pictures, books, poems, plays, television programs, newspapers and magazines, pictures, and in toy departments. And yet, most people say that they do not like or want war!

The Vietnam war appears to be the longest period of fighting conflict in the history of the United States. How the United States got involved is complex. It involves Japan, France, the "Cold War", an attitude towards communism, China, the role of the U.S. Congress, the role of several U.S. Presidents, alliances, and the desires and attitudes of the American people. A 3,000 page study (plus 4,000 more pages of documents) has been made by the Pentagon. This study tries to show how the United States committed itself to non-communist Vietnam, how the U.S. moved from "advising" the non-communist Vietnamese to actively fighting in the war, and why the war has dragged on for such a long a time.

Mentioned in the Pentagon Study are comments by Assistant Secretary of Defense John T. McNaughton, not about how but *why* the United States was involved in South Vietnam in 1964. In trying to give *several* reasons and to give each reason a level of importance, he used percentages.

70 per cent to avoid a humiliating U.S. defeat.

20 per cent to keep the South Vietnam and near-by areas from falling into the hands of the Chinese.

10 per cent to permit the people of South Vietnam to enjoy a better, freer way of life.

This all was to be done in such a way that the United States would not be questioned about the methods it used. Mr. McNaughton said that the United States was not really in South Vietnam to "help a friend." (Sometimes even the reasons for doing things change as one gets involved in the doing.) The *what*, the *how*, and the *why* of war are as complex as a human being!

We all know that some people protest the United States being in the war. Does the following sound familiar?

What War?

Over 70,000 American troops are involved in an undeclared war half-way around the world. It is a dirty little war. Both sides have resorted to the use of terror. One American officer did not get court-martialed for allegedly killing a priest under torture because the officer's enlistment time ended. An American gunboat captain misread his orders and shelled a friendly village, killing and wounding civilians. The mistake was suppressed by the military.

In the United States, the Americans are bitterly divided. One well-known author suggests that Americans fly a new flag "with white stripes painted black, and the stars replaced by a skull and crossbones." A national magazine calls the American actions "barbarism. . . bringing disgrace upon the American name and civilization." A black editor writes that it is "a sinful extravagance to waste our civilizing influence. . . when it [is] so badly needed right here [at home]." Opponents of the war include political leaders, members of the business community, and labor leaders.

An American general reports to a Senate Committee that the native population was opposed to the revolutionary government. Few people in government really think that stalling the revolution will bring freedom, peace, or democracy.

A few Americans want the war. An Assistant Secretary of the Navy orders a naval Commander to attack, under certain circumstances. The order is kept secret from the President. The same Assistant Secretary of the Navy instructs Henry Cabot Lodge that there is fear the war will end too soon. "You must prevent any talk of peace. . .," he writes.

A Senator makes a speech about China's large markets. "The Pacific is the ocean of trade in the future and most future wars will be conflicts of commerce." The senator justifies the American position because the United States is the "trustee of the civilization of the world."

A general reports that it might be necessary to kill half the population in order to save the other half.

The President prays for guidance. He concludes that it is our responsibility to uplift and to help people to live a good life.

Arguments rage at home. The President is reported as saying that if we pulled out, we would be humiliated before the world and that we would lose prestige with the Orientals. We have to face the issue of national honor and fulfill our obligation to the nations of the world.

Two American generals write home that the protesters at home were giving confort to the enemy and were prolonging the war. One said: "continuance of the fighting is chiefly due to reports that are sent out from America."

The leader of the revolutionary forces later says that his side had hoped that the American people would demand the end to the war. Not just because they would tire of the cost, in blood and money, but because "the basic [ideas] on which the American government was founded were being violated and denied in the [war]."

Sound familiar? Go back to the Philippines around 1900! Go back to the Assistant Secretary of the Navy, Teddy Roosevelt. Go back to President McKinley who said: "I walked the floor of the White House night after night until midnight. . . I went down on my knees and prayed Almighty God for light and guidance. . . And one night it came to me this way. . . . We could give the Philippines back to Spain but that would be cowardly and dishonorable. We could turn them over to other countries but that might hurt us in our business dealings. We could leave them alone but they were unfit for self-government. There was nothing left to do so. . . ."

CONCERN WITH WAR AND PROTEST

Concern with war and concern with protests over war are not new. Seventy years after the Philippines, the concerns are still with us. Only now we have the tools to get at what some of the protests might mean. Is it possible that people protesting war could be protesting for *different* reasons? Is it possible to support the war and still protest? Is it possible to say that one wants to stop the war and that this can be done by *escalating* (increasing) the war and *not* by pulling out?

Since 1961, the people of the United States have been *sampled* in order to try to find out what they think about the Vietnam War and what they think should be done. You have probably received "samples" in the grocery store—for example, when you are given one cookie as a "sample," you are being given a cookie that tastes like all other cookies. It has the same ingredients. By sampling a very small part, one can tell about all the rest. The odds are in your favor. If you like the one cookie, the chances are good that the other cookies will taste the same way. When people are sampled it means that a small group of people (say, 1,500) closely resemble the rest of the 100,000,000 adults in the country. The sample has to be selected carefully so that different ages, educational levels, occupations, geographic areas, sexes, and so on, are the same as though the whole population was broken into parts. If you get the right sample, you can predict what the whole is thinking. This is what polling is all about. The polls are usually reported from time to time in newspapers and magazines.

The taking of polls is hard. Social scientists have to be very careful about selecting samples. And they have to be very careful about the way questions are worded. For example, to think of Americans as being "hawks" or "doves" is just as misleading as any effort to label whole groups of people. In one poll a hawk was defined as anyone who believes the U.S. did right in trying to stop communism in Asia and who believes the nation should accelerate (increase) its efforts to win a military victory. Think. The definition has *two* parts. Is it possible to believe *one* part and not the other? Doves were people who thought the United States was wrong in getting involved in Vietnam in the first place and who want an immediate withdrawal (leave Vietnam). Think. Again there are two parts. The terms hawk and dove may not tell us much!

POLL TAKING

As a matter of fact, a survey of polls taken over the past ten years found that those people viewing the war as a mistake were split: almost as many favored escalation as withdrawal. Most of those opposed to the United States getting involved in the first place, actually wanted a stronger stand—even using military forces to invade North Vietnam.

And people answer according to events. When asked if they favored U.S. stopping of bombing, 40 per cent said yes; 51 per cent said no. One month later President Johnson announced a decision to halt the bombing. Polls found that 64 per cent of the people *favored* his decision; 25 per cent did not. The survey of polls taken shows that support of the President *rises* after he tries anything new or different—it makes no difference if his move is for escalation *or* withdrawal. People seem to support *some* action, no matter what.

Do you think most of the polls found the following?
1. The more attention a person pays to the Vietnam war, the more likely he will favor getting out.
2. College educated people are more likely to protest our staying in Vietnam than are people with less education.
3. Young adults seem to favor getting out of Vietnam while older people tend to want to stay there and win.
4. Women tend to want to stay in Vietnam and try to win. White males favor getting out.

Most people will guess that the samples over ten years show that the above describes how parts of the American population think. But, in each of the above four groups, the finding was just the opposite! People will say that it is common sense that women don't have to fight in the war so they would not oppose it as much as men. But sometimes common sense doesn't fit with the facts.

What the polls seem to have found out is that there are *two* parts of the American population that oppose the war. The first part is very small. It is made up of well-educated people who have the ability to be seen and heard. They object to the war because they think it is "wrong" and because they believe it is inhuman. The second part is much larger and is less educated than the average American. It doesn't speak much. It just appears to be growing tired of the war: "we haven't won and it doesn't look like we will" attitude. They feel that the sledgehammer can't crack the walnut.

Not to realize that there are two different groups opposing the war for two different reasons can cause confusion. The two groups are different. They don't communicate with one another. And the larger group doesn't like people to protest and dissent in the "streets." 63 per cent of those not favoring a continuation of the war didn't approve of the way objection to the war was made. Opposition to the war and opposition to active protest are *not* two different things! The polls suggest that protests in the streets may actually work against what the protesters say they want. Some argue that the protests do keep the issues alive.

WAR HAS CONCERNED MAN THROUGHOUT HISTORY

Writing almost 400 years before the birth of Christ, Plato, the Greek Philosopher, said:

But our. . . society. . . must be ready, if need be, to wage successful war. Our model community would of course be pacific (peaceful) but neighboring states not like ours might look upon our ways as an invitation to attack. While being sorry about the need, we shall have. . . a sufficient number of well-trained soldiers. At the same time we shall take every precaution to avoid war. The first cause is overpopulation; the second is foreign trade. Indeed competitive trade is really a form of war. . . peace is only a name. . .

Voltaire, writing in the 1700's, said that "patriotism. . . commonly means. . . that one hates every country but one's own. . . War is the greatest of all crimes; and yet there is no aggressor who does not color his crime with the pretext of justice. It is forbidden to kill; therefore all murderers are punished unless they kill in large numbers and to the sound of trumpets. Twenty years are required for a man to grow so his reason begins to make itself felt. Thirty centuries are necessary in which to discover even a little of his structure. An eternity would be required to know anything of his soul. But one moment suffices in which to kill a man."

Another writer in the 18th century said that "Our rulers have no money to spend on public education. . . because all their resources are already placed to the account of the next war. . ."

Americans also showed concern.

1783: Benjamin Franklin: "there was never a good war or a bad peace."
1793: Benjamin Rush wanted to establish a Secretary of Peace. Free schools would come under the Secretary's authority. The schools would stress the importance of human life. All military uniforms, titles, and equipment were to be abolished. There would be a Peace Office. Over the door would be a lamb, dove, and olive branch. The motto: "Peace on earth—Good Will to

Men." If there was a Secretary of War, why not a Secretary of Peace?

1815: First Peace Society founded in the world. New York City. Those who wage war find that the best thing being said when they are accused is "doing evil that good may come."

1815: Massachusetts Peace Society. By 1819 there were seventeen chapters throughout the land. Wars were said to be caused by false patriotism, passion for power, greed, love of excitement—only education could be a remedy. Jefferson became an honorary member. John Adams refused, saying: "Universal and perpetual peace appear to me no more or less than ever lasting passive obedience and non-resistance. The human flock would soon be fleeced and butchered by one or a few. I cannot, therefore, sir, be a subscriber or a member of your society."

1837: William L. Garrison gave space in the *Liberator* to the peace movement. He held that in no case could physical resistance be allowable either individually or collectively. Yet, when faced with the issue of slavery, Garrison approved the violence of John Brown at Harper's Ferry. (Moral issues at home forced some revision of thinking.)

1838: Ralph Waldo Emerson gave an *Address on War.* "All history teaches wise men to put trust in ideas, and not circumstances." He said you can't get peace by legislation but only through strong private conviction: ". . . the cause of peace is not the cause of cowardice. . ." A few years later he changed his position, saying that he did not want to give up a privilege such as the use of the sword or the bullet. "For the peace of the man who has forsworn the use of the bullet seems to me not quite peace."

1846: Henry David Thoreau refused to pay taxes to a government that tolerated slavery and war. In 1848 he published his essay *Civil Disobedience* in which he said that a government became a form of tyranny when it denied the right of the individual to be responsible for his own.

Mexican War: Theodore Parker, talking about war, said that "We can refuse to take any part in it; we can encourage others to do the same; we can aid men, if need be, who suffer because they refuse. Men will call us traitors; what then? That hurt nobody in '76. We are a rebellious nation; our whole history is treason.

A $500 prize was offered for the best essay on the Mexican War.

An *Address Movement* was started. British cities and American cities were "impaired" and exchanged views on peace. New York with Manchester, Philadelphia with Exeter. This was a protest movement with international ties.

The leader, Elihu Burritt, wrote that "Peace is a spirit. . . it is life, not a theory."

1848–1852: Four international peace conferences were held. The American writer Horace Greeley attended some of the meetings and found it unreal:

". . . suppose there is a portion of the human family who *won't have Peace*, nor let others have it, what then? If you say 'let us have it as soon as we can,' I respond with all my heart. I would tolerate war, even against pirates and murderers, no longer than is absolutely necessary to inspire them with a love of Peace, or put them where they can no longer invade the peace of others. But so long as Tyrants. . . say. . . as they now practically *do* say. . . 'Yes, we too are for Peace, but it must be Peace with absolute submission. . . a Peace which leaves the Millions in darkness, in hopeless degradation, the slaves of superstition, and the hopeless victims of our lusts.' I answer, 'No Sirs! on your conditions no Peace is possible, but everlasting war rather, until your unjust pretentions are abandoned or until your power of enforcing them is destroyed.' "

There were wars: The Crimean War, the Polish Revolution, the Civil War, wars to unify Italy and Germany. . . and others.

War seems to be like the weather. Everybody talks about it but nobody does anything about it. Well, at least we have started to bring the weather under control. Who knows, when peace is not just an idea and casualties are not just statistics — who knows?

STUDENT QUESTIONS

How would you define war?

Do you think that war is "natural" for man and that there always will be war? Or do you think that man learns the reasons for war and that these reasons can be changed? Do you have any evidence for your answers?

Do you think that just because something has existed for a long time that it is necessarily good?

In what different ways can one view the casualties of war?

In how many different ways do you encounter war in your daily life?

Can you give examples of how different people may do the same thing for completely opposite reasons? Why is it hard to assign motives to what a person does?

If you were asked to explain what the term "sample" means, how would you respond?

Can you think up a question that includes two parts and in which one could give different answers to each part? If one really wants information that is accurate, what must one think about in order to ask good questions?

When you hear the terms "hawk" and "dove," what do you think? Are there any other words that seem to place people into categories in an unfair way?

Can you think of situations in which the use of common sense might lead to doing the wrong thing?

Why do you think that it is important for people to be able to predict what other people think, want, and will do?

If you had to give *one* major reason which most people in peace movements use against having war, what would the reason be? And, if one had to give *one* reason why some people say that they want peace but it isn't the way things are, what reason would you give?

Would you agree with Theodore Parker that America's whole history has been one of treason? What evidence could you use to support or deny Parker's view of the whole U.S. history?

Can you give an example in which an individual was judged by what he did and not by what he said? What is a person saying when he comments: "I don't like the author as a person and therefore his books are terrible!"?

If you were to set up a Department of Peace, how would you determine who should head it, what it should do, and how it should be funded?

What is meant by the term "undeclared war"?

STUDENT ACTIVITIES

1. The written material contains information on wars in which the United States was involved, the total number of casualties since the Colonial period, the time spent at war, etc. Try to get the same kinds of information about two other "large world national powers" and determine similarities and differences when comparing the United States with the other two countries.

2. Try to prepare an opinion poll of your school. All the students in the school are to be considered the "whole" population. What must you do when:

    A. Trying to determine the questions to ask?
    B. Trying to determine a sample?
    C. Trying to interpret the results?

(Try to make your opinion poll deal with the issues of war and peace.)

3. The story dealing with the United States and the Philippines might make one think of some of the problems the United States has faced in Vietnam. Try to find *specific* ways in which the U.S. role in Philippines and in Vietnam are similar and *specific* ways in which they are different.

4. The material says that a person "meets" the faces of war in a number of different ways. Locate:
    A. Two books that deal with war.
    B. Two poems that deal with war.
    C. Two motion pictures dealing with war.
    D. One drama or play that deals with war.
Select one of the above and explain how it deals with war. What does it say? What message is it trying to get across?
Make a study: Go to a toy store and make a list of toys that have something to do with war. What different interpretations can you make from your findings?

5. Make a list of the "conclusions" which the opinion polls seem to make about how different groups of people in the United States think about the Vietnam War and how it should be handled. Assume that you are the President. Using the conclusions, what strategy would you use to get people to support your position?

6. Plato, John Adams, and Horace Greeley all had doubts about ways to get peace. Look at what they said (at different times in history) and try to see what they based their doubts on. How might the three have reacted to Emerson's idea that "all history teaches wise men to put trust in ideas, and not circumstances."?

7. Using specific information, people, and quotations, build a case which either supports or denies the view that most people speaking out for peace *did* put trust

in ideas. Can you give an example of two people who changed their ideas when they faced a situation in which they had to make choices? (Example: Garrison)

8. It has been said that the casualties of war go beyond those who are killed and wounded in a war. Use your imagination. Suppose that during the last one hundred years, the people on earth had lived in peace. What might our world be like? (Think about such things as health, food, jobs, population, research; and think about what problems having peace might pose for man)

9. The material on peace, war and protest makes the following points:
   A. That the American people who follow the Vietnam War closely and who keep up on what is going on, seem to favor *not* having an immediate withdrawal.
   B. That with the exception of a small, well-educated group, most college educated people are *not* in favor of having an immediate withdrawal.
   C. That the idea of a "generation gap" does *not* seem to be in evidence when people voice their views about the Vietnam War.
   D. Women, more than white males, seem to favor withdrawing from Vietnam.

   Given the above points, try to give at least two reasons why the people in each category might think as they do.

10. Using the material, (and other information) try to make a list of reasons people give for having war. Then try to figure out if the reasons are "born in" man or if they are learned as he grows up.

The case study involves the following inquiry concepts:

SYNTHESIZING INQUIRY CONCEPTS:

1. Inquiry can be both a process of knowing *and* a process of teaching.

2. Inquiry, as a process of teaching, implies that learning is most effective when the learner is actively involved in more than just listening or reading.

3. Most people engage in inquiry during their everyday lives but usually do not engage in thinking about the processes involved in inquiring.

4. Inquiry involves both affective and cognitive dispositions; i.e., a student must understand the need for objectivity in the search for knowing and be willing to engage in such an objective search. This is more difficult than simply accepting the "products" of someone else's search.

5. Knowledge and a general awareness of a problem or a desired action is an initial aspect of inquiring. Such knowledge and general awareness may be a function of "intuition", happenstance, or formal structuring by the students and/or instructor.

6. Once a problem has been identified and refined, it must be determined whether or not the problem is relevant; i.e., are people willing to work at resolution because the resolution has some meaning for them.

7. Inquiry is not a set, sequenced, step-by-step approach to problem solving. It calls for a number of mutually influencing activities which complement one another in data collection and use, in hypothesizing, in application.

8. *Both* deductive and inductive reasoning are used in inquiry. Each form of thinking rules work in association with the other in the formation and testing of concepts.

9. A statement of a concept addresses the use of data and how the data is related. There are different kinds of concepts based on different kinds of evidence and serving different kinds of functions.

Perhaps you are still confused. Indeed this is a complex process. The following chapters attempt to clarify Concepts, the Use of Content, and how to plan for inquiry teaching.

"Oink, oink!"

"Arf, arf!"

2

A CONCEPT OF CONCEPTS

AN APPROACH TO CONCEPTUAL TEACHING

Most of us assume that our teaching is going to make a "difference" to our students. Or why go through all the effort? And why put the students through all the hurdles?

This idea of making a difference, in turn, assumes a number of things:

1. The student will learn things in our classes that he would not just pick-up if he never had attended school. In other words, we have something unique that we offer.

2. The unique thing that we offer our students is worthwhile. For having undergone studying with us, what he has learned will be of value to him. He will be better off because of the experience.

3. Being better off assumes something about what kind of a person the student will be and assumes something about his being able to do some things which he would not be able to do if he had not taken our course. In other words, he will change. He will change as a person and this means that he will be better able to do certain things.

4. We can't teach everything. We must select those things that will help bring about the desired changes. Thus, we must select *what* is to be taught, *how* it is to be taught, and what kinds of experiences will assist in relating the what with the how.

5. Implied in all this, is the view that education is a *means* and not an end in itself. Even the teacher who says simply that a "student must know" this and that, if pushed, will come up with a reason. "If he knows this, he will be a better educated person. . . he will be happier and have a better chance of living a full life." Simple as this may appear, most reasons for studying anything assume a *use*. They assume that the student will be able to *transfer* (or use) what he has learned as he lives in the world about him.

If teaching really makes a difference, one must ask of himself and his course, what am I teaching that can't be got anywhere? Why is it worthwhile? Why did I select this to teach and not that? And, does what I am teaching and how I am teaching help a student to make use of it—help him to transfer it to a future situation which we may not even be able to anticipate?

If a teacher allows herself to think about what she is doing, these questions are constant companions—a co-partner with conscience, an integral aspect of professional integrity.

A good number of teachers insist that their role is primarily that of teaching facts. A student should learn all the names of the presidents in order. First name, middle initial, last name, dates of occupancy, and party. It is argued that if they don't know the facts first, students will never be able to understand government, politics, American history. The argument usually rests upon an analogy. "After all, one has to have all the material—the bricks and the wood—before one can build a house." And that seems to end it!

One can play with the analogy but the key issue is a rather simple one: Wasn't there an *idea* of the house *before* specific kinds of material could be selected and used? Or do we simply collect bricks and then say we are going to build a house? Obviously, it is not "either/or". A general idea of available materials may influence one's idea of a house, and a general idea of a desired house may influence one's idea about materials and material use. The point is a rather simple one: Discrete piles of unrelated facts or information do *not* have to be collected first. The brick-house argument is a cop-out.

We have not said that bricks are unimportant: Only that some idea of how they are to be *used* may assist in their collection and use; some idea of how things *relate* may help bring a clearer view of the things themselves as well as a clear view of how to use them.

If a teacher is really concerned with the use (transfer) of what she is teaching, she may have to ask herself which will prove most functional for the student: information or ideas? If she pursues this far enough, she may find out that her response may *not* be an either/or choice.

Two things to note:
1. Ideas are tools.
2. The whole is greater than the sum of its parts.

Ideas may be abstract; that is, they may go beyond actual experience but an idea *does* influence what one does. Thus, ideas have consequences. In a sense, ideas are as real as any fact. And, they may be of greater importance because people seem to act in terms of their ideas about a situation more than in terms of the facts of a situation. As one sociologist said: If a person thinks a thing is real, it is real in terms of how he behaves. Most of our real world is abstract. Our very use of language and communication systems indicates the permeating importance.

When we talk about teaching *concepts,* we usually mean that we are teaching verbal statements about ideas. We are teaching abstractions.

Why the concern with teaching concepts? The concern certainly is not new. Perhaps there is a growing realization that we can't teach everything. To think that we can come close to teaching everything is naive, simplistic, and could be considered humorous if the attempts were not so seriously undertaken. We must teach concepts *and* use facts in the teaching.

WHAT DO CONCEPTS DO?

Why the concern with teaching concepts? What do concepts *do* for us? How are they tools? How does teaching concepts help meet the problem of the accumulated and accumulating proliferation of facts?

Concepts:

1. Assist in mentally organizing individual and discrete pieces of information by relating them into "wholes" or umbrella ideas.
2. Help an individual to interpret, screen, discover, and incorporate new information and experience.
3. Help an individual to think and to make sense out of his worlds and out of the changes he encounters.
4. In verbal form, help people communicate with one another. They also pose some problems in effective communicating.
5. Act as cues which help people to recall specifics when needed.
6. Act in helping human beings to order experiences by relating and providing meaning among and between seemingly separate data and experience.

In other words, concepts are *tools.* They are not ends in themselves. They assist in transfer. And they assist in further learning. *And, they have consequences for individual and social behavior.* Whatever a concept is, it serves a number of functions. If a teacher looks at the functions served, concept teaching can assist in organizing and planning teaching. It can bring a focus to the use of content with teaching methods.

If a student knows the sources of concepts, how they are created, and how they can be effectively used in situations other than the classroom, he learns to have more control over his own experiencing.

CONCEPTS: FACTS WITH FACTS

But, concepts don't just exist. They are put together with facts and experience. The facts and experience are the raw material. As the raw material is organized and related, the concept emerges and stands for the organization and the relationships. In this sense the concept is abstract, and it is greater than the sum of its parts. It goes beyond just the facts. If facts don't speak for themselves, at least a concept tries to whisper. How the parts are put together to form a concept is called inductive reasoning: the moving from *particulars* to a broader, over-riding, and inclusive relationship of the particulars. How a concept is tested and checked in order to see if the particulars do lead to the stated relationship is called deductive reasoning.

Relating Ideas With Facts. Building and testing concepts is an activity that seems quite "natural." For example: We are alone in a house. A door slams shut. Fact: no one else is in the house. Fact: it is gusty and windy outside. Fact: a window opposite the door that slammed is open. Fact: the curtains are blowing helter-skelter. We know the door has slammed and we may well relate all four facts and conclude that the door was blown shut by the wind. The facts were put together in a very simple concept of cause-effect relationships in a specific situation. It is so simple and "natural" that we often are not aware of the thinking processes we use.

Sometimes concepts are much more complex and try to be inclusive of many facts and relationships; for example, Herbert Spencer's concept of social change approximating a physical theory of evolution.

But, in both cases, the processes are fairly similar. One observes, forms guesses, classifies and collects data, and describes relationships among and between the "parts."

The terms "understand" and "explain" suggest some kind of a *relationship* which satisfies or puts us at ease with a new experience or new information which previously had not fit in or been related to what we previously thought, believed, or knew. What we are saying is that satisfaction rests on our perceived consistent relationship of something with something else.

Teachers live with this idea of relationships and explanations. We are told that teaching begins with where the student is and this implies that the student brings something (experiences or information) *to* the learning process. How the student relates what he brings to the "new" which the teacher makes available is involved in the learning process. This is as true of adults as it is of a third grade youngster. When a problem is resolved or when our curiosity is satisfied, the explanation is accepted and meaningful to the extent that resolution or satisfaction occurs. Both resolution and satisfaction involve relationships of the past with the new.

To say, "I have the idea," is another way of saying, I see how these particular items are related. The new relationship is a concept which may suffice until new situations or new data are encountered which no longer allow the luxury of satisfaction.

CONCEPTUALIZING PROCESSES

Let us imagine how the relationships might take place. I see an electric box hanging over an intersection of roads. When the box shows a red light the vehicles moving in certain directions stop. Thus, a red light and vehicles stopping are two facts which I have observed. I check my observations for another ten minutes and it appears that when the light is red, vehicles stop. The light has changed four times in the ten minutes and the facts of red light and stopped vehicles appear related. I may then form a concept which states the relationship. At this *particular* intersection, when the light turns red vehicles stop.

Then I go to another intersection and notice a similar relationship between the light and the traffic. The concept stating the relationship is the same. Then, *I relate the two concepts* and come forth with a more *inclusive* abstract thought: Vehicles stop when there is a red light.

But, as this concept is emerging I run into some problems. A vehicle making a loud sound does *not* stop at the red light but goes through it. The new data makes the old explanation no longer satisfying. The moving vehicle with the sound was also colored red. Can I relate the data and say that vehicles making a loud sound go through the red light? Can I say that red vehicles can go through red lights? Can I say that red vehicles making loud sounds can go through red lights?

The red light and vehicle problem can be pursued to rather

minute and detailed conceptual levels involving electrical current (again, a concept), timing devices, etc. The point, however, is that concepts are never finalized unless one chooses to ignore observations and data and refuses to think through relationships. A statement of relationships or a concept is open to change as new experiences and new data are forthcoming.

MAKING WITH SENSE

When one works with a concept of a concept, he usually faces two major positions. Both positions make some fundamental assumptions regarding what it means to know. One position claims that all knowledge must resort at some time and place to *sense* data which is then conceptualized or related. The other position notes concepts as being real or independent of sense perception and that such concepts exist, in essence, *a priori* to, and separate from, empirical data. "Right" concepts thus conform to what is. What is, is independent of human effort.

What one means by concepts and by concept learning depends on which alternative position he accepts.

If learning is the conforming of the student to "what is" and if there is a right concept already determined, the curriculum offerings, data used, and the purposes of teaching *must* correspond. And student evaluation must be consistent with this correspondence.

If learning stems from sense perception and rests on "public" data and is the statement of the results of man's attempts to relate and test experience, then learning is the finding of meaning through relating. No "right" concepts exist independently of man's efforts. Learning then becomes a process for creating and testing concepts. Curriculum is geared to this process as is student evaluation. Thus a concept is *created* and tested, and not *given*. The alternative to this brings some degree of closure on attempts at social inquiry.

How is a concept created and tested? Let's follow the idea of the process involved in the red light and stopped vehicles experience and apply it (transfer) to another situation.

You and I can go into a room which we call a "kitchen" and which has in it a "white" stove and "white" "refrigerator", as well as a "white" "sink" and a "table" and some "chairs." The word symbols are important to us and provide a shortcut to thinking. We use the "stove" and the "refrigerator" and the "sink" without too much thought. One could say that you and I have a habit which connects the symbol with the item with a function. If someone tells us to "boil some water" it is highly probable that we would turn to the item called "stove" without going through all the relational procedures. The habit rules.

But suppose we observe a crawling youngster wobbling into the same room. He cannot talk and has a quite limited working vocabulary. To us, there are two upright objects (both "white," one a "stove" and the other a "refrigerator") but to the crawling youngster, the objects in the room do not have names either as objects or as objects of a certain color. Consequently, he crawls to one object (what we would call a "stove") and touches it. He feels what we would call "pain" and thus through an experience becomes aware of two pieces of information. The object is there, and when he touches the object the consequent experience is not pleasant. He may do this a second time and perhaps he makes an abstraction which relates *through his senses* the object and his being uncomfortable. The terms "hot" and "on" and "oven" are not part of the learning experience.

From the initial experience and from his initial empirical data, the child moves into a world of increased variables and new data. And he must relate all this into qualified and expanding concepts. For example, the data of place location, color, time, etc., may subsequently indicate that the object may not be painful *all* the time. The thinking processes are rather complex and did not directly involve any word symbols which might have described the experience. The word was *not* the object nor was it the experience. At this stage of learning the word symbol was not functional: it could neither assist nor impede the learning.

What we would have observed is the crawling youngster relating himself to sense perceptions and then abstracting the relationship.

But, someone might contend, he could have learned "later on" when given the concepts of "hot" and "on" and "oven." Granted, but the source of the concept did rest in sense experiences and could, at any time, be tested to see if valid. What we noted, therefore, was the *process* by which a concept was formed, the bombardment of new data which demanded that the concept be modified, and the fact that the concept could be tested with sense data.

A more sophisticated view of how concepts are derived may be noted in an actual classroom situation. The students note, through the senses, all the objects in the room and they are asked to list the objects according to the word symbol agreed upon. For example: "chalk" or "desk" or "student" or "plant." The list would then include all the objects in the room and should be rather extensive. The students could then classify in a number of different ways: color, size, shape, etc. Thus, classification of common characteristics can be meaningless unless there is *a definite reason for* classification. Supposing that the major classification desired involved "living" and "nonliving" objects. The differences between the two would be analyzed and then the objects put into the two different groups, say, according to those which needed food and protection in order to continue existing over a period of time. Once the category of living objects has been determined, the students could work within this category and note major characteristics of "animal" and "plant" life.

CLASSROOM USE

One may see possibilities for applying the above example of concept formation to actual classroom use. The following lesson plan is a specific application of the process actually done in a classroom.

In reviewing the lesson plan, please note:

1. The major concept has been identified by the teacher and becomes the major guide by which the teacher selects the pertinent data.
2. The major concept has at least 3 sub-concepts which can be derived by the students and then related to form the larger concept. The sub-concepts are anticipated (others may emerge) but these also help in suggesting both data and approach.
3. "Skills" or how to work with experience are included in the lesson plan in order to help in the planning of the use of such "skills." This is not left to chance.
4. General approach attempts to get at the experiences which the students bring to the class and the concepts which they might have derived without realizing the extent of what they are claiming.
5. The skills come into play in terms of how one might test a theory, hypothesis, or concept. Note the relating of data into a theory and then the question as to how one might test the theory.
6. Taking empirical data from other social groups (taken from Margaret Mead), how does this new data relate to the old? What happens to the theory?

The lesson plan includes: concepts, sub-concepts, skills, approaches, and specific data. It is a plan which attempts to put the skills to work in deriving a concept and then adding new data which force the original concept to be modified. Lesson plans are crucial in that the direction of the class, the types of data, and the use of data are not randomly approached. Such plans also can be shared and modified with other teachers and with students.

There is a great deal of security in knowing where one is going, why he is going, and how he plans to get there!

LESSON PLAN: MAN LEARNS TO BE

Major Concept:

Man learns his differences (his lessons are different).

Sub-concept 1: The world into which we are born ascribes to us a particular role.

Sub-concept 2: The roles each of us plays helps us to think that all people behave the same way.

Sub-concept 3: Roles are learned and thus unless all people learn the same way from the same lesson, the role will be different.

Skills to be introduced:

1. The making of a theory and the testing of a theory.
2. Words are man-made and substitutes can be found if helpful.

General Approach:

Trying out for a play; trying to get one of the roles.

1. Father　　3. Son　　5. Grandfather
2. Mother　　4. Daughter　　6. Grandmother

Note: The actor plays the role the author wanted him to play. The author has an idea and the roles lead into completing that idea: each as a *part* of the *whole* play. The actor learns his role and acts his role.

ACTIVITIES

I. Question:

What general characteristics should the above role have? In other words, how are fathers, mothers, sons, daughters, grandfathers, grandmothers *expected* to behave. For example:

father: work, discipline, decisions.
mother: children, gentle, more loving,
              etc.
daughter: dolls, shy, gentle, cries when
              hurt.
boy: active, loud.

II. Listing on the Board. Characteristics:

1. Gentle
2. Crying
3. Shy
4. Fighting
5. Hunting and Fishing
6. Raising children
7. Earning a living for the family
8. Cooking and keeping house
9. Making the major decisions
10. Soldiers

After the listing and after knowing that the students understand the meanings of the words, ask the students to give the first reaction as to whether or not they think this is male or female; father or mother.

List the responses next to each term: what conclusion would one draw?

Note: Here comes the idea of theory: (Guess about something)

Example: I fall over the waste paper container.
Theory: I did not see it.
Test theory: by answering "yes" or "no"

Example: I hold my nose.
Theories: something smells. . .
Test:

O.K. The fact that most of us agree on what a father and mother do; what the male and female do: what theory would you come up with? (Most males and females have certain roles to play: it is natural for males and females to behave this way, etc.?

III. New Guinea:

(locate on the map). . . . Three Groups of People (Fact Sheet).

Arapesh (A)	Mundugumor (B)	Tchambuli (C)
1. Both Male and Female are gentle and are motherly.	1. Both Male and Female are harsh and violent.	1. Men stay at home. Women work.
2. Both raise children.	2. Both slap and abuse children	2. Men wear adornments. Women are plain.
	3. Wives work in the fields and support the family.	3. Women support the community.
	4. Women and men fight each other.	4. Men dance and entertain.

Now: Taking the characteristics used before,if you were living in **A**, how would you answer? Living in **B**? Living in **C**?

    1. Remember what was said about roles and the author and what the actor does with his part.

    2. Remember that we talked about a theory and that you already had a theory about how men and women are supposed to behave.

    3. But now. . . we find other peoples behaving differently; the theory doesn't hold true.

What new theory would you now hold?

"KINDS OF CONCEPTS"

If the teacher is concerned with the student being able to use or transfer concepts derived and tested in class, the logical question arises: Are all concepts of equal "value" in the sense that they are and *will be* functional for the student? Are there kinds of concepts which are workers more than artifacts? Are some kinds of concepts more likely to be used than others?

The following terms and statements have been given the "label" of concept:

1. Columbus discovered America in 1492.
2. Democracy.
3. Good American citizens vote in elections.
4. When a change takes place in one part of man's activity, then changes in other parts of his living patterns are likely to take place.

Columbus Discovered America in 1492. Most people would call this kind of a concept a "fact." And, some people say that they "teach facts and not concepts." Let's take a look at it. If a concept organizes separate pieces of information and explains how the pieces relate, we find four distinct pieces of information being related: (1) a person named Columbus; (2) an act of behavior; (3) a place location; (4) a date. These four pieces of information are put together or related into the statement: Columbus discovered America in 1492. This statement also incorporates a large number of other data not mentioned but instrumental in the act.

Can we test this concept and see if it holds up? Sure. You check the records and sources and you find a man named Columbus sailing for the Indies in 1492. "Discovery" and "America" remain problems and refer to definition and application after the fact.

It should be noted that the concept Columbus discovered America in 1492 will never be repeated. Columbus will never again discover America in 1492. The concept thus becomes a

Unique and non-repetitive concept. It has happened and it will not happen again.

Democracy. As a single term, we are not told very much. Apparently the term democracy implies a host of data and relationships. But the data and the organization are not explicit. We have to view the term simply as a "cue" concept—it cues us into other concepts but, in and of itself, it denotes no explicit data or organization of relationships. In its existing form, the term does not lend itself to testing through any evidence. We would have to go beyond the term before we could get a concept we could teach.

Good American Citizens Vote in Elections. We find the statement not only describing people called "citizens" behaving in a certain way at a certain time but *also a judgment about the behavior.* This is a *value concept.* What would one have to do to test such a concept against and with data? In a sense, it is also a prescriptive statement. Obviously, it raises all sorts of questions: If one doesn't vote in elections, he is a bad citizen? What if a vote is cast without the voter weighing the issues? Is a vote an affirmation of a position? What if the citizen denies *both* alternatives presented him? And what about citizens who, for one reason or another, are excluded from voting?

When a Change Takes Place in one Part of Man's Activity, then Changes in Other Parts of His Living Patterns are Likely To Take Place. This statement of a concept is universal in that it does not qualify the term "man" nor does it qualify the nature of the change. It is not restricted and it is repetitive. That is, it is *general* and *repetitive.* It is open to being tested. One can determine whether or not and to what degree the concept works. There is no value judgment as to whether or not the concept is good or right and no judgment as to whether change is good or bad. There is no judgment as to whether the relationships are good or bad. It makes a general descriptive statement about experience and is open to be checked and modified through data.

If concepts are to be tools and are to be used in situations outside and beyond the school and classroom level, what kinds are likely to be most functional for the student?

UN AND GR CONCEPTS

A Unique and Non-Repetitive concept is probably of little transfer value as is. A UN concept may be used to construct and to test concepts but its very nature does not lend itself to transfer use.

A Generalized and Repetitive concept (GR) includes more than one unique phenomenon and is open to repetition. It is difficult to imagine a GR concept being built or tested apart from UN concepts. But the transfer target would be the generalized concept.

The term "democracy" does not help us in its present form.

And the teacher must wrestle with the ethics involved in teaching concepts that do not lend themselves to data and to testing. Do we simply ask students to take our word? If so, what do we do with a colleague who exercises the same privilege but with whom we disagree? Where is the court of appeal?

We would argue that a teacher should concern herself with GR concepts that are open to sense data. Knowing that we never have all the data, a GR concept is never taught as a given but rather as something to be tested and modified when data and situations so indicate.

One part of a teaching strategy might place emphasis on having students differentiate between various types of concepts as well as know what we mean by the term "concept." We have talked for years about having students differentiate between fact and opinion. It seems quite natural to move from this to the area of kinds of concepts.

DO GR CONCEPTS HAVE DIFFERENT LEVELS OF GENERALIZABILITY?

It is recognized that UN concepts are unique and non-repetitive. But, not all GR concepts deal with *all* people in *all* situations. Not *all* GR concepts are universal.

Some GR concepts deal with all people in all places in similar situations. *Some* deal with *some* people in *some* places in *some* situations. There are levels of GR concepts. For example, note the differences in the following statements:

When x, y, z exist there will be riots.

When x, y, z exist in the United States, there are likely to be riots.

When x, y, z exist in New York State there are likely to be riots.

When x, y, z exist in New York City there are likely to be riots.

When x, y, z exist in the Ocean Hill-Brownsville area there are likely to be riots.

X, y, z existed in Ocean Hill-Brownsville, New York City. There were riots.

You can see that we moved from a large, inclusive — universal —

statement of relationships into more and more qualified situations and eventually ended up with a UN concept. A number of UN concepts (Hough, Watts, Ocean Hill-Brownsville, Hartford, Detroit) allow us to move into different levels of generalizable and repetitive concepts.

In the use of social studies, most UN concepts come from history. By themselves, they do not lend themselves to being of transfer value. But when related into various levels of GR concepts, they begin to expand their potential use.

Most of the GR concepts we have — at least those supported by data — come from the social and behavioral sciences. *No GR concept is assumed to be absolutely valid under all circumstances.* Thus, when teaching GR concepts, one is always ready to modify and qualify — even discard — a concept when new data and situations warrant the change. A GR concept is *probable* and not an absolute, unchanging "knowledge pill."

GR'S WITH UN'S

A high school teacher planned a lesson on the environment and listed the following GR concepts. Notice how each GR concept cannot be said to be true unless one can support each statement with factual instances — UN concepts. The latter are also listed by the teacher as examples of many more UN concepts available to validate or reject each GR concept.

GR CONCEPTS DEALING WITH ENVIRONMENT

1. People cause pollution and only people can stop pollution.
2. Only when things are noticeable or obviously bad in the sense that a number of people are adversely affected, do people's energies become focused on addressing the problem.
3. Pollution knows no class, cultural, or political boundaries.
4. Americans assume that continued economic growth is equated with qualitative improvement of the people and the nation. Pollution challenges this assumption.
5. Making decisions in a complex society involves considering consequences. The solution of one problem with technology gives rise to other new significant problems.

UN CONCEPTS FOR POSSIBLE USE IN TESTING AFOREMENTIONED GR CONCEPTS

1. Air pollution costs between 14 and 18 billion dollars a year in direct economic loss.
2. The demand for electricity has doubled since World War II.
3. 500,000 tons of garbage are collected each day in America.
4. Every second, two million gallons of sewage and other wastes are poured into out waterways.
5. Solid wastes increase at the rate of 4 per cent per year— approximately the same rate as our Gross National Product.
6. World population will double in the next thirty years.
7. Highways and new suburban tracts take up 100 million acres of land each year.
8. 100 million pounds of herbicides have been used in Vietnam.

Relating GR concepts with UN concepts is a necessary condition for teaching students how to use social science data and how to inquire. But these are not sufficient conditions for teaching. Planning for inquiry teaching and learning involves not only selecting concepts and testing them but also deciding how the content will be ordered and what materials will be utilized in the teaching of specific concepts.

B.O.'S: DON'T YOU WISH YOUR FRIENDS. . .

BEHAVIORAL OBJECTIVES WITH CONCEPTS

The most conventional and the most far out social studies teachers both assume that what is learned by their students has some utility—that somehow education is functional. One will claim that all students must learn UN concepts about the presidents, *not* as an end in itself, but because one must know his heritage to be a good citizen. The other will claim that everything a student learns should be transferable to the real world—practical, useful.

No matter which position one takes, he still encounters the question of How do I know I am doing what I say I am doing? And, for that matter, How do I know what the student has learned because of his and my efforts?

If concepts are mental constructs, what evidence does one accept in determining whether or not the student has grasped the concept? The student can repeat the statement of the concept. Is he simply saying that he is able to put in sequence and repeat sounds? It's like the father who asked his daughter what she learned in school that day. "I learned Einstein's theory." "Oh," queried the father, "what is it?" The daughter proudly said: "$E=MC^2$." "Well, what does it mean?" the father asked. The daughter did not know. "What you learned," concluded the father, "is simply to repeat certain sounds upon cue."

The move toward having Behavioral Objectives (B.O.'s) attempts to address this problem. As a result of encountering the instructional experiences, what is a student able to *do* — what is he able to do that is observable and measurable? In other words what kind of evidence does the teacher and student have that the student has learned certain things? The use of B.O.'s is an attempt to become more objective and less subjective about evaluation.

A behavioral objective is related to purpose. Purpose is, in turn, *related to the mental constructs or concepts which are applied to data and experience.* The B.O.'s allow us to determine whether or not the relationship holds up.

A B.O. is a stated objective having three characteristics:
 1. *What the student is expected to perform.*
 2. *Under what specific conditions the performance is to take place.*
 3. *What criteria for performance are acceptable evidence.*
For example:
> Given a list of ten stated social studies objectives, the student will circle the expected performance, will underline the specific conditions under which the performance takes place, and will "box" the performance criteria in each of seven of the listed objectives.

Student will circle. . . will underline. . . will "box".

Given a list of ten stated social studies objectives.

". . . each of seven. . ."

The use of Behavioral Objectives finds different levels of performance much as there are different levels and kinds of concepts. Some B.O.'s ask for strict recall and/or definition. Others may ask a student to compare/contrast, analyze or synthesize according to specific criteria, or transfer specific concepts to a new and unique situation. Stated Behavioral Objectives depend upon desired outcomes. We are not implying that the *only* valid objectives are those that can be stated and used in behavioral terms. Rather, they do provide a means for checking on how effective planning and implementation prove to be—information which should be helpful to both teachers and students.

Inquiry is related to how people learn and function. The instructional role of a teacher includes: identifying purposes, planning how instruction is to take place, implementing the plans, and evaluation of whether or not—or to what extent—the purposes were achieved. This book is not a methods book in the usual sense. Recognizing that "methods" encompass a great many of related activities—motivation, interaction analysis, specific techniques and strategies, etc.—our *primary* focus is on relating content *with* method, in broadening a content base for inquiry.

After having read, studied, and used the chapter, students will indicate their understanding and knowledge by being able to do the following:

B.O. 1. Given a situation in which a person insists that social studies students must have the facts first before working with inquiry and with conceptual teaching, the student will identify four assumptions being made about learning and subject matter.

B.O. 2. The student will write one example of each of the following: (1) a social studies UN concept; (2) a social studies GR concept; (3) a social studies value concept; (4) a social studies GR concept which cannot be tested by empirical data; and (5) a social studies GR concept that can be tested with empirical data. The examples used in the chapter cannot be used.

Note: If you and your classmates do the objectives, you might want to analyze what each objective infers a student "knows." What other alternatives are there for making such inferences?

"Once upon a time there was a kind and benign dictator . . . ."
By Paul Peter Porges. Copyright © 1971 Saturday Review, Inc.

3

PLANNING FOR CONTENT USE

GAMBLING WITH OPTIONS

A social studies teacher's planning must involve the use of content and, specifically, the use of data. It has been argued that education is primarily concerned with two related activities: conceptualizing and concepts — inquiring and the results of such inquiring. It is rather obvious that neither the teacher nor the student must re-invent the wheel. This is to say that he is not the only one who is inquiring or who has inquired. Other people, many more sophisticated in the processes of inquiry, have come up with findings or concepts about how data and experience relate and form a basis for prediction.

Granted that not all the findings or concepts are equally valid or hold the same levels of probability allowing the same base for figuring the odds for predicting. Not all findings find the same basis for the "chances" involved in assessing consequences. Because of the uneven levels of probability involved, some are tempted to dismiss the whole thing as not being very useful to human functioning. The question, however, is simply put: Does one decide to "gamble" indiscriminately with his life and with the lives of others or does one intentionally seek the odds that provide a better chance for allowing choices among alternatives? If one wants the better chance, it is almost an imperative that he confront the findings, concepts, and data stemming from the academic disciplines — in the case of the social studies, from the social science disciplines.

The teacher thus faces two major problems: (1) The teacher must be aware of the processes and products of past inquiry; (2) The teacher must work with such data in planning for students to *use* content. It may be heady but all teaching somehow and in some way stands at the bar of content.

This chapter deals with the very practical dimensions of the teacher's use of content in planning the students' use of content.

69

Three teaching situations are presented. Each is real in the sense that each takes into account what the teacher brings to the task in terms of his own background and how he utilizes different approaches in planning.

Each situation brings focus to the content the teacher has available, how this content becomes a *data bank* for teacher planning, and how the data banks might be used with students.

It should be pointed out that the data is given to the reader. The raw material is included with addressing the problems of use. There is a great deal of data in the data banks. Not all of it is predigested and prerelated. In a very real way, it puts the reader in the same situation faced by teachers: it raises some of the same frustrations. This is done on purpose and with purpose. Selecting and using content involves inquiry on the part of the teacher: purpose, inquiring processes, application. If social studies teachers wish to initiate students into the fraternity of "discovery" and "inquiry" then it seems a logical necessity to affirm that one practices what he teaches.

We have assessed the context within which the individual teacher builds a rationale for teaching social studies. The rationale implies the broad goals. The goals, in turn, suggest the concepts to be considered and the objectives to be approached. The concepts and objectives help guide both the teacher and the student in the use of content.

The struggle with evolving a rationale perhaps takes one to an even more basic question—a question asked for centuries— *Why?* It would seem that the determination of the *What* somehow implies that the *Why* has been identified. If not, one ends up with a series of random activity. This random type of activity in the teaching of the use of social studies has been referred to as the *Four H* approach: *H*unch, *H*ope, *H*ush, and *H*oorah. The teaching effort is premised upon a number of hunches, it is implemented with fervent hope, it is not exposed to public view, and loudly "hoorahed" when hunch and hope seem to have paid off.

Most of us do not think very much about thinking. We get confused by the unexamined illusions we accept as givens. Our so-called reasoning usually ends up as a way of finding arguments for continuing to believe as we already do and leads us to a form of "primary certitude." The struggle to evolve a rationale forces one to do some thinking about thinking—an effort that would seem to be a basic ingredient in teaching and learning. At the very least, a rationale raises some key questions, forces a realistic assessment of the situation, identifies a range of alternatives and choices, and exposes the value judgments one makes for himself—and others. If worked at, a rationale can serve as an analytic instrument which assists in integrating the teaching effort so that there is a view of the whole and how each part is in a web of mutually influencing interaction—a view of teaching as a synthesized system. While also helping in generating new ideas, new methods, new materials, and speculative frameworks, the most vital function of a rationale is that it provides a guide to action, a thoughtful and thought out base for deciding what one can and should do.

In a book that is of value for social studies teachers, Berelson and Steiner wrote, "How people come to know and interpret their world is fundamental to the understanding of human behavior, since behavior, as distinct from sheer motion, is action that takes the environment into account."[1] According to the authors, the starting points are a philosophical assumption that all knowledge of the world depends on the senses, and an empirical finding that the facts of sensory data, by themselves, are insufficient to produce a coherent picture of the world. If we interpret correctly, behavior is purposeful and the human being creates his purposes by relating "facts" with ideas, and thus evolves a coherent picture of himself *with* his world.

The starting point for a teacher is to recognize that teaching is done on purpose and with purpose. The purposes somehow focus upon relating ideas with facts. How this relationship is constructed, implemented, and evaluated hinges upon the intended *uses* of study as deemed most worthwhile by the teacher. As we have seen, few, if any, would view an approach to social studies at the secondary level without concern for the uses beyond the subject matter itself. In other words, teaching and learning are *means* and not strictly ends. Ideas have consequences. The sociologist W. I. Thomas commented years ago that if a man thinks a thing to be true, for him it *is* true and he will act accordingly. And, if ideas have consequences, then the facts that we select and use also have consequences. The skills used to retrieve and to process all sorts of data also play a vital role.

The three primary areas for teacher planning thus are: (1) ideas, (2) data, and (3) skills. Although the term "content" has often been used to denote only the data area, it becomes rather obvious that the term actually covers the functional *relationship* of all three areas: ideas, data, skills.

---

[1] Bernard Berelson and Gary A. Steiner, *Human Behavior*, Harcourt, Brace and World, Inc., New York, 1964. p. 87.

We have used the term "idea" interchangeably with the term "concept." Rather than worry about definitions at this point, it might be prudent to think in terms of what ideas or concepts *do* for us:

FUNCTIONS OF CONCEPTS

1. Concepts assist in helping to mentally organize experience. All of us are constantly bombarded with information and the experiences encountered through just plain day-to-day living. The experiences may be direct or vicarious — picked up through media, books, conversation, and/or classroom lessons. The way we organize this bombardment is to somehow form ideas or concepts that relate and fit experience into "wholes." We abstract experience and organize what has been abstracted into concepts.

2. Concepts assist in screening and selecting what information and experience is to be used from among the deluge we encounter day-to-day. In a sense, concepts serve to sift facts.

3. Concepts also assist in searching for additional information and experience. When a concept becomes disorganized and not helpful in forming a consistent and coherent picture or fails to solicit desired responses from the "world out there," one may be driven to modify, drop, or reorganize.

4. Concepts assist in establishing predispositions to act and react. This involves the affective world of attitudes and values. We find the "affective" and "cognitive" domains not discrete and unrelated aspects of behavior but rather mutually influencing — much as ideas with facts are in transaction.

5. Concepts assist in patterning experiences and thus allow for predicting ongoing relationships. How much of our actual behavior is based on mental organizations that allow us to predict?

Ideas and the *use* of ideas are at the heart of teaching. Emphasis upon this realization takes the form of what is called "conceptual teaching." Each subject area such as social studies, language arts, mathematics, science, and health, have certain organizations of human experience, or concepts, which are taught because they are felt to be important *tools* for the young to have when coming to grips with their many worlds and with their society in particular.

Concepts are usually indicated through symbols—through language. There are declarative concepts, imperative concepts, interrogative concepts, "open" concepts, "closed" concepts, hypothetical concepts, value concepts. What concepts should one teach from the various social studies disciplines—from history, geography, anthropology, sociology, psychology, political science, economics?

Let's take a critical look at some teaching efforts that were actually made with secondary school students. In reviewing the planning and lessons, try to determine what concepts were used, what *kinds* of concepts were addressed, whether or not there was historical or social science data used, and whether or not the methods used allowed inquiry and discovery. And ask yourself what kind of preparation the teachers, themselves, had to have in order to attempt what they did.

SITUATION ONE

The teacher is working with an 11th grade "average" class in American History. The school social studies curriculum calls for American history at the 5th, 8th, and 11th grades. The flow of the courses at all three grade levels is essentially the same: starting with the Age of Exploration, and moving chronologically up through the various periods—with leaps and luck one might get past the Reconstruction Period in one of the three excursions. The detailed course of study presented a political approach: administrations, laws, governmental changes, wars, and some references to economic factors. The students had taken World history (emphasis on Western Civilization) during the 10th grade. Occasionally the course of study related back to previous study (Columbus, mercantilism, the French Revolution) but the attempt to synthesize was negligible. The class had gone through the "Triangular Trade," the Colonial "laboratories," the examples of friction leading to a separation from the "Mother" country, and were now involved in taking another look at Richard Henry Lee and the help Adams and Franklin gave Jefferson as he penned the Declaration of Independence.

Before the class one day, the teacher was asking the usual types of questions. And, getting the usual types of responses.

"What," he asked, "are the self-evident truths mentioned in the Declaration?"

All men are created equal.

All men had rights —— unalienable rights given by the Creator.

The rights included life, liberty, and the pursuit of happiness.

He looked around the class. "Any questions?" he asked. It was a rhetorical move, one that allowed him to move into how one secured such rights.

But, one student raised her hand. "I think most of us already know what rights were self-evident, but, she asked, "why were they self-evident? I don't think they're self-evident today."

"Well, everyone at the time knew ——"

One of the boys in the row by the window laughed. "Not everybody knew it. We had a war didn't we?"

The "why" question bothered the teacher. He was accustomed to dealing with the "what" variety. There were several issues on the table and he decided to ad-lib and move from the prepared script. Calling them "hangers," he wrote on the board the issues as he saw them:

What are the self-evident truths today? Are they the same as in Jefferson's time?

Why did Jefferson call them "self-evident?"

A hand went up. "Why not put down that the people of the time must have taken some things for granted?" The textbook said that Jefferson did not invent the ideas. What did Locke have to say? And, there must have been others besides Locke. These, too, became "hangers." Then the teacher asked the students how they could go about trying to resolve what had been left hanging. It would be nice to report that the students overflowed with enthusiasm, with creative ideas, and with scholars' curiosity and dedication of effort. They did not. With no malice aforethought, the students had succeeded simply in maneuvering the teacher away from the prepared script. It had been a game without substance and the teacher knew it.

Between classes, he jotted down the hangers which he had scrawled on the board. Three minutes of surging humanity moving from one classroom to another didn't allow much time to pull together what had happened, and he soon found himself again talking about Lee, Adams, and Jefferson and asking students to tell the "truths" that were so self-evident.

He sat next to a first-year English teacher at lunch. She was telling some of her colleagues about her current love affair with Hamlet—it was a kind of private affair because few students had shown any great feeling. "Tomorrow," she said, "I'm going to take *one* small thing and stay with it for one full period. I'm taking the quote 'His liberty is full of threats to all', and I'm going to spend the entire period teaching it."

Another teacher did a little digging. "You should be able to have at least half of a class be able to *memorize* it during the period."

The social studies teacher found himself back in the "why" arena: Why study literature in the first place? Why Shakespeare? Why Hamlet? Why memorize? And why *this* particular quote rather than another? Why? And, in a moment of diogenesian thinking, he had to turn the same questions to himself: Why study history in the first place? Why American history? Why the Colonial Period? Why memorize, and why the sweat over "self-evident truths"? In the midst of all the frenzied "teaching" activities — study hall, activity assignment, hall duty, bus duty, record-keeping, homeroom, lunch duty, and periodic supervision of detention halls — what was he really trying to do with those moments in the classroom which all these other activities "allowed" him to have?

Well, the kids had to have some knowledge of their heritage. Why? So they could be better citizens. Oh? What do better citizens *do*? Vote intelligently. How's that? Make choices with some pertinent information, see options, take part in decision-making, be effective in determining ends *and* means, act with some informed restraint in terms of seeing how the pieces fit together, recognize the value judgments being made, approach community living with some reason and rationality ——.

You moved away from the heritage bit, didn't you? Yes — but all the above takes place in some sort of framework which is at work on making decisions. You know, the "every man his own historian" bit. Anyhow, one *uses* history to help make history — it tells one where he has been, what he can do, and what he might do. History is really a record, and at times an analysis, of human experience.

Every historian has a frame of reference. He's not exempt from his *own* times, his *own* experiences, thus in a way history is an extension from the present aimed at forging the future.

Oh? Then a study of American history provides a framework for certain human experience, a sample of human experience within a certain time and place? Then Colonial history is a smaller sample — more limited time, place, and situation? And, the Declaration ——?

Why memorize? Does it assure helping a citizen function? Evaluate information? Reason? Predict? Make choices? Act with understanding and appreciation of human behavior?

What specifically did the social studies teacher want to accomplish with the self-evident truth hangers? Somehow, and in some way:

> To get the students to be sensitive to consequences of the habitual attitudes and meanings attributed to words.

> To have students become aware of the fact that there are implicit assumptions or unexamined mental habits that influence what individuals or generations think, feel, and do.

> To have students become aware that the most significant development in Western culture over the last four centuries has been the rise of science. It influences man's way of looking at himself, his society, his government, his way of organizing human activity.

> To have students recognize that major ideas go beyond national boundaries.

> To have students become sensitive to the ideas active today in challenging one to review his habitual ways of thinking.

Given that the above things were viewed as the important outcomes he wanted, he also recognized that another "given" was the fact that he had to work within the existing curriculum and he thus had to *use* the Declaration of Independence — its time, place, and message — as a *means* to accomplish the outcomes. The key question: Why did Jefferson believe that there were self-evident truths in the 18th century?

However he approached the study, he wanted the students to get away from the simple attitude that all scholarship was just a matter of applying common sense and then disciplining oneself to memorizing. He wanted the approach to be useful beyond just the time period studied — useful, if possible, in assessing contemporary affairs.

He knew that the textbook would help frame a general context but not much more. And, he knew that just as the Declaration of Independence was a means or *vehicle* for helping him get to the main purposes he had in mind, so he would have to find additional means or sub-vehicles related to the issues the Declaration raised. Initially, this would have to be *his* responsibility as a teacher. Perhaps once the students got into it, they might help but at this point the responsibility was his. As he played with possibilities, he grew increasingly aware that this called for a completely different approach to planning: a shift from having a set script for what *he*, the teacher, would do to having a script that would depend, in part, on the students and what they were able or willing to do. There was a risk in all this. The old type of security would be gone. He would have to be flexible, be sensitive to student feedback, be willing to make decisions "on-the-spot" rather than firm up set strategy the night before. It would take more planning than the usual. It also meant that he, himself, had to do a different kind of homework. A lot of this he didn't know, and this would make him vulnerable to those who demanded the standard answers.

At this point, he had determined: (1) the large goals he wanted to work toward; (2) the fact that he would work from the existing curriculum which meant he didn't have to clear a lot of things with the department chairman or the principal; (3) he would have to locate materials to be used with the students; and (4) he would have to continually revise his plans as he went along. He gave himself a week to try a different approach. If he bombed, it would be just with the one class. He could make up the lost time, if necessary.

It became obvious to him that he couldn't really establish a teaching strategy until he had some familiarity with the material related to the 17th and 18th centuries. The large goals he had determined acted as a sifting base. The dust came off some books he had used as a student in college which, up until now, had little apparent relevancy to the topics as listed in the curriculum guide. He needed all kinds of data which might be used as vehicles with the students. It was reassuring to know that when he knew what he was looking for, all sorts of data seemed to be available. He recorded, on 5″ × 8″ cards, a data bank indexed according to topic, idea, time, and key people.

DATA BANK

> "A society is possible in the last analysis because the individuals in it carry around in their heads some sort of picture of that society. . ."
>
> (Mannheim, *Ideology and Utopia*)

> ". . .the 18th century view is still at the bottom of our view of life — especially in the United States."
>
> (Crane Brinton, *Shaping of the Mind.*)

> "I perceive," said the Countess, "philosophy is now become very mechanical." "So mechanical," said I, "that I fear we shall quickly be asham'd of it; They will have the world to be

in great, what a watch is in little; which is very regular, and depends only upon the just disposing of the several parts of the movement. But pray tell me, Madam, had you not formerly a more sublime Idea of the Universe?"

(Willey, *Seventeenth Century Background*)

"On the level of simple directions, commands, descriptions, the difficulty is not great. When words mean 'look out!,'. . . communications is clear. But when we hear words on the level of ideas and generalizations, we cheer loudly, we grow angry, we storm the barricades — and we do not know what the other man is saying."

(Chase, *Tyranny of Words*)

"Our interpretation of any sign is our psychological reaction to it, as determined by our past experience in similar situations, and by our present experience."
"How far is our discussion itself distorted by habitual attitudes towards words, and lingering assumptions due to theories no longer openly held but still allowed to guide our practice."

(Ogden and Richards, *The Meaning of Meaning*)

"When men believed that fixed ends existed for all normal changes in nature, the conception of similar ends for men was but a special case of a general belief. . . But man is not logical and his intellectual history is a record of mental reserve and compromises. He hangs on to what he can in his old beliefs even when he is compelled to surrender their logical basis."

(Dewey, *Human Nature and Conduct*)

Ways of thought are not themselves subject to scrutiny — they seem so natural and inevitable. But, people do think in terms of certain categories having particular types of imagery. E.g.: *Esprits simplistes* — minds which assume simple solutions to problems are different from those who assume the general complexity of things. . . pertinent to any situation. "The representatives of the Enlightenment or the 17th and 18th centuries. . . largely. . . *esprits simplistes.*"

(Lovejoy, *The Great Chain of Being*)

What is the task of philosophy in the 20th century? It is to assimilate the impact of science on human affairs — to provide a system of ideas that will work to make an integrated whole of our beliefs about the nature of the world and human values.

(Kaplan, *The New World of Philosophy*)

The classical Chinese literati found the Golden Age in the past. At best, all the present could do would be to hang on to the values, order, etc. of early sages. Nature was seen as indifferent to which man must adapt—a contrast with the Western view of man coming to control his environment. The Chinese view suggested an immutability of things, a permanence of human and physical nature—change had to be avoided.

In the Christian view, there is a convergence to time—a concern with the process of "becoming" as it moves towards an ultimate of "being." This relates to a view of historical change, a teleological point of reference: the goal of perfectability, an idea of progress.

(John Marcus, "Time and History,"
*Comparative Studies in Society and
History, Jan.* '61.)

A popular phrase during the 17th Century was *Climate of Opinion.* Words are indicators of the accepted "climate" of opinion:
13th Century: God, Sin, Grace, Salvation, Heaven
18th Century: Nature, Natural Law, Reason, Perfectability, Science.
19th Century: Evolution, Progress, Individualism, Science.
20th Century: Relativity, Process, Adjustment, Function, Science, Complex.

(Becker, *The Heavenly City of the
Eighteenth Century.*)

"Let me trace in some detail the reaction of science upon man himself, and consider briefly some of the effects of every major scientific discovery. The obvious effect is technological; it is the visible and impressible movement from discovery through. . ., toward the establishment of greater comforts of life. . . . But every truly great scientific discovery launches also another trend, much less apparent and more subtle in its progression phase to phase through human culture. The discovery, acting as a *fact* in initiating the obvious movement [technology] becomes the lever of an *idea* in the other. It clamours to be understood. . . .

Results as challenging as these cannot fail to have a profound effect [ending] in new views on the nature of the universe, the relation of man to the universe and the relation of man to man.

Ethics, sociology, politics are ultimately subject to infestation by the germ that is created when a discovery in pure science is made."

(Margenau, *Age of Science.*)

Lazarsfeld's study: (common sense and uncommon evidence)
1. Better educated men showed more psychoneurotic symptoms than those with less education.
2. Men from rural backgrounds were usually in better spirits during their Army life than soldiers from city backgrounds.
3. Southern soldiers were better able to stand the climate in the hot South Sea islands than Northern soldiers.
4. White privates were more eager to become noncoms than Negroes.
5. Southern Negroes preferred Southern to Northern white officers.
6. As long as the fighting continued, men were more eager to be returned to the States than they were after the German surrender.

The teacher then developed the following hand-outs, which he called "data banks," for the students:

TIME LINE

(A) Francis Bacon (1561–1626)
(B) Galileo (1564–1642)
(C) John Locke (1632–1704)
(D) Isaac Newton (1642–1727)

TIME LINE

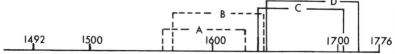

FRANCIS BACON (1561–1626)

Probably most of us know Bacon for his works *Novum Organum* (1620) and *Advancement of Learning*, and his name has become synonymous with the inductive method in science. . . and philosophical thought.
   A. His inductive method moves from observation of the particular to generalizations which deal with only

probability. He did not apply a priori reasoning to support indubitable "truth."

(1) In a very real sense Bacon was striking at Aristotle and his logical heirs, the Scholastics. Aristotle derived his universal truths *before* the application of intensive inquiry to the phenomena themselves. Bacon contrasted his own inductive method with the deductive one of Aristotle (and the 13th–17th Centuries.)

Bacon wrote:

"There are two ways, and can only be two, of seeking and finding truth. The one, from sense and reason, takes a flight to the most general axioms, and from these principles and their truth, settles once and for all intermediate axioms. The other method collects axioms from sense and particulars, ascending continuously and by degrees so that in the end it arrives at the most general axioms. This latter is the only true one, but never hitherto tried."

(*Novum Organum,* Bk. 1, xix.)

B. The crucial question for scientific method seemed to Bacon to be the problem of obtaining a major premise that would correspond to the facts. He criticized Scholastic science for not doing this. He wrote:

"The syllogism consists of propositions, propositions consist of words, words are symbols of notions. Therefore if the notions themselves (which is the root of the matter) are confused and over-hastily abstracted from the facts, there can be no firmness in the super-structure. Our only hope therefore lies in a true induction."

(Spedding, Intro. *Novum Organum*)

FOUR IDOLS

Bacon attacked what he felt to be the method of the Medieval science. To challenge the method he felt that he had to uproot "false notions" and "prejudices" that led to hasty generalizations, and which, in a sense denied our noting the exceptions. Bacon felt that the mind of his period was possessed by four "idols" and these idols he attempted to expose.

IDOLS OF THE TRIBE:

The human understanding is of its own nature prone to suppose the existence of more order and regularity in the world than it finds. . . For what a man had rather were true he more readily believes. Therefore he rejects difficult things from impatience of research; sober things, because they narrow hope; the deeper things of nature, from superstition; the light of experience, from arrogance and pride, lest his mind should seem to be occupied with things mean and transitory; things not commonly believed, out of deference to the opinion of the vulgar. . .

IDOLS OF THE CAVE:

The Idols of the Cave take their rise in the peculiar constitution, mental or bodily, of each individual; and also in education, habit, and accident. . .

IDOLS OF THE MARKET-PLACE:

. . . the most troublesome of all: idols which have crept into the understanding through the alliances of words and names. For men believe that their reason governs words; but it is also true that words react on the understanding . . . words stand in the way and resist change. . . The idols imposed by words on the understanding are of two kinds. They are either names of things which do not exist (for as there are things left unnamed through lack of observation, so likewise are there names which result from fantastic suppositions and to which nothing in reality corresponds. . .

IDOLS OF THE THEATRE:

But the *Idols of the Theatre* are not innate, nor do they steal into the understanding secretly, but are plainly impressed and received into the mind from the play-books of philosophical systems and perverted rules of demonstration . . . the corruption of philosophy by superstition and an admixture of theology is far more widely spread, and does the greatest harm, whether to entire systems or to their parts.

1. In your words, express what Bacon meant by each of the four idols.
2. What would you assume to be the scientific method to which Bacon was protesting?
3. What sometimes happens when we "name" something we do not understand?
4. Bacon's attitude towards the "play-books of philosophical systems" implies a distaste for what?

      A. What is a system?

      B. What is the meaning of the term "innate" and what is your reaction to the idea of innate ideas?

  5. Discuss what was going on in the world during the time in which Bacon lived (1561–1626) . . . be sure to include the "New World."

Review of Bacon:

  1. To what was he opposed?

  2. In what century did he die?

  3. In what general way did he classify the sources of why people have false notions?

IDOLS OF THE TRIBE:

1. Human Nature to assume:

      A. More order than there is. "*The* Cause of Juvenile Delinquency" or, Manifest Destiny.

      B. To get an idea and then look for support. (What would be the opposite of this?)

      C. Wishful thinking — man believes what he would like to believe.

      D. Man is impatient — looks for quick answers — *deep thinking often gives rise to serious doubts.*

      E. *Man wants an absolute* — to see change about him makes everything transitory. . . and he equates this with being *meaningless.*

      F. Easier to "go along" with the crowd.

IDOLS OF THE CAVE:

1. The experiences of just living — education, habit and environment.

      A. Man is born into *different experiences and accepted habits* . . . these become his "presuppositions" — accepted without thinking.

IDOLS OF THE MARKET-PLACE:

1. Recall by quoting from Stuart Chase. *Tyranny of Words* — simple commands can be understood but not words dealing with ideas. (These provoke emotion. . .)

      A. *Words resist thinking and change:* (Two ways . . .) it,,, and then the word becomes "it" and what we admit we don't understand becomes real . . . and exists. (Can you give me an example of this?)

IDOLS OF THE THEATRE:

1. Accepted world-view which discounts the "evidence" it uses — accepted as a whole and then we deductively move from this . . . example, a world-view in which we look for evidence by which to support it.

What was going on during Bacon's lifetime?

1. 1517 and what not?
2. 1588
3. 1603 — James the 1st: Divine Right . . . "I'll harry them out of the land."
4. 1620 — Puritans. . . .

Test on Wednesday . . . up and through Bacon's Four Idols . . . see the summary sheet.

GALILEO: (1564–1642)

1. While Bacon was more of a philosopher than a scientist, Galileo laid claim only to the latter category. He faced two intellectual problems:
   a. On what structure should an intellectual science be built?
   b. What criteria should be used to replace Aristotelian thought?

2. Consequently, we again see an attack on a priori reasoning — an attack on Aristotle, and an attack on the Scholastic thought. Perhaps his greatest contribution was the insistence that naming a thing is not necessary a causal factor and need not lead, therefrom, to an understanding of relationships. And, of course, most of us realize that his use of the telescope, his observations of the heavens, confirmed Copernicus's hypothesis that the sun was the center of the Universe. These conclusions eventually challenged man's concept of himself. "The tidy Aristotelian Universe, with man on earth as its physical, as well as its moral center, was destroyed."

3. Such challenges as emanated from Galileo shook the Church and most of us are familiar with his appearance before the Inquisition and, at the age of 70, his eventual disclaiming of his theory. He had challenged the "authority" basis of the Scholastics — and it had crushed him. . . but not his ideas.

JOHN LOCKE: (1632–1704)

1. Locke tangled with the question of the source of ideas: Where do ideas come from? Most of his contemporaries believed, that we start life with a certain number of "native ideas and original characters" and that these ideas, "being in our

minds from their first beginnings, are antecedent to all experience and must have been implanted in them by God
himself.''

    a. Locke wrote: "The dogmatists call all their pet ideas
       innate, hoping thereby to induce us to accept their
       opinions uncritically. They even try to justify them-
       selves by claiming that criticism of the doctrine of
       innateness destroys 'the foundation of knowledge and
       certainty,' but actually it is their own dogmatism that is
       destructive of knowledge.''
       (1) Locke claimed:
          (a) The mind at its beginning is an empty surface—
             the "tabla rosa."
          (b) All ideas come from sensation or reflection
             (the objects of sensations) and our minds are
             the source of ideas.

NEWTON: (1642–1727)

1. The most significant scientific figure to appear was Newton and his ideas permeated the century of American settle-
ment. A mathematician, Newton worked with gravity and
optics and concluded that mechanical explanations of all
phenomena could be expressed in mathematical terms.

    a. Bacon gave the new science its method; Newton gave
       it a basis for generalization—the concept of a mechan-
       ical natural law; that the universe and man was ruled
       by natural law.
    b. From this point it was an easy step to the belief that
       man could discover these laws and by living in accord-
       ance eventually arrive at perfectibility.
       (1) It followed logically that the way to learn the laws
          of nature was by education.
       (2) Education could train the mind to perceive and
          understand God's eternal will—and the heavenly
          city on earth.

The entire move in the changing "world view" was perhaps
best expressed by René Descartes, when he wrote:

    "It is possible to attain knowledge which is very useful in
    life, and instead of that speculative philosophy which is
    taught in the schools (Scholasticism) we may find a practical
    philosophy by means of which, knowing the force and action
    of fire, water, the stars, heavens, and all other bodies that
    environ us, as distinctly as we know the different crafts of
    our artisans, we can in the same way employ them in all
    those uses to which they are adapted, and thus render our-
    selves the masters and possessors of nature." (Discourse
    on Method)

The teacher admitted that this type of data gathering and

planning took a big chunk out of precious little time. But, he also admitted that for the first time the idea of teaching was becoming fun—fun in that it was whetting his *own* curiosity, his *own* intellectual interests, his *own* learning. He said: "For a long time I honestly felt that much of the academic work I did at college had little or no value for teaching. It was not until I started thinking of teaching the *use* of social studies—in my case, history—rather than teaching history *per se* that I realized what resources were available. Looking at it this way, I find that the existing curriculum structure need not strangle me or the students. If I see it as a means, as a tool, it opens up a whole new ball game and I can dip into political science, sociology, economics, current events—you name it. It sounds silly, but I am starting to like teaching after all these years. It's like starting to be a student again but a student with a purpose. . . ."

He admitted that when he had pulled together all the resources and had organized his data bank around the self-evident truths base, he had doubts about whether or not the students could handle such material. It was heavy stuff, especially for high school juniors. It was too much. They would never be able to understand it. He'd be lucky if two students in the whole class would be able to see how it all related. He was asking them to do things he hadn't done at college! Was this really it, or was he saying that he wasn't sure he could teach it: not sure if he understood the relationships he hoped the students would grasp? Was it that he feared the students wouldn't understand or that he couldn't teach it? Both?

He knew his basic intent was sound. Marie Boas Hall had written in the Thirty-Fourth Yearbook of the National Council for the Social Studies (*New Perspectives in World History*) that "Historians have long taught that the eighteenth century was an age in which ideas mattered. . . The intellectual ferment of the Age of Enlightenment rested. . . upon the achievement of seventeenth-century science." He had come across this in his data gathering. If he needed some authority to justify the attempt, he had it. From the same source he also gathered that the main thrust of 17th-century science was Newtonian science, which fed a world viewed to be subservient to man, a world made "comprehensible and reasonable."

Fine. But having good intentions, some data, and assurance about the basic academic direction was one thing. Teaching it was something different. What is exciting and challenging to one person in the wee hours of morning often loses some of its brilliance in the full light of day.

To synthesize in his own mind what he was trying to do, he outlined a "model" of the whole. A relatively simple thing that tried to put everything into perspective, the model was for his use and would not be shared with the students.

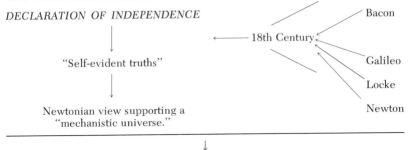

Culminating assignment for students: Write a "contemporary" statement about "self-evident truths" and the "rights" of man. Compare/contrast with positions stated in the Declaration of Independence.

SUMMARY OF 18TH CENTURY "THOUGHT" OR CLIMATE OF OPINION:

(1) A world of natural law . . . by no means denuded of a God but rather enhancing his scope by showing a mechanical universe — governed by laws — by constant relationships.

(2) If there were laws, man could discover them, hence an underlying optimism and a faith in the natural law . . . in reason to discover the natural law, and hence the perfectibility of man and society — the Utopia, the heavenly city on earth — thy kingdom come, thy will be done, on earth as it is in heaven."

(3) Thus equipped with laws that are discoverable; a reasonable faculty with which to discover, man and society could assume *progress* — progress towards conformity with natural law, conformity with God's design.

(4) Progress implied a future orientation — change — tomorrow.

(5) What the 18th century saw was a different source of knowing God. Man was made in God's image, hence man with his rational faculty (the ordering of his rational relationships) could find the larger model, the rational and ordered God.

(6) As Brinton points out in *The Shaping of the Modern Mind,* "In the widest terms the change in the attitude of Western men towards the Universe and everything in it was the change from the Christian supernatural

heaven after death to the rationalist natural heaven on this earth, now . . . or at least very shortly." The new, modern doctrine of progress. The idea of God was not done away: deism embraced the "newtonian World Machine" arguing for their "chilly" and distant God from a First Cause and design proves a designer theses.

(7) This then, the seeds of *The American Dream*.

IN ACTION

Here's what he did. He put *all* his accumulated data on ditto sheets so that the data bank could be passed out *en toto* to the students. The first data was a complete quote from Hall but he made no effort to sequence, categorize, or in any way relate the data. The students would discover the relationship.

Imagine several purple-pages of dittoed material on which are quotes and information: Mannheim, Brinton, Willey, Chase, Ogden and Richards, Dewey, Lovejoy, Becker, and so on plus a time-line, words, and data sheets on Bacon, Galileo, Locke, and Newton!

With a self-righteous feeling almost bordering on *Noblesse Oblige*, he passed his gift out to the unsuspecting students.

He should have known better. They didn't appreciate all the work he had done. He should have passed out twenty-eight pacifiers instead. Waste of time. . . It bombed!

What are you giving us all this stuff for?

What did all the dittoed material have to do with what they were studying?

The "hangers"—the questions put on the board last Friday—the things we didn't know? Oh.

An "A" student wanted to know why the class was no longer studying history.

A comedian asked of his colleagues that they take note of the paper drive being held on Wednesday.

With some anger and much frustration, the teacher turned the period into "seat work." Each student was to list the words or terms on the hand-outs that he didn't understand. The lists would be handed in at the end of the period.

The lists were collected at the end of the period. Two students had listed four words, one had stopped at twenty-two unknowns.

At lunch he shared a copy of the material with a colleague and lamented the intellectual bankruptcy he had witnessed in class.

The colleague hefted the material, glanced through it, and said, "You talk about overkill! No wonder they reacted the way they did. Hell, I don't even know what to do with all this. You've got a lot of information. When do you plan to teach?"

He had brought a gift; The kids had rejected it. His ego was wounded. But, like it or not, his flip colleague had a point. The teacher had worked things out in his *own* mind and learned; but this was not synonymous with teaching. He had worked out the ingredients but had not spent time assessing the next step: planning for teaching — planning for learning.

The next day he started off with Willey's quote: the countess, clock universe, the replaced sublime nature. The class discussed the quote for a few minutes.

Then the teacher threw out the statement that the "world is like a clock." If a small clock was a model of the universe, what did it suggest about the universe. Slowly the students warmed up to the issue:

A clock has a predetermined purpose.

All the parts had a purpose — to help fulfill the big purpose.

A clock was designed.

There must be a designer, a planner.

Each part, small as it is, is important to the whole thing.

If it were planned, there must be ways ("laws") saying how things should be done so the thing can operate.

The laws would work even if the parts didn't know about the laws.

After listing these things on the board, the teacher posed another issue: If one bought the simile and all that it *implied*, what would it mean for human purpose: All humans? individuals? social class? role of society, state, church?

"You mean to tell me that that was the way people looked at the world?" a student asked. Another student responded: "Not only then but one of these things (goes through the ditto material) says that we still accept this way of looking at things today." She read aloud Brinton's words.

It started. I don't look at the world that way! How do you look at the world? Not waiting for a response another student jumped in, You mean that self-evident meant this kind of a thing? It was common sense — people just took it for granted.

The teacher made an assignment: Finish the statement "The world is like a _____." Tell it as you see it but be sure to do the same thing with it that we did with the clock. Explain what it implies.

The students appeared to like this. One was overheard saying as he left the room "Ah, the world is like a Merry-go-Round on a trip. . ."

One student nodded his head as he walked past the teacher. "Not bad. . . ."

The next day they picked it up again and it became clear that there was substantial confusion about what the world was like, what could be called "self-evident" today, the importance of what people take for granted: Dewey was used, Chase was used, and one student brought up Bacon's "Four Idols" and the class spent the rest of the period trying to find specific examples of each Idol.

Another assignment was made: Read Lazarsfeld's conclusions from his study of the American soldier and just jot down your own reaction "to this social science study that took substantial time, effort, and money to make."

The next day, the response to the Lazarsfeld "findings" was what one would expect. Students thought it was absurd to spend time researching into the obvious: everyone knew that bright people were "oddballs" and had more "hang-ups" than the average guy; farm-boys were more used to roughing it than city-boys, army life wouldn't have been as much a change; naturally people accustomed to hot weather wouldn't mind it as much; it didn't take much brains to want to get away from the fighting and want to come home while the war was on. There were some questions about the black privates and preferred officers but the questions were directed more at trying to justify rather than take issue with the findings. One student said "social science research is kind of stupid. It's like studying poor people and then saying that we have poor people!" Another: "Why spend money trying to find out things that anyone would know if he just took time to look around!"

The teacher informed the students that the findings given from Lazarsfeld were just the *opposite* of what the research showed. There was discussion about the teacher being "dishonest" and "tricking" them. The students didn't seem willing to get into the "just looking around" common sense issue. The teacher pointed this out to the class. He then handed out a reprint of the article appearing in the Philadelphia *Evening Bulletin* which had appeared at the time of Sputnik. They reviewed briefly the Sputnik issue—an issue ancient to the students. The students were asked to take each major idea put forth in the article and, under each idea, try to determine what the writer seemed to have taken for granted —what ideas he just accepted as being true, as being self-evident. Some structure was given:

Example: ". . . that ours were the best schools in the world."
   (1) there is a *single*, world-wide standard by which to measure schools.
   (2) there is a specific purpose that is the same for *all* students.
   (3) . . .
"The news [of Sputnik] shocked many Americans. . . who had depended. . . that ours were the best schools. . ."

". . . college professors. . . complaining about the schools for some time. . ."

". . . the persons running the public schools — the principals, superintendents, Teachers' College faculties and state education officials. . ."

". . . sugar-coated education. . ."

What ideas are taken for granted about such things as:
   Purpose of education
   Cause and Effect
   Who "runs" the schools
   Education and "pain"

They spent the period wrestling with the hidden assumptions. Near the end of the period a student asked why they were doing such things in a history class. "It is fun. . . but, you know, so what?" This opened up a chance to do some synthesizing about self-evident truths, common sense, and, as a student put it, "Big ideas are often built from a number of little ideas that aren't even checked or thought about. If the little ideas are wrong, the big ones don't make much sense."

The next class session was a review of some of the things the students had hit (without too much of a thud) in their previous world history tour. Using the list of key words during the 13th, 18th, and 19th centuries, there was an attempt to reconstruct some of the major things going on during the respective centuries. One thing became apparent: the students "knew" a large number of descriptive phrases (e.g. "Middle Ages") but didn't have a grasp of how pieces fit together. It was a review period. An assignment was made which asked that students take the quote from Ogden and Richards, interpret what they thought the authors meant, and then try to figure out words or phrases used today that seem "fuzzy." Example: Individual, purpose, exact, certainty, cause-effect.

The students ran into all sorts of trouble. Some picked up

Chase's quote from *Tyranny of Words* and tried to work it in. Some just didn't understand. The class played with how words stand for ideas, and often influence ideas, and that sometimes people react unthinkingly to words and not ideas. The teacher called attention to Becker's list again and asked that the students try to "guess" what seemed to be going on since the 18th century. They worked with Hall's quotation from the NCSS Yearbook. Science—and whatever the idea of "science" meant—seemed to be a major idea at the time the Declaration of Independence was written.

A larger rendition of the time-line appearing in the dittoed material was put on the board. It covered a time period from 1492 to 1776. The line focused upon four people: Bacon, Galileo, Locke, and Newton. The students had become familiar with the Four Idols and used them to review some of the things going on in class during the past few days. Aside from this, the students didn't know about *Novum Organum*, tied Galileo to a telescope, Locke to Jefferson "in some way," and Newton to an apple.

Given the hand-outs on the four persons, a few days were spent trying to determine what contributions, if any, each had made toward building an idea of science. Bacon: deductive and inductive reasoning and the problems encountered in putting relationships into words; Galileo and Aristotle; Locke and the role of the senses with ideas; and Newton's "natural law" which, if understood, would help man to understand himself, God, and purpose and ways of social living.

The teacher then dittoed off his *own* summary sheet and gave it to the students partly as an attempt at synthesis and partly as a way of putting to work what they had been studying. Students were asked to find *specific* information which would either support or deny the seven ideas included in the Climate of Opinion, as listed on the summary.

The culminating assignment: Rewrite the second paragraph of the Declaration of Independence from a contemporary (current) climate of opinion.

At the conclusion of the effort, the "A" student was upset. Why didn't they just continue studying history instead of getting into philosophy, science, language and "things like that." Fair enough, as the students hopefully learned, words stand for ideas. Each idea usually takes a lot of little ideas for granted; now, "What about the idea of 'history'. . . does it, too, have a number of 'self-evident' truths? If so, how would one find out about them?" If anyone were interested, the teacher said that he would be willing to help explore this area.

In reviewing the processes used and in trying to "go to school" on what the teacher tried and what worked or didn't work and to what degree, the teacher made several points:

SELF-EVALUATION

1. *He had tried to do too much too fast.* "If I had to do it over again, I would try to make a transition from the old style or approach to the things I wanted to try. Kids have expectations—right or wrong—which raise all sorts of problems when a teacher tries to change the content or approach. I think I'd share with the students what I was going to try to do—the big ideas, the role I hoped they would play."

2. *Determining in advance specific things, usable concepts, that would come out of a study* "helped open the door to all sorts of information. It causes problems though. I had a tendency to want to use too much information—an intellectual conspicuous consumption type of thing."

3. *Having multiple materials and a lot of information is not teaching.* "The whole thing fell apart that first day. I shot way too much at them somehow hoping that by osmosis or something, everything would be learned. Having content is necessary. But, not sufficient; you've got to do something with it. Teach."

4. *He recognized the need to set teaching priorities.* "All the data we used—the quotes, the words,—everything, I thought was exciting and great. But I wasted a lot of time too. Some things could have been used in passing. For example, the work of assumptions and common sense I would approach differently—it cluttered things unnecessarily. Oh, good stuff but not used well in view of what I was trying to do. Other things I would spend *more* time on, slow down, go into depth; you know, savor it a bit."

5. *Relationships are not given but made.* "There are times when I, or with the class, should have tried to synthesize more. We had a number of hangers within the big hangers and I should have done something with them."

6. *Large, over-view planning is important. Day-to-day planning is vital.* "Every class session is information that has to go into planning. Kids give you feedback one way or another and this means you've got to take it into account

in what you do next. You make decisions along the way. This takes time."

7. *Question:* Would you have handed out all that material at one time if you had to do it over again? *Response:* "Not on your life. That material was my security blanket. No, I would give out material but bit-by-bit so that nobody got overwhelmed; and so we could make better use of the material by zeroing in without a lot of other things getting in the way."

Question: Wouldn't that structure things into a tight box? *Response:* "No, not necessarily. It would depend on what we did with it. The material itself doesn't have to box you."

Question: What about your role as a teacher? You still seemed to be the "take charge" person. You still gave direction. *Response:* "Yes, but it was a different type of 'taking charge' and a different type of direction giving. You can take charge in the sense that you have resources, questions, suggestions, and so on; you can take charge of opening up opportunities. The same thing with direction. You can give a set direction or you can help direct opening up directions. I'm not saying it well—you got a role to play. But, it's not a teller. You work your butt off getting materials, clarifying, pushing ideas, and weaving things together with them. It's hard. You've got to be thinking and working all the time. And you've got to be willing to learn."

Question: What about content? *Response:* "You've got to have content. Whatever you mean by it. I think one reason we don't connect with kids is that our content itself is ludicrous. Three times through that American history scene. I'm not talking about the need for the old packaged content but there is a need to recognize that new information, new knowledge, even if not used as content, still forces the teacher to reorganize what he already uses."

Question: Would you try it again? *Response:* "Yeah. If I don't plan to reach the retirement age. Let's face it, it takes time (and that's one thing 'ole Charlie the Children Checker doesn't really have). Seriously, in that one class, I doubt if I can go back to the old routine. They know what it could be like; You get a taste of steak. And I used parts of what we did in that one class with my other classes— only parts but they liked it. Or, seemed to. *I loved it.* But, the whole thing just isn't set up for this type of teaching."

Question: Was it a success? From your own point of view—that one class, was it successful? *Response:* "Compared to what? Everybody assumes the old routine is successful. It's almost axiomatic—like we were studying with the kids. A lot of things are taken for granted. Nobody asks me if my other classes are a success. Were the kids able to use the ideas? Yes—in varying degrees. Did they get a more firm understanding of the complexity of the Declaration of Independence and for that matter the base of American history? Yes. Did they become more aware of thinking and of what different ways they could use information? Yes. Will they sock the old college boards? I have no idea. Some will and some won't, but I have a funny feeling that doesn't tell very much about teaching or curriculum. A bright kid can psych it out and do O.K. regardless of us. I don't know how to answer your question."

Question: How many school days did you actually take to do this thing? *Response:* "Seven. I had planned for a week but it took seven school days. That's a total of about five hours. Maybe we ought to think in terms of hours and not days and this might change curriculum approaches."

Question: How would you make up the time taken from the regular course of study? *Response:* "If teaching is cramming in a lot of the usual, it is easy. Summarize the text into fact sheets and cram. But, tell them it is cramming. Even the old routine is not known for its effective and efficient use of time. I'm just waiting for the day when the old—when American history is programmed. A kid takes it and finishes it. Then, maybe, we'll have the time and energy to teach."

Review Situation One and develop a chart depicting the sequence of what the teacher went through. You might want to try to determine what he was trying to do in terms of concepts and skills and you might want to list your own "hangers" at this point. And what would you do with the data bank if you had the 11th grade class—how would *you* plan?

SITUATION TWO

In this situation you will be provided with an assortment of information, ideas, questions, and activities. Assume that you are teaching an "average" senior class in Current Issues or a 9th Grade course in "civics." Noting the differences in planning as evidenced in Situation One, use the material to provide a teaching "umbrella" around the issue: "The Media and The Government."

As you work with the material, keep a process log of your own functioning. This would include establishing some criteria for selection and use, some strategy (teaching and/or content) for categorizing information, the use of a number of skills in your own efforts, the kinds of concepts to be used, etc.

This may be done individually or in groups. It is interesting to note the substantial number of alternatives that will emerge. And it will be interesting to compare the differences, if any, between what is prepared for seniors and what is prepared for 9th graders.

After preparing the umbrella, plan *one* specific one period lesson plan *other* than an introduction or summary. You may wish to analyze the different lesson plans prepared by your colleagues.

DATA BANK: THE MEDIA AND THE GOVERNMENT

"The best Things, when perverted, become the very worst: So Printing, which in itself is no small Advantage to Mankind, when it is Abus'd may be of most Fatal Consequences."

(Pamphlet, 1712)

"Here we have 'America's Greatest Menace' to the free press, in the eyes of your profession, eyeball to eyeball with 'Censorship Unlimited,' according to my crowd."

(Vice-President to Associated Press Managing Editors' Association in Honolulu, 1970)

Adlai Stevenson: "one-party press"

Franklin D. Roosevelt: "newspaper barons"

John F. Kennedy: "reading it more, but enjoying it less"

Thomas Jefferson: "even the least informed of the people have learnt that nothing in a newspaper is to be believed."

James Madison: "Could it be so arranged that every newspaper, when printed on one side, should be handed over to the press of an adversary, to be printed on the other, thus presenting to every reader both sides of every question, truth would always have a fair chance."

Poor Richard: While free from Force the Press remains, Virtue and Freedom chear our Plains And Learning Largesses bestows, And keep unlicens'd open house. . . .

If William James was right in commenting "What holds attention determines action," then concern with media is justified in a democratic society. Who *should* determine what is reported, how it is reported, when it is reported, and in what format? Responses vary. When the "what" is acceptable or liked, those adhering to the particular "what" will fear any sort of censorship. When the "what" is disapproved, all sorts of questions about accountability, responsibility, and function arise.

Should media admit biases?
Should the individual citizen have more alternatives open in regard to what, how, when he will see, hear, read, . . . learn? What should the relationship be between government and public information? We are aware that translators do more than just "translate," that they help create the message. Do media simply report the "facts" or do they become active participants in creating what is perceived "to be"? Should there be a public standard for evaluation of the power and functioning of print and electronic media?
How would one establish a standard? How would one enforce a standard?

Most people are not concerned with the concept of media freedom.

Most people think that the mass media already has too much freedom.

Most people think the press and electronic media should print "good" news instead of "bad" news.

Most people think that the media should "help the government, not criticize it."

Most people favor governmental or some public monitoring of media.

Most Americans trust T.V. more than other media.

When one leaves the school and stops his formal schooling, his education continues. Learning does not stop. Mass communications provides a means of continuing education. Electronic media, and print media select certain information to report, choose topics, and present alternatives in an effort to educate the public. What one "knows" and how one behaves is in part a product of mass communication.

In what ways are public education and education of the public similar?

Is there a difference between propagandizing and reporting, indoctrination and teaching?

Are media reporters and teachers objective?

Is there a difference between interpreting and opinionating?

What kinds of things are involved in determining how and what one selects to teach or report?

What about the guarantees of the First Amendment? Are the guarantees unconditional? (Does the First Amendment apply to teachers?)

Dictionary: Objectivity is the state, quality, or relation of being objective and objective means "uninfluenced by emotion, surmise, or personal prejudice." Deals with that which is based on "observable phenomena, presented factually."

Kent Cooper (AP, 1943): the ideal of impartial, objective news "the highest original moral concept ever developed in America and given to the world."

Walter Cronkite: "Maybe it is impossible to be 100 percent objective, because of emotions, but I don't share the philosophy that it is good to resort to personal opinion because we cannot be 100 percent objective."

Bill Moyers: "Of all the great myths of American journalism, objectivity is the greatest. Each of us sees what his own experience leads him to see."

Marshall McLuhan: "Societies have always been shaped more by the nature of the medium by which men have communicated than by the content of the communication."

History: Press's view toward Presidents:
1800, Connecticut *Courant:* "Neighbors will become enemies of neighbors, brother of brother, fathers of their sons. . . the air will be rent with the cries of distress, the soil soaked in blood, and the nation black with crimes." [If a certain candidate were elected]

1830's: "Ambition is his crime. . . intrigue is his native element. He governs by means of corruption, and his immoral practices will redound to his shame and confusion. His conduct in the political arena has been that of a shameless and lawless gamester."

Governmental uses of the Press:
1831: President asks Congress to have the Post Office Department refuse to transmit newspapers and publications "intended to instigate the slaves to insurrection."

1863: Burnside issued order: "On account of the repeated expression of disloyal and incendiary sentiments, the publication of the newspaper known as the Chicago Times is hereby suppressed."

1918: Minnesota: It is unlawful "for any person to print, publish, or circulate in any manner whatsoever" anything "that advocates that men should not enlist in the military or naval forces of the United States or the State of Minnesota."

1798: ". . . if any person shall write, print, utter, or publish, or shall cause or procure to be written, printed, uttered, or published, or shall knowingly and willingly assist or aid in writing, printing, uttering or publishing any false, scandalous and malicious writing or writings against the government of the United States. . . or the said President. . . ."

(U.S. Statute)

1509–1547: King took absolute control of the press: over who had a press and over what was to be printed. ". . . the Long Parliament (1640–1660) did not hesitate to copy this precedent of a tyranny they had overthrown."

Jefferson, in a letter written in 1807, suggested that a newspaper could be made more useful by dividing the paper into four chapters: Truth, Probabilities, Possibilities, Lies. Truth would be quite short and report only confirmed facts. Probabilities would be interpretations justified by facts in Truth. Possibilities and Lies would be for those who would rather have lies for their money than the blank paper.

Henry Ward Beecher: "Newspapers are the schoolmasters of the common people" The newspaper is seen as an endless book. . .

AP and UPI provide 100 percent of non-local news and commentary to local newspapers and TV stations.

Readers screen out and evaluate that information which appears to be of value.

Newspaper readership increases with the rising occupational status of the family head, with increased education, and with greater activity in voluntary organizations.

In a sample of metropolitan newspapers (excluding New York and Washington), of 83 stories: 13 were concerned with violence, crime, or war; 33 were local stories; 38 dealt with domestic national stories; and 12 dealt with foreign stories.

Most metropolitan newspapers carry a range of opinions as reflected in syndicated columns.

80 per cent of newspapers originate in the same geographical area in which the reader resides.

Newspapers lead in informing voters about local elections.

Television leads in informing voters in state and national elections.

People feel that television gives a clearer understanding of issues in national elections than does the press.

Vice-President Agnew:
"How is network news determined? A small group of men, numbering perhaps no more than a dozen, decide what forty to fifty million Americans will learn of the day's events in the nation and the world."
"Those really illiberal, self-appointed guardians of our destiny would like to run the country without ever submitting to the elective process as we in public office do."

Charles L. Bennett, *Daily Oklahoman,* warns: Better communication need not necessarily result in better understanding. "Information becomes useful only when organized, analyzed, and rationalized. This requires self-disciplined, unemotional thought, and, too often, it's far easier to dismiss the day's news with an emotional, all encompassing reaction and let it go at that. . . public discussion becomes public argument, recrimination, and name calling."

Government officials often view the media as potential help. To be elected, to gain financial support, to move policies into practice, the voter must be reached in a positive way.

Sometimes communication efforts are designed to hide ideas rather than to share—aimed at gaining acceptance more than at securing a way of mutual persuasion.

Before the quill, before nations, governments, big-business, mass education, communication was in a "speech world."

The media usually do not see their role as an arm of any administration. "A journalist owes nothing to those who govern the country—everything to his country."

If people are involved in decision-making, they must have valid information. Free speech and press is designed to serve such a purpose and is protected by the Bill of Rights.

A democracy stakes all on the premise that right conclusions may come from many tongues and not through authoritative selection. (Judge Learned Hand)

It is sometimes easy to ascribe programs to a single source (President, Media) and not to take into account the events, time, and number of related factors including one's own frame of reference.

In three-quarters of the states, reporters have no more right than average citizens to withhold information demanded by a court subpoena, grand jury, or legislative committee. They are compelled to disclose all information, written or oral, relevant to the issues. They may be held in contempt if refusing.

Washington, Jefferson, Jackson, Lincoln, *Teddy* Roosevelt, Wilson, Franklin Roosevelt, Truman, Kennedy, Johnson, and Nixon faced serious problems regarding the function of the media.

Resources: Leo Bogart, "Newspapers in the Age of Television" *Daedalus,* Winter, 1963.

Herbert Brucker, "Can Printed News Save a Free Society?" *Saturday Review,* October 10, 1970.

Herbert Brucker, "What's Wrong with Objectivity?" *Saturday Review,* October 11, 1969.

W. H. Ferry, "Masscomm as Educator," *American Scholar,* Spring, 1966.

Abraham S. Goldstein, "Newsmen and Their Confidential Sources," *New Republic,* March 21, 1970.

Bernard Hennessy, "Welcome Spiro Agnew," *New Republic,* December 13, 1969.

John Tebbel, "Studying the Mass Media," *Saturday Review,* February 14, 1970.

Richard L. Tobin, "The Coming Age of News Monopoly," *Saturday Review,* October 10, 1970.

"What Does Walter Cronkite Really Think?" *Look,* November 17, 1970.

Case Study: C.B.S.: "The Selling of the Pentagon."

When a person reads the printed word, he remains pretty much an individual. He selects the parts on which he wishes to concentrate. He can stop and contemplate and, if necessary, reread. He may raise questions, challenge, and in a broad sense, carry on an intra-dialogue.

Television engulfs the viewer. The viewer is surrounded with integrated appeals made through more than one of the senses. It is one way, a synthesized "whole" that hits one with immediacy and allows no opportunity for the viewer to interact, to pause long enough to initiate an intra-dialogue, to go back over, to separate the technique from the message.

In 1943 a Commission of Freedom of the Press (chaired by Robert Hutchins) was appointed. The committe's report was made in 1947. Recommendations included: Other media should have the same constitutional rights as the press receives under the first amendment; repeal of legislation prohibiting expressions favoring revolutionary changes in institutions where there is no clear and present danger that violence will result from the expressions; government should use the mediums of mass communication to inform the people of facts regarding policies. (If private instruments are unwilling or unable to supply facilities, the government should employ mass communications of its own. . .)

After getting deluged with all sorts of facts, opinions, interpretations, questions, quotations, sources, and floating ideas, you probably feel as a number of students do: that it all may be interesting, but so what? One could learn the material as is. That is, one could try to memorize what a pamphlet said and when, what the vice-president said in Honolulu, match quotations with people's names, figure out a scheme for learning all the facts (i.e., "most people favor governmental or some public monitoring of media"), matching historical dates and happenings (Minnesota, 1918. . .), what the 1943 Commission reported, etc. But, after all this work — all this "learning" — one would still be faced with the question *so what?*

ORGANIZATION

Whatever else teaching and learning might be, they have, as a basic ingredient, *organization.* Organization implies a sense of purpose, relating diverse experiences, to that purpose, ways of processing the relationships between experiences and the purpose, and somehow making the effort in a form that *makes* sense. In planning for teaching, organization is a crucial if not the most crucial factor in the entire process.

In trying to work out your own process log, how would you respond to the following?

1. At what point did you determine your major goals — before going through the material, after going through the material, while going through the material? All three?

2. As you worked with the material, did you find yourself modifying your initial goals?

3. Did you have to relate data in order to form concepts or were the concepts obvious in the material? In other words, did you work with the material and *induce* relationships called concepts?

4. To what extent were you conscious of GR concepts in contrast with UN concepts?

5. As you worked with the material, were you aware of questions that you raised? Did you try to explore the questions at the time or were they left hanging? Did you have a system for recording the questions?

6. Did you evolve a *system* for categorizing and classifying the different kinds of information in the material? What criteria did you use? (Facts, time, quotes, issues, topics, people, ideas?) Did you find yourself wanting to evolve a sort of "cross-indexing" system?

7. Did you find yourself synthesizing as you went along or did the synthesizing take place after most of the work was done? Did the synthesizing raise questions about the way you categorized the material?

8. Did ideas for student activities come after the "organization" or did possible activities pop up at different times? Did you have any system for recording activity ideas?

9. What role did your own subjective feelings play in your approach and use of the material? Did you find some quotations, etc., turning you off because you didn't like the content or the person? What part did this play in your effort?

10. Were you aware of the skills you were using in the process of relating and generalizing? Can you describe the skills and how they were used? In other words, to what extent did you monitor your own approach?

11. In trying to work out a single class period lesson plan, what problems did you encounter? (Concepts, skills, material, activities, consistency, motivation, over-all method?)

All the questions related to your use of the material are not just nice exercises. They embrace many of the variables involved in conceptualizing, inquiring, and the use of generalizing skills. These are the same variables faced by students when they encounter new experiences and new data. An *awareness* of the processes one is using allows for more effective self-monitoring, more effective functioning. Even being aware of the attitudes and values one brings, and with which one creates meaning, is a vital aspect of learning.

It should be rather obvious that learning is not a neat, logical, step-by-step, sequenced activity. In a real sense, learning is a systems approach to experience with each part relating with other parts—transacting, mutually influencing, modifying. If such things as goals, concepts, skills, data, material, values, etc., are constantly influencing one another, organizing for teaching becomes more complex than just having bodies, books, and bugles.

SITUATION THREE

Two teachers were teaching a "unit" on India to sophomore students. The unit came under a section of the curriculum called "Non-Western Studies." The unit included addressing U.S. aid to India following World War II. The Peace Corps was mentioned as being a part of such aid—aid designed to improve health and sanitation as well as to upgrade education. Peace Corps workers were seen as spending up to two years in countless small Indian villages trying to bring about change.

The following three mini-case studies were duplicated for use with the students. The ideas were adapted from Anthropological Studies, and reworked for secondary students.

CASE STUDIES*

CASE STUDY ONE

An extension worker was teaching ways to "midwife" in a small village. She informed the midwives in one class that they should not cut the umbilical cord with an unsterilized sickle. The worker explained that unless the sickle were sterilized, there could be a disease called tetanus. The villagers attributed tetanus to an invisible flying insect called Jam. If Jam touched a baby, the baby would die. The worker did not discard the villagers' notions about tetanus and Jam. She told the villagers that Jam might touch the sickle or other cutting instruments used. Since Jam was invisible and no person could see the flying insect when it touched things, everything should be put in boiling water before use. This way, Jam's danger would be eliminated. The worker believed that they would not sterilize the instruments unless they saw the act related to Jam. If they sterilized the instruments, eventually tetanus would not be a danger. The need for the belief would disappear.

CASE STUDY TWO

Small-pox vaccination was to be introduced to the villagers. The villagers believed that small-pox was caused by a disease goddess. Smallpox epidemics had grown and caused much fear. The disease goddess was not easily placated. Despite the offerings made by the villagers, the disease persisted. A few villagers decided to risk the vaccination approach. The villagers watched with concern the children who had received the vaccination. They knew that pox marks and fever were signs that the goddess was residing in the body. Ceremonies would be performed in her honor. The vaccinated children became feverish. The goddess was in the body! Ceremonies were performed, the fever died down, and thus the

°Source: Mildred S. Luchinsky, "Problems of Culture Change in the Indian Village," *Human Organization*, Spring, 1963.

goddess had left—never to bother the child again. The villagers were impressed. Had the worker simply told the villagers that smallpox was caused by a virus, the villagers would have thought that such blasphemy would only bring the wrath of the goddess.

CASE STUDY THREE

Villagers used the fields as latrines. Two extension workers wanted to build indoor (covered) borehole latrines as a move to improve sanitation. The womenfolk in the village agreed that there were good reasons for building such latrines. But, there was one major reason why the use of the fields should *not* be changed. It seemed that the daily trips to the fields allowed a time for the womenfolk to meet and to chat with friends whom they otherwise had little occasion to meet. Young women of high caste who were strictly confined to their homes during the daylight hours disapproved of the indoor latrine project. To build indoor latrines would be to challenge the custom of *purdah* (seclusion of women) because there would have been a need to provide other means for women to socialize. The custom could not be interfered with. Thus, the indoor latrine project failed to get off the ground.

Note: Some of the extension workers' colleagues believed that it was wrong to introduce medical and sanitation changes without challenging the traditional beliefs held by the villagers.

Using the case studies as vehicles or means for study, both teachers made lesson plans for their use.

LESSON PLAN ONE

Goal: To get students to realize that some foreign aid is wasted.

Concepts to be taught:
1. American aid to underdeveloped nations is not always appreciated.
2. Archaic customs and superstitions blind people to chances for better health.

Skills to be used:
1. Reading
2. Critical thinking

Approach:
Pass out the three case studies which are to be read as an assignment.

In class, initiate discussion by asking the following questions:

(1) What is a midwife?

(2) To what did the villagers attribute the cause of tetanus?

(3) Why were the villagers concerned about Jam?

(4) What approach did the extension worker try?

(5) What did she think would happen to the villagers' belief?

(6) What did the villagers think caused smallpox?

(7) Why were some villagers willing to try vaccination?

(8) What did the extension worker have to be careful *not* to tell the villagers?

(9) What was *purdah*?

(10) What did the village women feel to be more important than sanitation?

In-class assignment: Write an essay telling if you agree or disagree with what the extension workers' colleagues said about introducing change.

Using the case study and the lesson plan, please answer the following questions:

1. The teacher planned his lesson. Yes No

2. The teacher used specific data in his plans. Yes No

3. The teacher had an objective in mind for using the case study. Yes No

4. The case study might be appropriate for social studies because it included such things as a study of other customs, anthropology, social structure, and social problems. Yes No

5. The teacher could indicate what he was doing and why he was doing it. Yes No

6. The teacher seems to assume that "knowing" specific details is logically connected with his goal and concepts. Yes No

7. The lesson plan put emphasis upon recall.   Yes No

8. The lesson plan did allow for students to relate and to think.   Yes No

9. The questions in the lesson plan implied certain "set" and "correct" answers.   Yes No

10. The lesson plan provided an opportunity for skills development.   Yes No

11. The lesson plan has a built-in mechanism for evaluation.   Yes No

12. In terms of classroom management, the teacher knew where he wanted to go, the students knew what was expected of them, and there was flexibility in the use of time.   Yes No

13. Given all the above factors, would you consider the lesson plan to be a good one?   Yes No

Given a chance to talk with the teacher, what three questions would you ask? (Please place the questions in *rank* order of importance).

1.
2.
3.

LESSON PLAN TWO

Goal: To have students realize that social change efforts are like teaching: to be effective you have to start where people are.

Concepts:
1. The ways by which people approach health and disease must include not only the latest knowledge but also an understanding of how health and disease is part of a "whole" cultural context.
2. Efforts to bring about change involve, even in medicine, people's values and beliefs.

Skills to be used:
1. Identifying specific information.
2. Generalizing with information to *inductively* form a concept.

3. Deductive reasoning. (Giving specific information which supports or denies the selected concepts).

Approach: Pass out the three case studies which are to be read as an assignment.

A. Share with students an article from the *New York Times* (June 6, 1971) on the psychological dimensions of pain.

B. Review previous work dealing with the view that effective foreign aid "should" be directed at helping people to help themselves. Anchor this with the Chinese proverb: "Give a man a fish, you feed him for a day; teach him to fish and he can feed himself for a life-time."

C. Pose issue: When one attempts to change another, what types of things should he take into account? (About himself? About the people asked to change?)

D. Activity:

(1) Given the three cases studies, the students are asked to determine what specific *similar* things appear to be part of *each* different case study. Example: In all three, there is an effort to change. Students do this individually. When completed, the class will try to relate the similarities into a larger, encompassing "idea."

(2) Students are to take each of the concepts above and test them with the data in the three case studies.

(3) Using the statement about what the extension workers' colleagues said, the students are asked to try to determine what *assumptions* the colleagues have about human change.

Assignment: Think of a possible change in your community which customs and beliefs might make difficult to bring about. (How would you go about trying to bring about the possible change?)

Using the case study and the lesson plan, please answer the following questions:

1. The teacher planned his lesson.   Yes   No

2. The teacher used specific data in his plans.   Yes   No

3. The teacher had an objective in mind for using the case study.   Yes   No

4. The case study might be appropriate for social studies because it included such things as a study of other customs, anthropology, social structure, and social problems.   Yes   No

5. The teacher could indicate what he was doing and why he was doing it.   Yes   No

6. The teacher seems to assume that "knowing" specific details is logically connected with his goal and concepts.   Yes   No

7. The lesson plan put emphasis upon recall.   Yes   No

8. The lesson plan did allow for students to relate and to think.   Yes   No

9. The questions in the lesson plan implied certain "set" and "correct" answers.   Yes   No

10. The lesson plan provided an opportunity for skills development.   Yes   No

11. The lesson plan has a built-in mechanism for evaluation.   Yes   No

12. In terms of classroom management, the teacher knew where he wanted to go, the students know what was expected of them, and there was flexibility in the use of time.   Yes   No

13. Given all the above factors, would you consider the lesson plan to be a "good" one?   Yes   No

Given a chance to talk with the teacher, what three questions would you ask? (Please place the questions in *rank* order of importance).

1.

2.

3.

Granted, there are a number of things we don't know about the situation in which both teachers were working with the same material: students, community, time factors, teacher background, discipline, etc. So, no attempt is made to say that this lesson plan was "good" or that one is "bad." Besides, we don't know what in fact transpired in class with the students—and this may be the real test of a lesson plan.

Each of the two lesson plans seemed to have a number of the same ingredients and yet they were different. It is the difference that raises fundamental questions about teaching organization and planning.

REVIEWING SITUATIONS

In *Situation One*, we have noted the processes a teacher went through in attempting to modify his teaching. Having a substantial amount of data is a necessary but not sufficient base for teaching. Planning is an ongoing process which means "going to school" on what happens during the implementation of the plans. It takes time, effort, and an attitudinal willingness toward "risk" to approach teaching in this manner. And the institutional structure seems to limit or set perimeters on what one can and cannot do.

Situation Two is a data bank. You are asked to monitor your own *processes* and in so doing try to evolve an awareness of the factors involved in conceptual teaching, inquiry, and skill development. Organization is seen as a conceptualizing activity demanding the use of data and skills. The affective domain—emotions, attitudes, values—play a vital part of the processes used.

In *Situation Three*, there is a structure involving concepts, data, questions, activities, and reading checks. It provides one type of organization.

The case studies and the two "similar" lesson plans raise the issue of quality as part of planning. It is not enough to simply say: "I've planned a lesson" or, "I use case studies" or, "I use a conceptual approach to teaching" or, "I place emphasis on skill development." There is more to it than this and, as professionals, we should be willing to move into more sophisticated efforts.

You will notice that in all the situations, history has a chance to be used. In all areas, the social sciences and findings from the social sciences are put to work. The Situations are taken from American history, World history, Current Issues, and Non-Western courses. The approaches to teaching raise the same issues. Only the data and vehicles differ.

Where do we go from here?

You probably have several questions at this point. For example, all the examples assume some availability of data which broadens the concept of "content." How does one get this data? Where are the sources? Obviously, one builds data banks over a period of time. And, the sources are plentiful as we will try to indicate. You may be wondering if you will be expected to teach this way. Hopefully, better! But, this too takes time and effort and a willingness to try, get feedback, and try again. We believe that if a teacher can do what he expects his students to do, then teaching will be sound and exciting. If not, it becomes a game of hide and seek. One learns to do by doing.

More pragmatic questions lead us to the next section. Does one decide on the concepts he wants to teach first and then look for material? Or, does one pick a topic and then try to find both concepts and materials? Or, does one find the material and then determine the concepts and skills to be developed? As you might expect, the response is: Yes. And, no.

We will try to develop this in the next section.

"What a cheap trick! Is it any wonder I'm anti-Semitic?"

4

INQUIRY PLANNING STRATEGIES

THE TACIT UNDERSTANDING

There is a tacit understanding among social studies teachers that materials are the tail that wags the dog—or stabilizes the kite —depending upon how you look at it. And this is not to fault anyone. There is very little time allowing one to: (1) set up broad goals, (2) establish objectives that are logically consistent with the goals, (3) determine concepts and more specific, measurable objectives, (4) devise an effective system of student evaluation, and (5) *then* go searching for just the right materials or vehicles which will carry one effectively through his classes. Most of us will argue that the concepts we teach must be academically accurate: amenable to empirical testing. The natural source for such academically accurate concepts would be the disciplines feeding the social studies. We can and do get findings from the scholars working in history and the social sciences. The findings, or concepts, are sometimes so broad that one thinks of them as "commonsense" concepts. They sometimes seem to escape the artificial confines we have labeled disciplines.

For example, following is a list of concepts reported from scholars working in their respective discipline areas. We are reporting the concepts and will let you ponder the discipline source.

Discipline

1. Continuous change has been a universal condition of human society. _____

2. A society exists in the minds of its members and occurs only when there is interaction among members. _____

3. Each culture tends to view its physical habitat differently—a society's value system, goals, organization, and level of technology

determine which elements of the land are prized and utilized.

4. Practically all significant differences in human behavior (and among human populations) are understandable as learned cultural patterns rather than as biologically inherited ones.

5. The larger the society, the more an individual must rely upon group membership; uniting with others increases the self and the chances to "move" in decision-making.

6. The study of human experience allows man the possibility of a wider range of choice. The study offers no immutable laws, givens, or inevitables upon which to make decisions.

7. Man is a flexible and "becoming" creature. Through the experiences he encounters he learns a complex of roles, understandings, and expectations.

8. Man moves from isolated and self-sufficient communities to a growing interdependence: more trade, migration, diffusion of ideas and practices, and importance of relative location and situation.

9. Every cultural system is an interconnected series of ideas and patterns for behavior in which changes in one aspect generally lead to changes in other segments of the system.

10. As a minimum condition for its existence a society establishes authoritative institutions that can make decisions which are binding on all the people, provide for resolution of dissent, and effectively enforce basic rules.

When the findings become more specific, we find them in the "if"–"then" context: *if* x, y, and z exist under conditions a and b, *then* d will *probably* happen. At this point most practitioners become impatient. We want the concepts and say that we recognize the complexity involved but are unwilling to recognize the difficulty faced when trying to simplify. We seem to grasp for meaningfulness with a demand for simplicity. We can get thousands of findings from history and the social sciences but they cover a range of probability and are always conditional and limited. In other words, the highly universal GR concepts set a model. We want more concepts and we want them to be *both* universal and *specific*. Recognizing that the social sciences are relatively young and that wishful thinking seldom adds much to the furtherance of sound research, our quest may remain valid but our expectations have to become more realistic.

FACTS OF LIFE

The "tail that wags" includes the teacher coming face-to-face with some facts of life. In most school systems there is a broad social studies curriculum which lists what we call "administrative topics"; such topics set broad limits or boundaries for the data to be used. For example, a teacher may find that American history will be taught at the eleventh grade. This means that whatever data a teacher uses must somehow relate to a portion of human experience, to a place and time, and to a *specific* group of people called Americans. Granted, this is extremely broad. But within this framework, there are sub-administrative topics such as the Age of Exploration, The Colonial Period, The Age of Jackson, The Progressive Movement, and others. Many school systems provide this administrative structure within a context established by state departments of education.

Thus, in many cases the topics are "givens." Seldom do the givens go beyond broad listings. Seldom are concepts, student objectives, activities, and methods to be used "given" the teacher. Such things are left, theoretically, to the professional. To be sure, the administrative structure may list some broad goals such as Learning the American Heritage, Fostering Good Citizenship, Developing Critical Thinking, and so on. On occasion one will find more specific value goals mentioned, such as "Developing an appreciation for the free enterprise system." However, generally what is done within the broad framework is determined by the professionals. In other words, given the framework of American history and the Colonial period, the teacher or a group of professionals then determine the concepts, student objectives, methodology, and activities.

It is at this point that the tacit understanding seems to be operational. The administrative topics imply certain materials. The standard textbooks support the understanding. Thus, materials come first. *Then* the teacher grapples with what to do with the materials: what ideas or concepts to teach, what students should know, what kinds of activities should help the student to know. This, in turn, suggests evaluation procedures.

The broad framework called American history, and even sub-topics such as the Colonial Period, *could* be approached in a number of ways. For example, within the American history and Colonial Period framework one could work with such things as economic theory and development, social class structure, the fine arts, science, history of ideas, even such areas as ecology, minority groups, industrialization, agriculture, social organization and change, value systems, and culture blocs.

In many cases, social studies programs stay anchored with a political base — kings, legislative functions, governmental policies, revolutions, war. Most teaching materials support such a base. If one were to approach the colonial period in American history with a focus on the history of ideas, this would pose substantial problems just in terms of planning. What student materials would one use? Some would argue that an effective way might be to broaden the concept of American history to a more psychologically liberating concept of American studies. Then train teachers by letting them major in some aspect, allowing in-depth knowledge of the subject matter, and thus allowing one to *start* planning with concepts, with student objectives, and then adopt and adapt materials for student use — a process made easier because the teacher himself is familiar with a wide range of possible materials that could be used as vehicles to transport students to concept development and use. We find a similar type of thing taking place in NonWestern Studies where the trappings of tradition aren't quite so binding. We find this also in some contemporary approaches to geography, in which the conventional view of geography as an inventory of physical patterns is being replaced by emphases on functional relationships and inter-relationships among phenomena in terms of time and space. But, here the common impression of geography parallels what one finds in the American history framework.

Funded social studies projects in the areas of the social sciences have run into similar difficulties. A teacher may be trained in sociology or anthropology, may have a wealth of disciplined findings at his command, may be able to note different kinds of materials, and may be able to determine specific student objectives. When he arrives on the school scene he may encounter the Administrative topics subsumed under American and World history which professional colleagues allow to imply certain "right" and "necessary," and *available*, materials. The available materials tend to reign. The castle is secured by a manned drawbridge of Administrative topics and a moat of sub-topics which reinforce the medieval way of life behind the walls.

THE CONTENT PREPARED TEACHER

Let's pursue the idea that a teacher has a sound academic background in the area of prejudice and race relations. The teacher is assigned to teach American history. The sub-topics such as "the Colonial Period" run chronologically. Assuming that he and his colleagues view these as administrative and *not* teaching areas, what happens to his approach to teaching if he first decides on the concepts he wants to work with, on the specific objectives he wants to attain, and identifies some student activities he believes would be sound?

RACE RELATIONS

CONCEPTS TO BE USED
(TEACHER AND STUDENTS)

UNIVERSAL GENERALIZED AND REPETITIVE
(GR) CONCEPTS:

1. Individual human beings differ from one another.
2. When any group of people live together over a period of time in relative isolation, clusters of similar traits are developed.
3. Biologically, individual human beings throughout the world have the same basic physical and neurological equipment. Variation within the human species is minor.
4. Physical differences do *not* cause differences in religion, habits, beliefs, emotions, or intelligence.
5. The culture of any society consists of *learned* patterns of behavior.
6. The most effective and efficient mechanism for perpetuating cultural differences is segregation. Restricting opportunities for shared experiences reinforces cultural patterns.

7. The question of differences in intelligence is complex. It deals with a number of interacting factors. All major racial stocks are represented in the broad range of human intelligence.

8. When people formulate a stereotype of other people and cultures, they treat the others in terms of the stereotype. The reaction of the stereotyped leads to a circle of self-fulfillment.

9. A "culture of discrimination" makes discrimination a way of life which is perceived to be both natural and right, thus seldom subject to question.

10. Social change necessitates the *unlearning* of old behavior patterns as well as the learning and practicing of new behavior patterns.

11. Social and political justice has nothing to do with the chemistry of chromosomes but with the interests, attitudes, and values of human groups.

12. The more any proposed change is perceived as threatening traditional values, the more likely people are to resist.

13. People most likely to push for innovation are those who are in some marginal relationship with society. Impetus to alter social factors seldom originates with those in control of the social structure.

14. Group boundaries in every society are maintained through some system of social reward and punishment.

15. Societies have ethnic and race related boundaries. The boundaries vary according to the ranking and the power of groups in preferred positions.

If the teacher were asked what he hoped his students would get out of the study, he would be likely to respond that, at the very *least*, he would want his students to know the above GR concepts. They are *universal* statements about humans and to the best of his knowledge there is little contradictory evidence. In a sense, the fifteen GR concepts become his large "goals." He is now faced with the problem of teaching and this includes determining more specific (place, time, numbers, situation) GR concepts—concepts that may not be universal but are at least applicable to a major portion of the American experience. He must also determine what students should do (activities) which will contribute to their learning. And, somehow, he is faced with the problem of having what he is teaching fit into Administrative topics.

He plans to give the fifteen concepts to his students and ask them to test the concepts to see if they can come up with *any* data, from *any* time and *any* place which challenges the validity of the GR concepts. He plans to explain to the students what is meant by a universal GR concept.

He then identifies some introductory activities for the students:

INTRODUCTORY ACTIVITIES

A. Students may address the question of whether a comparative study of other societies may assist one in understanding how social boundaries are effected and the role of such boundaries in determining one's chances in life in a particular situation.

B. Given such things as biological factors, ethnic background, religion, language, wealth, education, and length of "tenure" as a citizen, students are asked to determine combinations of diversity that can make up the American. What role does race play in determining the group boundary of an American? Does the American group boundary provide the same rewards and punishments for all group members? What role does race play in determining the group boundaries according to rewards and punishments?

C. Students are asked to test the validity of two or more concepts when studying the Civil Rights Movement in the United States during the 1960's. With an emphasis on Dr. Martin Luther King, students may address such things as: leadership techniques; strategies; resistance; situational targets; flexibility of movement; and the fundamental idea that one does not try to change individual attitudes first but rather modifies the social situation so that behavior is modified and then attitudes are rationalized.

D. Given the above concepts regarding discrimination, students are asked to determine a strategy for effecting change directed at reducing prejudice and improving race relations. The student should be aware of building upon accomplishments of the civil rights movement and of the need to identify basic factors in the current situation. The strategy might focus upon: how old behavior patterns are unlearned; identification of advantages underlying new patterns; the types and sources of leadership—the functions leadership serves; the considerations of leaders and organization; the difference between initiating and implementing change.

E. Students may be asked to determine specific examples of institutionalized racism and explain how the students are directly and/or indirectly influenced by the examples.
F. Given such labels as: Hippies, Middle-Class, Bureaucrat, Blacks, students may be asked to identify the characteristics which form a stereotype form of classification.
G. Students may be asked to diagram the circle-reasoning involved in the self-fulfilling prophecy.

From the fifteen GR universal concepts and the several introductory activities, the teacher determines some administrative topics of his own which sets a framework for more specific concepts, data, and activities: a framework, as well, for trying to determine appropriate materials.

TEACHER'S ADMINISTRATIVE TOPICS

1. Perspectives of the issues.
2. The idea of "race" and racial "differences."
3. Social Class stratification and race relations.
4. Economics as it relates to race relations.
5. Family patterns and race relations.
6. Politics, urban crisis, and race relations.
7. The problem of leadership: pressures and decisions.

Given the above, the teacher now addresses more specific concepts, more specific student objectives, more specific desired student activities, and questions that may help relate to the issues.

PERSPECTIVES OF THE ISSUES

CONCEPTS

1. American history has a major thread of social relationships between the races—a thread of shared interactions which shaped what people believe about themselves, others, and which gave form to behavior and to the consequences of such beliefs and behavior.

2. Technological changes influence the extent and nature of social relationships.
3. Any single act of emancipation or legal "freeing" does not automatically erase deeply ingrained attitudes, beliefs, and behavior.
4. A caste system intertwined with a social class structure suggests an "underclass" system in which the usual avenues of mobility are denied to caste occupants.
5. When people formulate a stereotype, they treat others in terms of the stereotype, and the reaction of the stereotyped leads to a circle of self-fulfillment.
6. The concept of culture is used in racist arguments. This "explanation" suggests change strategies which place the correction of racial injustice on the *next* generation.
7. America, as an experiment, is in the process of being conducted.
8. Protest movements in the '50's and '60's were led by clergymen, lawyers, college students — people who had individually achieved but who were still perceived as members of the American underclass.
9. There is no single causation prompting civil disorders or widespread violence. Oppression and discrimination may be *a* causal factor.

SPECIFIC STUDENT OBJECTIVES:

1. The student is able to define the following terms:
   - (1) "free" Negro
   - (2) social class
   - (3) social caste
   - (4) social mobility
   - (5) channels of mobility
   - (6) underclass
   - (7) Multiple causation
   - (8) "real" income
   - (9) self-fulfilling prophecy
   - (10) stereotype
2. The student is able to list four behavioral characteristics of: (1) a slave; (2) a "free" Negro; (3) indentured servant.
3. The student is able to chart the increase in Negro population from 1619 to 1860.
4. Given the following lists of dates and happenings, the student is able to identify the specific issue being addressed in each citation.
   - (1) 1793 — Cotton Gin
   - (2) 1807 — Thomas Jefferson
   - (3) 1863 — Emancipation Proclamation

      (4) 1865 – 13th Amendment
      (5) 1868 – 14th Amendment
      (6) 1870 – 15th Amendment
      (7) 1875 – Federal Civil Rights Act.

5. The student is able to list four characteristics of a "culture of discrimination."
6. Given that all human beings belong to a single species and given that discrimination is learned behavior, the student is able to explain how this may lead to not addressing the problem of racial justice.
7. Given that urbanization and industrialization have enabled Negroes to move out of what had traditionally been "their place," the student is able to identify the specific impact of: (1) WW I; (2) WW II; and (3) the G.I. Bill as enabling this move.
8. The student is able to cite four reasons why attributing current upheaval and riots to an oppressed class is poor social science analysis.
9. The student is able to list four variables which social scientists feel differentiate black Americans today from their parents, grandparents, and enslaved ancestors.

SUGGESTED STUDENT ACTIVITIES:

1. Given: "The 1950's laid the setting for drastic social change in American race relations. The 1960's were a decade characterized by alterations in the laws governing race relations, the role of race in politics, and even in economic relations between the races."
   Students are asked to determine *specific* examples which either support or deny the above "given."
2. Students are asked to retrieve "hard" data (empirical facts) and to construct a fact sheet concerning areas of discrimination. Using *only* this information, each student is asked to build *both* an argument supporting a culture of discrimination and an argument suggesting ways to lessen a culture of discrimination.
3. Using the data on white and non-white income, education, and the information from Brink and Harris's *Black and White*, the student is asked to analyze the findings and to explain how this might *increase* dissatisfaction among black Americans.

4. A little knowledge is a dangerous thing: Students are asked to take each of the following and explain the danger implicit in the quotation:

   4.1 "If they're brought up in those dreadful slums without a father in the home and with crime and drugs all around, you can't expect them to be like us, can you?"

   4.2 "But he's an exception."

   4.3 Asked the question: "All in all, compared with three years ago, do you think things for people such as yourself and your family are better, worse, or about the same?" Only 5 per cent of the blacks said things were "worse."

5. The historically minded student might be asked to take historical figures such as Jefferson or Lincoln, or may take an historical event such as an amendment or civil rights act, and analyze the factors at work in positions taken.

THE IDEA OF "RACE" AND RACIAL "DIFFERENCES"

This area of study is divided into two sub-areas:

    Area One: Race

    Area Two: Racial Differences.

AREA ONE

Concepts

1. The repeating of facts and findings does not assure learning.
2. Prejudice is not synonymous with disliking. Prejudice involves taking liberty with the facts.
3. There are many unsolved and perplexing questions about the genetic diversity of human populations.
4. Once one admits a diversity in human populations and *differentiates* such diversities, it is often tempting to start *ranking* differences according to value judgments.
5. It is questionable whether "race" can be used as a scientific concept. The descriptive term becomes increasingly meaningless in that it allows little base for analysis.
6. 30,000 years ago, our ancestors who were active in hunt-

ing and collecting, lived in small groups scattered over the globe. The groups lived in a variety of environments and displayed differences in physical features.

7. A clue to studying human variation is found in "clusters" of traits which seem to hang together and which seem to provide broad divisions of mankind according to distinctive physical characteristics.

8. Skin pigmentation, teeth, nose, eyes, hair, body build, blood types, are discrete and measurable differences. Intelligence and temperament are *not* of the same order.

9. Every race has demonstrated a capacity to learn anything produced by any other race and can breed with any other race thus demonstrating a universality. There is genetic diversity without specialization. Developed differences can be pooled and repooled.

10. Certain differences in capacity for solving certain kinds of problems exist between individuals and between populations. What a group lacks in one ability it compensates with another—the same mental processes are involved in executing different skills.

11. There is no race incapable of developing *high* civilization. This is more a matter of motivation than ability.

12. Some abilities have slight advantages over others in specified circumstances but every population has practically a full range of abilities the same as it has a full range of blood groups.

13. There is no absolute ranking of blood groups and there is no absolute ranking of different manifestations of intelligence.

14. A common capacity to learn is shared by all members, there is a beneficial pool of genetic diversity on which the species as a whole can draw. Diversity allows opportunity to meet environmental challenges.

Specific Student Objectives:

1. The Student is able to define the following terms:

   (1) Race
   (2) Genetic Diversity
   (3) Differentiating
   (4) Ranking
   (5) Intelligence
   (6) Cluster Traits
   (7) Breeding Population
   (8) Melanin
   (9) Perception
   (10) Non-sequitur.

2. The student is able to list four discrete and measurable ways by which one can differentiate between members of the species.

3. The student is able to identify two problems encountered when one moves from differentiating to ranking.

4. The student is able to discuss two logical problems involved in moving from discrete and measurable differentiation to questions of social policy.

5. Given: Many anthropologists have stopped using the term "race" as a scientific concept. The student is able to: (1) Identify one function of a scientific concept; (2) explain how "race" does or does not fit such a function; (3) give two uses of the concept "race" which go beyond a scientific base.

6. Given the broad categories of "White," "Black," "Yellow," and "Red," the student is able to give at least one specific example in which the internal diversity of one category makes it malfunction as a way of analyzing human differences.

7. Given the "dubbed races" Hindu, British, Aryan, the student can identify at least one problem encountered when attributing the concept "race" to each.

8. The student is able to explain how the definition of race as "a group of mankind, members of which can be identified by the possession of distinctive physical characteristics" is a cultural definition rather than a biological definition.

9. The zoological concept of "breeding population" suggests that certain genetic characteristics become relatively "fixed" within a given population. The student is able to identify two problems when making the transfer to the human species.

10. Races and breeding populations do not seem to present satisfactory categories or units for explaining human variation. The student is able to explain trait "clusters" as an alternative.

11. Given the question: Why should we not all look alike?, the student is able to develop two theories which both support a similar picture of the human species some 30,000 years ago.

12. The student is able to:
   (A) give one example where "chance" may have produced physical differences among the groups.

(B) give one example of the difference between "selection for" and "selection against" in terms of adaptive physical characteristics.
13. Assuming that physical traits are functional, i.e. help man in his adjusting to his environment, the student can identify two reasons either supporting or denying the view that the most advantageous skin color in most circumstances is "a pleasant medium-brown, tending towards *café au lait* rather than cocoa."
14. Given the categories of hair shape, nose, body build, the student is able to identify: (1) adaptive merit in specific circumstances; (2) how such categories cut across conventionally accepted racial classifications.
15. Motor ability, temperament and intelligence are "adaptive" in the same way physical traits are considered functional. The student is able to give two examples of difficulties encountered when attempting to view intelligence as a discrete and measurable trait.
16. The student is able to give two examples of how blood types cut across conventional ethnic and racial classifications.
17. The student is able to identify three positive functions served by the variation found within the human species.

Possible Student Activities:

1. Given the list of concepts, the students as individuals or as a class, may evolve strategies for determining the validity of one or more of the ideas listed.
2. Given a conventional view of "race," the students might be asked to establish specific criteria allowing for analytical discrimination. (The difficulties encountered in attempting this within the framework of a conventional view raises some basic issues).
3. Assuming that the human species spread out over the globe and adapted to various ecological influences, students can:
   3.1 Use a map to determine climatic zones and identify skin pigmentation of inhabitants prior to the age of discovery in order to determine any correlation between pigmentation and climate.

3.2 Build a case indicating that eyefolds, teeth, and body builds are a form of adaptation.

3.3 Assess the relationship of blood types with disease, diet, and with the conventional view of races.

4. Students can be asked to react to:

4.1 The suggestion that genetic diversity of a significant kind within the human species is regarded by some as tantamount to being a fascist.

4.2 Assuming, for the sake of argument, that one intelligence is determined to be inferior to another, it is plausible that the higher intelligence should control the life chances of the lesser intelligence.

4.3 In questions of "race relations," *perceived* differences are more important than actual genetic diversity.

4.4 What a race (however defined) *does*, depends more upon motivation than upon ability.

AREA TWO:

Concepts

Most of the concepts listed below are taken from Professor Jensen's work. If concepts exist to be "tested" and not swallowed, Jensen permits an excellent opportunity to raise a number of issues.

1. Negroes as a group—as opposed to any single individual Negro—test out poorly compared with whites or Orientals on that aspect of general intelligence (g.) that involves abstract reasoning and problem-solving.

2. The ability measured by I.Q. tests, is largely inherited, a matter of genes and brain structure, and no amount of compensatory education or forced exposure to culture will effect substantial improvement in I.Q.

3. Studies of matings between cousins of normal I.Q. reveal they produce larger numbers of retarded offspring than are produced in nonfamily random matings.

4. Studies of identical twins reared apart from one another found that the separated twins averaged only six points apart by I.Q. Any two people in the total population, chosen at random, will be on the average 18 points apart. Nonidentical siblings reared in the same household are on the average 12 I.Q. points apart.

5. Studies of adopted children reveal that intelligence relates more closely to natural parents than to adoptive parents. Other studies indicate that the closer people are related, the more similar are their I.Q.'s. Environment is *not* the deciding factor.

6. "Race. . . is actually a 'breeding population'. . . the population is not closed but there is a well known probability of greater mating within this population than outside it."

7. 400 major studies involving racial differences all indicate "that in the standard distribution of I.Q. throughout the population the Negro is 15 points lower than the white. Only 3 per cent of the Negro population exceed an I.Q. of 115; in the white population 16 per cent exceed 115. In the white population 1 per cent exceed 140; a sixth of that exceed 140 in the Negro population.

8. Children of Negroes in the highest income class of our society will average lower in I.Q. than white children of the lowest class.

9. The Coleman study found American Indians coming out lower on all environmental indices than American Negroes; yet scoring higher on I.Q. and scholastic achievement. Disadvantaged children of Taiwan do as well as children of white middle-class parents in the United States.

10. Many different abilities are subsumed under the term intelligence. The abilities valued and most pragmatic in American society are the ones measured by the I.Q. test.

11. The findings reported refer to larger group populations and *not* to individuals — not to individual genius, ability, and talent. The group findings should not stand in the way of providing opportunities for individual achievement and reward.

12. 80 per cent of the variability in intelligence can be contributed to inheritance; the other 20 per cent to environment.

Specific Student Objectives:

1. The student is able to identify one assumption basic to each of the following reactions to Jensen's views:

(A) "Fight racism. Fire Jensen."

(B) Jensen's receipt of postcards emblazoned with swastikas.

(C) Reading of Jensen's article into the Congressional Record.

(D) Offer of $100 to anyone who could predict a man's intelligence by observing his features.

(E) A study of leading psychologists in which those favoring environmental influences over hereditary influences were liberal in their political views and those favoring heredity over environment were conservative in political outlook.

(F) The argument that I.Q. tests were culturally unfair and loaded with factual material that only certain groups in our society could know or respond to.

2. The student is able to: (1) explain the "liberal egalitarian's" concern with Jensen's views; (2) identify the basic premise upon which federal social policy (education) has been built.

3. The student is able to: (1) identify the argument of criticism in each of the items listed below and (2) identify Jensen's response to the criticism in each item:

(A) Effectiveness of I.Q. tests.

(B) Influence of teacher expectations.

(C) Bettelheim and Bloom's kibbutzim study.

(D) Army Alpha tests.

(E) Relationship of nutrition with intelligence.

(F) Separation of black genes from white genes.

(G) Inability of science to take a position.

(H) Unfairness of raising the issue at such a critical time.

4. The student is able to differentiate between "Level 1" and "Level 2" in Jensen's series of tests given to students to determine learning style, and is able to make one inference about education from Jensen's findings.

5. Given the following two ideas the student is able to relate the two ideas to the "fear" of Jensenism which involves the *non sequitur* method of arguing.

(A) Certain differences in capacity for solving certain kinds of problems exist between individuals and between populations. What one group lacks in one ability it compensates with another—the same mental processes are involved in executing different skills.

(B) Some abilities have slight advantages over others

in specified circumstances but every population has practically a full range of abilities the same as it has a full range of blood groups.

6. The student is able to defend or deny that Jensen's belief that ". . . It is unjust to allow the mere fact of an individual's racial or social background to affect treatment accorded to him" is in opposition to the position he has taken regarding the dominance of heredity over environment.

Possible Student Activities:

1. Given that Jensen has "added little that is new" to the old nature vs. nurture controversy, students can be asked to analyze:
   (1) The variable of "timing" as it relates to the furor of reaction to Jensen's article.
   (2) The *nature* of the response received from many of his professional colleagues.
   (3) The fear involved in having "an open market-place of ideas."

2. Jensen's words — "Compensatory education has been tried and apparently has failed" — and his conclusion that school systems must be set up to allow a diversity of programs that match the abilities and readiness of youngsters, raise some issues in regard to social policy. Students can be asked to determine the extent of governmental efforts to effect "compensatory" education as compared with other educational funding, determine what kinds of alternative programs schools might establish if agreeing with Jensen, and assess the political, economic, and social ramifications if such programs were implemented. (Does Jensen raise, indirectly, the basic issue of the purpose(s) of education?)

3. Students can be asked to prepare for analysis and debate the following issue:
   "Should science be used only to serve the values of a society or should science also be used to help modify the values of a society by exposing the values as unsubstantiated if necessary?" (Is there "good" science and "bad" science?)

4. Students can be asked to: 1) outline the data supporting Jensen's position; 2) outline the data used to challenge

this position; and 3) pose empirically based questions for both the support and the challenge.

5. Students can be asked to assess the means by which one's position can be attacked—means such as character assassination, guilt by association, use of data, emotional argument, etc.—and apply this to an analysis of the reaction to Jensen.

SOCIAL CLASS STRATIFICATION AND RACE RELATIONS

Concepts:

1. It is easier to agree upon desired ends than on *means* to be used in reaching the desired ends.
2. The concept of "evil" usually rests in a moral perspective. The premise that evil is caused by evil denies that evil may be more complex and may even be caused by something good.
3. Social evils are inseparable from other conditions, both good and evil.
4. Parents' concern for the perceived welfare of their children—a conventional social good—is a factor sustaining *de facto* segregation.
5. Programs aimed at improving the lot of subordinated racial groups must recognize that racism is a popular attitude and not the prejudice of a small conspiracy.
6. Racism is seldom pure. People who are racist in some areas may support racial equality in others.
7. Racial antipathy is a social class issue in which visible genetic factors are used as clues to a person's position in the class structure.
8. Concrete action, not statements of abstract rights, are crucial to integration campaigns.
9. School integration affects the white family in the determination of the family's role in defining the social position of children.
10. The family is the most conservative of all social institutions. Society is stratified and parents are anxious to pass on their stratified status.
11. The study of attitudes is often a recording of myths and platitudes.

12. The school district influences the housing market. The school district becomes a vital part of assessing residence values.
13. Neighborhood schools reinforce the class system. Segregated schools produce segregated neighborhoods because the white demands push house prices higher than that afforded by all but a small part of the minority.
14. Suburbias are "Balkanized" into a patchwork of small, jealous, proud municipalities which resist involvement in concerns of the larger encompassing metropolitan area.
15. The white's defense against integration is to move, and the general movement is to the suburbs, which are well adapted (though costly) to the maintenance of class distinctions.
16. Many programs to improve education of black children involve the unequal allocation of resources on the basis of race—the policy that prompted the 1954 Supreme Court decision.
17. Anything motivating prosperous white parents to withdraw support from public education weakens education as a force in social mobility thus favoring a more rigid class system.

SPECIFIC STUDENT OBJECTIVES:

1. The student is able to define the following terms:
   - (1) de facto
   - (2) de jure
   - (3) sanctions
   - (4) Balkanized
   - (5) social mobility
   - (6) stratified society
   - (7) "Equality plus"
2. The student is able to identify the following:
   - (1) Supreme Court Decision, 1954.
   - (2) Title VI, Civil Rights Act, 1964.
   - (3) Coleman Report
   - (4) "neighborhood school" concept.
3. Given the quote from a real estate broker that "You don't just buy a house, you buy a school district," the student is able to cite two situations which tend to support the quotation.
4. The student is able to explain a relationship between each of the following:

(1) "visible genetic factors" and stratification.

(2) the role of the family as ascribing student social position.

(3) the role of the school district in family social position.

5. Suburban areas have been referred to as "Balkanized." The student is able to report on (1) the historical factors and problems of the Balkans, and (2) the similarities and differences between the current suburban outlook and that of the Balkans.

6. The student is able to identify:

(1) two specific moral arguments to support integration.

(2) two specific functional arguments to suggest focusing concerns on areas other than desegregation.

(3) pre-scientific arguments used to argue against integration.

7. The student is able to give one specific example related to the question of integration in which two people can have the same idea but for different reasons.

8. The student is able to list at least three functions of a public school in which one function applies to student learning, one function to family concepts, and one function to property value.

9. Given the fact that metropolitan school districts may have less money per student than suburban districts but more total funds, the student is able to list three specific undertakings that would be economically feasible and geared to attract and retain white students.

Possible Student Activities:

1. Students can be asked to prepare a ten minute talk on not putting energies into desegregating the schools — a talk that could be given by both a conservative and a liberal. The students can then be asked to cite different reasons for reaching the same conclusion.

2. Students can be asked to determine the source of the term "Balkanized" when used to refer to American suburbia, trace the history of the Balkans, and note the problems which stem from the Balkan type of situation.

3. Students can be asked to research and discuss the meanings of the term social class and to differentiate between "class" and "caste." The discussion can include address-

ing "cues" of social class position in terms of family, living location, and group association.

4. Students can be asked to defend or attack the view that when whites give up on a school district and move, more than students are taken away.

5. Students are asked to build an argument for either putting *more* emphasis upon school desegregation or *less* effort on concern with using the schools to help bring about school integration.

6. Most people think of schools as simply being concerned with educating the young. Using the student's own school district, the student can be asked to get specific information related to the functions played by the school for: property values; business interests; religious organizations; family self-concepts; and the individual student.

7. Right or wrong, there is *de facto* segregation. Such segregation must serve some purposes or the ways to circumvent it would not be so evident. For those seeking equality, integration became a prime objective because segregation has long been an instrument of inequality. The student is asked: What practical improvements can be made within a *de facto* segregated situation?

8. Students can be asked to do mini-research and reports on such things as: Federal sanctions and the politics of school desegregation; the Supreme Court Decision of 1954; antiracist and anti-injustice proponents feed the old myths of racism; Title VI (Civil Rights Act) and statements made by public schools when securing federal monies (check own system); federal fiat, federal funds, federal guidelines, and who gets what and how.

4. ECONOMICS AS IT RELATES TO RACE RELATIONS

Concepts:

1. The economic status of Negroes has improved but the gap between whites and Negroes has remained relatively constant.

2. Unemployment rate for Negroes is about twice that of whites, regardless of age, sex, or economic climate.

The 2:1 ratio is stable for adults but low when noting the disparity among teen-agers.

3. The unemployment rate for Negroes at the height of prosperity is greater than the rate for whites during recent recessions.
4. Despite some increase in "professional" openings, nearly half of Negro males work as laborers, janitors, porters, busboys, and similar service jobs.
5. 40 per cent of Negro females are doing unskilled and menial housework in one form or another.
6. The increase in Negro women employed in white-collar jobs is significant but it also reinforces the dominant role of women in the Negro home.
7. Dead-end jobs, lack of economic security, and irregularity of employment for the Negro male show little hope of modifying the structure and function of the Negro family.
8. Half of the poor in the United States living in metropolitan urban centers, live in ghettos. 60 per cent of the Negro poor are under 21.
9. Unemployment appears to decrease as youths mature.
10. National statistics do not reflect the statistics of the ghetto areas.
11. To substantially improve the situation will take large outlays of funds. Whether we can afford this is a matter of choice, not necessity.
12. Trying to find summer employment for Negro youth is a form of riot control and teaches such youth that the only way to be heard is to resort to violence.

Specific Student Objectives:

1. The student is able to differentiate between:
   (1) income and "real" income.
   (2) unemployment and labor-force drop out.
2. Given that the war-on-poverty impact on unemployment is referred to as a "feather pillow," the student is able to give three specific pieces of information supporting the view *and* three specific pieces of information which could be used to challenge the view.
3. The student is able to:
   (1) explain statistics as a way of gathering and interpreting data.

      (2) give one specific way in which statistics can prove of help.

      (3) give one specific way in which statistics can be misleading unless used with care.

      (4) explain whether he would use whole numbers (100,000) or percentages (2%) if he were trying to convince another of major improvements.

4. Given that family incomes have risen proportionately as much for Negroes as for whites and that family purchasing power has risen about $120 per year since 1960 for Negroes and $220 per year for whites, the student is able to:

      (1) identify the factor of per capita income with average size of Negro and white families in making comparisons.

      (2) identify the factor of inflation in assessing real improvement.

5. The student is able to cite the percent of increase of Negro males in the professional and technical occupations and the per cent of Negro females in white-collar occupations. The student is able to indicate: (1) one implication for education, (2) one implication for the Negro family.

6. Assuming it is silly to train a segment of the population for skills when there is no demand, the student is able to indicate how such a situation feeds the vicious cycle of self-fulfillment.

7. The student is able to give three examples of possible programs which could address youth employment without a substantial increase in public funding.

Possible Student Activities:

1. Students may be asked to compare national unemployment statistics with specific data from areas such as Watts.

2. Students may be asked to trace the origins and problems encountered in the Manpower Development and Training Act and in the Neighborhood Youth Corps.

3. Given the data listed below, the student is able to: (1) interpret the data as supportive of economic gains made by blacks, (2) locate other data that specifically challenge the initial interpretation.

(1) Since 1960 over one quarter of a million families have been removed from the poverty category.
(2) The percentage of Negro women doing domestic work has dropped since 1960.
(3) The proportion of Negro women employed in white-collar jobs has risen from 18 to 24 per cent.
(4) The Negro male employed in professional and technical jobs has increased from 4 to 6 per cent.
(5) Since 1961 Negro family income has risen.
(6) From 1961 to 1965 Negro unemployment rates declined from 12.5 to 8.3.
(7) Negro family purchasing power has increased at the rate of $120 per year between the years 1960 and 1965.

4. Students may be asked to note specific differences between comparisons of Negro with Negro and relative comparison of Negro with white in terms of economic improvement.
5. Students are asked to note the significance of categories such as: male, female, age, per capita, and residential area in terms of planning ways of meeting the situation.
6. A mini-research problem which students can undertake might be an in-depth case study of a ghetto area (such as Watts or Hough) with an emphasis upon economic factors. The case study could include an analysis of perceived causal factors in the summer riots.

5. FAMILY PATTERNS AND RACE RELATIONS

Concepts:

1. An end to formal discrimination would not necessarily assure the full integration of the Negro into American life.
2. The structure and functioning of the Negro family is *unique* in American society and differs from the traditional white Anglo-Saxon "model."
3. The family is the basic unit for socializing the young, and the functioning of the basic unit is crucial in determining societal expectations learned by the young.
4. The Negro family is a continuity of the forces found in the uniqueness of the American institution of slavery.

5. Black males still live within a framework of a "psychology of slavery" and find a semi-freedom with the traditional role of male being denied him.
6. To give a black male status as a husband and father requires basic changes in patterns of Negro education, training, and employment.
7. Whites cannot "give back" old values. This becomes increasingly evident as the larger society encounters new value systems. The whites can work to change the situation in education, housing, and jobs but only the Negro can evolve family structure and functioning.
8. All people are a product of historical continuity.

Specific Student Objectives:

1. The student is able to list three reasons attributed to causing the uniqueness of the Negro household.
2. The student is able to identify two examples of how expectations differ for the black and white male in American society.
3. Given the American institution of slavery, the student is able to cite six specific factors which influenced the role of the black male and female.
4. The student is able to relate the areas listed below to the concept that the Negro family has an "enduring sickness."
   (1) crime rate   (4) unemployment rate
   (2) illegitimacy rate   (5) school drop-out rate
   (3) divorce rate
5. The student is able to identify two functions served by desertion.
6. The student is able to define and/or explain the following terms as they relate to the Negro household:
   (1) Psychology of slavery
   (2) "black Anglo-Saxon"
   (3) "marry down"
   (4) patriarchial
   (5) matriarchial
   (6) Poor man's divorce
   (7) Male role
   (8) Female role
7. The student is able to discuss critically the following issue:

As the black family strives for "old" family patterns, the white family is encountering "new" emerging family patterns. Traditionally held (American society) male and female roles are undergoing change. What problems does this pose for the family as the basic socializing unit in the society and for identifying the expectations of the society?

Possible Student Activities:

1. Students are asked to determine the diversity of male and female roles as evidenced by other cultures and to address the issue of whether or not there is such a thing as the "natural" male role in social functioning.
2. Given that American slavery was different from contemporary slavery found in different parts of the world and from ancient forms of slavery. Students are asked to research the precise differences in the various forms that slavery takes.
3. Students are asked to determine the specific expectations of the male role as defined by the American institution of slavery.
4. Using contemporary declarations from the "lib" movement, students are asked to identify different roles for the male and female and to relate such changes to family structure and functioning.
   a. Given the data below, students are asked to give two completely different interpretations to the same data.
      (1) About 25 per cent of Negro families are headed by women who have no husbands.
      (3) The divorce rate among Negro families is 5.1 per cent, compared to 3.8 per cent among whites.
      (3) Six per cent of all female professionals are Negroes while approximately one per cent of all male professionals are Negroes.
   b. Using the different interpretations, students may be asked to determine which explanations fall within the self-fulfilling prophecy.
5. Students interested in drama, literature, or humor might welcome an opportunity to give specific examples of how the Negro male role was treated. The Negro female role?

6. POLITICS, URBAN CRISES, AND RACE RELATIONS

Concepts:

1. What is described as the urban crisis is in reality the beginning of a national political crisis.
2. One of the unquestioned traditions of American political life has been that of rule by the majority.
3. Disruption is a political technique. Perhaps the most important domestic issue is whether outvoted minorities can find peaceful and productive ways of meeting their needs.
4. Although individual citizens are urged to be active in affairs of community and nation, in practice, participation is generally limited to organized interest groups or lobbies. Legislation tends to favor the interests of the organized.
5. It is likely that the poor and the black (and other minorities) will probably be outvoted by the majority and that under the present structure of American government there cannot and will not be a solution to the problem of the cities. The basis of failure is built into the most important political and economic institutions.
6. In the past, minorities had to rely on the morality and good will of the majority for a form of charity.
7. Perhaps the most important reason for urban crisis is the structure of American democracy and the concept of majority rule.

Specific Student Objectives:

1. The student is able to define the terms listed below and is able to relate each term to one aspect of the urban crisis.

   (1) One man – one vote
   (2) proportional representation
   (3) ghetto
   (4) subsidy
   (5) gerrymandering
   (6) reapportionment
   (7) majority rule
   (8) pluralistic democracy
   (9) progressive taxation
   (10) school equalization payments
   (11) disruption
   (12) seniority system

2. Given that the problems of poverty, segregation, and municipal decay are subsumed under "Urban Crisis," the student is able to indicate relationships between the problems and (1) the national economy and (2) the responsibility of government to handle the "by-products" of economic processes.

3. The student is able to list two reasons why most voters are not inclined to allocate cities the funds and powers to deal with poverty and segregation.

4. The student is able to give two examples which support *or* deny the position that many Americans tend to separate their view of governmental participation in the economy not in terms of ideology but in terms of "self" and "generalized other."

5. The student is able to give three possible reasons why federal, state, and local governments have not absorbed the responsibility for the problems of poverty, segregation, and municipal decay.

6. For *each* of the statements given below, the student is able to identify one implication for the functioning of political processes.
   (1) Subsidies are generally provided on the basis of power, not merit.
   (2) American democracy allows affluent minorities to "propose and the majority to dispose."
   (3) Legislation tends to favor the interests of the organized.
   (4) The poor and the black are caught in an almost hopeless political bind.

7. Given that disruption is a source of power and is instrumental in proposing and disposing through inconvenience and threat, the student is able to:
   (1) define and give examples of disruption.
   (2) give one example of disruption in American history that is no longer viewed as antisocial activity.
   (3) give two examples of ends secured through disruption.
   (4) give two disadvantages in using disruption as a political tool.

8. The suggestions listed below are aimed at eliminating or lessening minority lack of access to decision-making processes. For *each* suggestion, the student is able to identify one way the suggestion might help and one way the suggestion might hinder such access.

(1) extension of one man one vote to all levels of political activity.
(2) abolishment of the seniority system in legislatures.
(3) replacement of appointive officers with elective ones.
(4) funding by government of all election campaigns.
(5) governmental financing of independent public-opinion polls.
(6) governmental financial aid to encourage political organizing.
(7) giving of increased power to the courts and Cabinet departments.
(8) extension of progressive income tax principles to federal funding programs.
(9) proportional representation by race, income, or occupation.
(10) Use of majority rule in the final step of a two-step process.
(11) Gerrymandering existing political boundaries to assure minority groups being majority groups in their own bailiwicks.
(12) Encouragement (no financial punishment) of minorities to establish own institutions if their demands are diametrically opposed to institutions reflecting majority opinion.

Possible Student Activities:

1. Using the concepts of majority rule, gerrymandering, and seniority and given a "political entity" of 100 people of whom 11 are black, 22 are poor, 42 are under the age of 21, 70 live in a greater metropolitan area, and 30 in nonindustrial areas, the students are asked to determine how they would use the concepts to assure that the "affluent minority proposes legislation and the majority disposes it" within the framework of a majoritarian democracy.
2. Students are asked to do a study of the historical development and functioning of the Electoral College and to identify the issues inherent in its functioning.
3. It has been argued that *majoritarian democracy* seemed to have worked prior to the Civil War but that the present pluralistic society demands a *pluralistic democracy*. Using specific historical data, students may expand this view.

4. The Federal Constitution can be studied by the students to determine what specific references are made to the relationship of government and economic institutions, to government and individual citizens, and to government and *group* activity.

5. Students are asked to study the Bill of Rights and then write a Bill of Rights for minority groups. (What kind of political structure would assure minority group rights?)

6. Students are asked to select one of the following terms and, using specific data, report to the class the implications for assuring or denying its importance in securing a government of, by, and for "the people."
   (1) one man one vote
   (2) proportional representation
   (3) gerrymandering
   (4) majority rule
   (5) principles basic to progressive taxation.

7. Using the American historical experiences, students are asked to identify how disruptions (protests, uprisings) were used as an instrument of inconvenience and threat. Specific incidents can be studied in terms of: what prompted the action, who took part, counter-reaction, and the results of the disruption. Advantages and disadvantages may be assessed.

8. a. Students are asked to write a "position paper" from the frame of reference of the majority non-ghetto, non-minority oriented American voter. The position on such things as: role of government, responsibility of economic institutions, role of individual taxpayer, general responsibility for the urban crisis, majority rule, and political processes should be included.
   b. Using the same basic arguments as developed in 8.a., students are asked to write a position paper from the same frame of reference but addressed at putting a man on the moon.

9. Students may be asked to come up with a viable set of alternatives to the majority rule concept, anticipate specific negative reactions to it, and then plan a strategy for encountering the reactions.

10. Bertram Gross has argued that professional economists, using only economic analyses, have excluded other relevant social science expertise in the formation of national

policy (*Annals*, March, 1970). Michael Springer, in the same journal, maintained that political scientists have given concern primarily to formal governmental institutions—rarely to lobbyists, participants in mass movements, and unorganized citizens. Students may be asked to assess whether political and economic activities can be separated in structure or function when addressing a situation such as the urban crisis. Students are asked to discuss how economic and political factors relate.

THE PROBLEM OF LEADERSHIP: PRESSURES AND DECISIONS

Questions (To be used for synthesis and classroom discussion)

1. What factors in the civil rights movement over the past twenty years are said to have paved the way for today's climate—factors for which Roy Wilkins and the N.A.A.C.P. claim some credit?
2. Wilkins has been characterized as a "pontiff," his statements as "encyclicals," his "theology" that of integration, his "church" the National Association for the Advancement of Colored People. What would lead to such characterization? To what extent is the characterization accurate or inaccurate?
3. As situations change, so do the expectations of followers. What problems did this pose for Wilkins? How might this influence his role of leadership?
4. Those opposing Wilkins claim that integration is dead as a talking point, that Wilkins is an "Uncle Tom," that Wilkins has "betrayed" the blacks, and that the 1954 arena was vastly different from that encountered in the late '60's and to be encountered in the '70's. What is the basis for the opposition? With what arguments does Wilkins counter?
5. How did Wilkins reflect the "Horatio Alger syndrome" in his own career and why would this enrage the young critics?
6. Using the history of the N.A.A.C.P., the composition of its board of directors, its tax-exempt status, its tie-in with foundation support, range of membership, social-class orientation, the charisma of Wilkins, and the control

exerted by Wilkins over internal policy, what arguments for its being a *de facto* arm of go-slow Federal policies can be developed? How might the arguments be countered?

7. As a leader, Wilkins recognized that a program of opposition is no longer enough and that new programs must emerge as changes are effected. He recognizes that the N.A.A.C.P. offers young people nothing spectacular. As a leader, what options are open to him? As a leader, what considerations must Wilkins give to the relationship between "internal" and "external" factors?

8. When the fight for the unsegregated world is won what realizations will appear?

9. Eldridge Cleaver is said to be a figure at the heart of the American scene. How would one relate his interwoven roles as "old con," writer, politician, agitator, culture hero, and fugitive to the pulse of the American scene?

10. In what segment of American people does Cleaver feel the greatest change is taking place? What would prompt Cleaver to claim that "Their revolt is deeper than *single-issue* protest."? Would this influence the strategy which a leader like Cleaver might use?

11. Cleaver's realization that it made no sense to continue in isolation from white power bases and that political organization was necessary, differs in what way from the stance maintained by Roy Wilkins? The political alliance with white radicals made Cleaver and the Panther party vulnerable to what accusations from nationalist rivals?

12. The parole authorities had told Cleaver he was selfish and that he should look beyond himself and relate to other people. Cleaver claims to have developed a social conscience, to have been involved with others, and to have addressed social problems. How does one account for the differences in perception between Cleaver and parole authorities?

13. A leader develops an image which conditions expectations for his followers as well as for the opposition. How might such an image limit the flexibility required of leadership roles?

14. Richard Gilman, writing in the *New Republic,* suggested that he did not know what truth for Negroes is — that the "old Mediterranean values" were no longer useful frames

of reference or guides to discourse and that he must "stand back and listen, *without comment* [to the new voices]. What were the "old Mediterranean values"? What changes seem to be taking place?

Possible Student Activities:

1. Students may be asked to write a short historical development of the National Association for the Advancement of Colored People.
2. Students may be asked to build a case for Wilkins and the N.A.A.C.P. *and* a case *against* Wilkins and the N.A.A.C.P. with references to:
   (1) Basic assumptions.
   (2) "Ends" in view.
   (3) Change strategies.
   (4) Role of Leadership.
   (5) Changes in the general "climate" or situation which pose specific roles for leadership.
3. Students may be asked to be specific in identifying the following names and terms:
   (1) mechanics of power
   (2) non-negotiable demands
   (3) old-time liberals
   (4) white power structure
   (5) Supreme Court Decision, 1954.
   (6) Thurgood Marshall
   (7) negotiation and litigation
   (8) Horatio Alger
   (9) militant
   (10) integration/ segregation.
4. Students may be asked to outline the sequential phases of Cleaver's career and, at each phase, note specific incidents, or events, or movements happening in the larger "climate" of the American scene.
5. Cleaver and Wilkins offer a number of similarities as well as some crucial differences in effecting change strategies. Students may be asked to compare and contrast the two in terms of charisma, life-styles, assumptions regarding change, nature of relationship with whites, and ends in view.
6. Students may be asked to read and compare any two of the following:
   (1) King, *Why We Can't Wait*
   (2) Cleaver, *Soul on Ice*
   (3) Hoffman, *Woodstock Nation*
   (4) *Biography of Malcom X*

7. It has been said that "an effective leader must know what *he* wants, what his followers want, what his opposition want, and how to organize with flexibility and timing. Most of all he must know that leadership is a temporary affair. . ." Students are asked to apply the above to Cleaver.

Several things become obvious. The teacher appears to have a firm grasp on his subject matter and knows his goals, his concepts, what he wants the students to be able to do, and what activities appear to be helpful in achieving his ends.

At this point, he starts to look for and select materials that will help in accomplishing what he views as his ends. In terms of his own background, his ideas and plans did not come from a void. He must have done some reading and thinking. However, there is a difference between what one used for his own preparation and what one selects to use as teaching vehicles. Some interesting questions about materials are also raised: must they always appear in written form or can there be films or records or tapes or cartoons? Can some materials be reworked for student use? What about fact sheets, case studies, legislative reports?

It is also obvious that not *all* the concepts, objectives, and activities would apply equally well for all students. As the teacher identifies materials, he might modify and change other parts of his planning and even delete a substantial portion if necessary.

In this particular case, the teacher has some basis for selecting and using material. He does not use material simply because it is there.

To be honest, few teachers use this approach. It requires a solid background in some academic area and it assumes that there is time to do this, or even part of it. It is provided as an example of how materials don't *have* to wag the curriculum or teaching.

And, in reviewing the concepts, objectives, and activities would you say that the teacher's approach fits into American history? How? Are there parts of his planning that allow *direct* relationship with the conventional sub-topics? And, if you had to select materials, what specific materials would you identify and use?

UNPREPARED BUT WILLING

Let's get down to the way it usually is. A teacher is told that she is expected to teach a certain topic or theme. In many cases, the teacher has some generalized feelings about that which she is expected to teach but little else. No extensive background in the particular area, no elaborate plans, little time to adequately prepare, and some forty-five minutes a day to fill with some enlightened learning. If seduced by the system and structure and if not willing or able to do more than emote the expected cliches, she will probably still get by. But, if conscientious and if wanting to do more than share a shabby ignorance, what does she do?

Suppose, for whatever reason, that she wants to teach about "Violence in America." And suppose that she is working with students within the framework of American history. What procedures, then, might she follow in selecting, planning, and using content related to violence? She is well aware that the term "violence" offers little help in and of itself. What is to be covered? What ideas are important? What data might she use? How can she go about planning?

The following is one approach that might be used. The approach is broken down into parts:

Part One: She finds *one* article dealing with violence.

Part Two: She determines the implicit and explicit concepts appearing in the article.

Part Three: She then raises questions — her own — which stem from the article: questions that may assist her in planning specific student experiences and desired student outcomes.

Part Four: The teacher then tries to anticipate student questions — those that students might raise in terms of other studies, the local situation, interests, etc.

Part Five: Specific student objectives are then tentatively determined.

Part Six: The planning of activities and the determination of materials.

CONTENT SOURCE AND OUTLINE

The article selected for use as a base is David Brion Davis's "Violence in American Literature," which appeared in *The Annals*, March, 1966. Why this one? First of all, violence as seen through literature provided a breadth and did not narrow down findings to a specific situation, time, or place. Such breadth would allow students to relate their previous studies in American history and literature. Secondly, *The Annals* is a journal of The American Academy of Political and Social Science. If one needed an authoritative base, the acceptance and printing of the article should assure a sound academic approach. The author had excellent credentials, having been published in such journals as the *American Historical Review, Journal of Negro History,* the *New England Quarterly, Mississippi Valley Historical Review,* and others with similar standing.

The article is read straight through in order to get the general flavor. Two ideas seemed to permeate:

1. Violence in American literature is *not* new. It tends to reflect historical conditions and circumstances.
2. Twentieth century American writers have appeared to push an anti-rationalistic view, an approach to violence as a symbol of reality and a regenerative or creative force on the American scene.

The two ideas provide a start. The second reading is done with an eye toward outlining the content used in the article.

OUTLINE

Overview: For over 160 years American literature reflects a fascination with homicidal violence:

(1) *Charles Brockden Brown* (first serious novelist) provides three forms of violent characters.
(2) *James Fenimore Cooper,* excitement, pursuit, and bodies of Indians and Renegades.
(3) *Edgar Allan Poe,* crime, suspense, and sickness.
(4) *George Lippard* (most popular American writer of the mid 19th century), abuse and murders.
(5) *Herman Melville (Pierre* and *Billy Budd),* plots turn about homicide.
(6) *Nathaniel Hawthorne,* homicide and abuse (*The Marble Faun*).
(7) *Mark Twain, A Connecticut Yankee in King Arthur's Court* ends in mass slaughter. Huck Finn witnesses murders.
(8) Ambrose Bierce, Stephen Crane, Jack London.
(9) F. Scott Fitzgerald, Ernest Hemingway, John Steinbeck, James T. Farrell, Robert Penn Warren.

Note: One can also compile a list of important American writers whose works contain little bloodshed: William Dean Howells, Henry James, Edith Wharton, Sinclair Lewis, John Marquand. "It would be naive to conclude that the frequency of fighting and killing in American fiction is proof of an unusually violent society."

". . . *There can be no doubt that the treatment of violence in American literature reflects certain historical conditions and circumstances.*"

Violence and the Mass Audience

(1) Violence is marketable.
(2) Many of the themes and situations of the best 20th century "pot-boilers" dealt with "moral insanity, monomania, sex, sadism," violence of the South, dehumanizing effects of the North urban centers; one speculates about a "trickle up" process finding refined literature coming from trash.
(3) Desire of the mass public for literature on violence.
    a. Better explained by limited attention span of the average reader than by theories of repressed aggression and vicarious release.
    b. DeTocqueville (1830's) talks of the mass market not being conducive to literature of nuance, understatement, and delicate pleasures.
    c. DeTocqueville's theory: democratic audiences feed on exaggeration, strong emotion, striking effect.
(4) To hold attention of the ordinary reader or that of the educated, a story must be full of suspense, surprise, and startling contrasts.

"Violence is the cheapest means to a change of pace"

American Themes

1. ROMANCE OF THE AMERICAN REVOLUTION

    1.1 Before the Civil War, most popular theme.
    1.2 Much historical writing on the Revolution exorcises its radical spirit—nation was conceived in violence and its birth accompanied by mobs and confiscations. A burden remained on the people to validate rebellion against lawful authority.
    1.3 By the 1820's and 1830's there was unquestioned allegiance to the Founding Fathers, whom "they saw as legendary demigods." The cause of liberty lay not in further rebellion but in fidelity to the true spirit of Washington and Jefferson. Anything threatening this was a betrayal of tradition: "Change was justified as a removal of corruption and a restoration of former purity."
    1.4 The above views left a deep imprint on literary treatments of the Revolution.
        1.4.1 War of the Revolution: Not a challenge to sovereignty but a struggle between peers— symbolized by good and bad brothers. Bad brother is an agent of enemy power; good brother has the sanction of a Washington-like father.
        1.4.2 Tacit agreement that American society is characterized by a "weakness of authority as an unregulated competition for power."

1.4.3 Villains in early American fiction were seldom a bad father or wicked king. . . the hero did not strike a blow against evil authority but rather defeated the renegade brother — the Tory — the ruthless competitor who defied the "sacred rules of the compact."

This "fed" a widespread fear of factionalism and anarchy and prompted a desire to identify one's interests with a tradition of self-sacrificing unity.

2. THE WESTERN HERO

2.1 Social unity might conflict with the self-sufficient and omnipotent individual — celebrated from the Age of Jackson to the Robber Barons.

2.2 Putting the hero in the vacant spaces of the West allowed aggressive self-reliance to be a constructive and wholly natural force. (Cooper's Ishmael Bush — "When the law of the land is weak, it is right that the law of nature should be strong")

2.2.1 Cooper's Leatherstocking tales provide the ingredients: Individualistic hero, isolated, solitary, far removed from complexities of adult love — from family relations, or vocation: "the perfect fulfillment of the preadolescent mind."

Instead of shaping lives to distant goals, they lived in the present, according to an understood code of natural justice, good natured generosity. Stripped of family ties, clan grudges, etc., the encounter was with the elementary struggle for survival.

2.2.2 Cooper's Deerslayer tells an Indian that the world is large enough for both but if not. . . "The Lord will order the fate of each of us." Deerslayer slays the Indian Mingo, dying, and with admiration, the Indian calls Deerslayer "Wahkeye" — finger lightning, aim, death, great warrior.

2.2.3 Owen Wister's classic finds the Virginian earning the manly characteristics — fighting, killing, and winning Molly Wood — a vehicle to adorn the hero and a vehicle to reveal his conscience and tenderness.

3. INDIANS AND NEGROES:

3.1 1799 — Charles Brockden Brown's Edgar Huntley tomahawks an Indian after overcoming religious scruples.

3.2 1837 — Robert Montgomery Bird's *Nick of the Woods* finds a father boasting that his son had killed his first "brute."

"When we recall that for some two centuries Americans were engaged in a continuing racial war, it is not surprising that so much fictional violence should center on the red man. To kill an Indian was a ritual that sealed one's claim to the rights and privileges of the white man's civilization; it was a symbolic acknowledgement that American freedom and wealth depended on the sacrifice of the aborigine's blood."

3.3 From colonial times, the American mind associated the Negro with violence—fears of the Southern slaveholders, debates in state legislatures and in the Constitutional Convention, tracts, and sermons.

 3.3.1 Prior to the Civil War, American fiction found the Negro to be *non*violent.

  Pro-southern writers, sensitive to abolitionists, portrayed slaves as content, loyal, etc., disrupted only by Northern meddlers. When a Negro showed violence it was in defense of his master or mistress.

 3.3.2 Beginning of 20th century with a tightening of segregation and racial tension brought "historic phobias" to the surface in popular literature.

  Thomas Dixon, Jr.—*The Clansman* (from which *The Birth of a Nation* was made) depicted the KKK "knowing" that Gus had abused a white girl, showed violence toward Gus and sentenced him to death.

  Richard Wright's *Native Son.* Bigger Thomas accidentally kills a white girl. At his execution he claims that "What I killed for must've been good! "and his lawyer, Mr. Max, said ". . . it was his way of living."

  William Faulkner in his *Light in August* takes Joe Christmas as an abstraction seeking to be a human being.

4. VIOLENCE AND ANTIRATIONALISM:

American literature is part of Western literature and has been currently influenced by a complex shift in thought and values —a shift we can call "antirationalism."

 4.1 Violence is (according to Mr. Max) an "act of creation."

 4.2 The roots for this view are deep, to the 18th century revolt against rationalism, an antidote to classic virtues of prudence, decorum, moderation.

 4.3 Mechanistic psychology threatened man and his moral autonomy. Romantic writers turned to the spontaneous impulse as a source of truth, goodness, beauty.

 4.4 Nineteenth century thinkers, Marx, Bakunin, Nietzsche, Jean Arthur Rimbaud, George Sorel, joined in attacking sentimentality and the cult of tender-hearted idealism—often putting forth the view that violence is a regenerative and purifying force. Thus:

4.4.1 Social radicalism merged with romanticism.

4.4.2 The novel became an instrument of aggression.

4.5 The two sides to the new literature of violence taught:

    4.5.1 All traditional ideals are illusions or instruments of class oppression. Society is ruled by brute force.

    4.5.2 Man is irrational, an animal, moved by deep, destructive impulses, irresistible and self-expressive; hence, creative.

    See Freud

          Social Darwinism

          "Lessons" of WWI and the Totalitarian regimes following.

4.6 *Twentieth century literature finds violence to be the essence of reality and thus opposes abstract ideals, myths, and institutions.*

4.7 Theme of violence as reality takes a variety of forms:

    4.7.1 Steinbeck, *In Dubious Battle,* man's spontaneous outrage at oppression; *Grapes of Wrath,* Tom Joad killing a policeman; *Of Mice and Men,* George killing Lennie, the giant half-wit, depicts the nature of class struggle. *We find sentimentality being more hard-boiled: dreams being punctured and illusions destroyed.*

    Farrell and Hemingway symbolize the brutality of the world to which one must be resigned.

4.8 Violence can also stand for the supreme moment of truth:

    4.8.1 Hemingway—*The Sun Also Rises*

4.9 Violence can be a nightmarish burst of life:

    4.9.1 Marc Chagall's painting of the falling angel or Picasso's "Guernica."

4.10 Violence can be a vehicle of unrelieved dehumanization:

    4.10.1 Herbert Selby, Jr.

5. America's view of images of violence as reality appear to be part of an international disenchantment with the view that life is essentially decent, rational, and peaceful.

    5.1 However, American writers bring a synthesis between rebellious antirationalism and the native tradition of the individualistic hero who "proves" himself through violent acts.

        5.1.1 Compare Cooper's Deerslayer and Hemingway's Robert Jordan; Melville's Ahab and

Faulkner's Joe Christmas; Wister's Virginian and Spillane's Mike Hammer; the conspiratorial Tories and the Communist subversives.

5.1.2 The antirationalistic philosophy and the individualistic hero has been moved from the open seas or prairies to the dense urban society in which only the brutal survive.

6. ". . . the treatment of violence in our literature has grown increasingly ominous for a people who profess to believe in peace and human brotherhood."

CONCEPTS

Not having any bank of concepts related to violence prior to working with the article, the teacher draws a number of concepts from the material itself. At this point she is *not* concerned with determining which concepts, if any, she will use in her teaching. This approach simply opens up options not previously held.

1. Violence in American literature reflects historical conditions and circumstances.
2. American writers have incorporated antirationalistic philosophies with the individualistic hero who uses violence as a regenerative or creative force.
3. Current literature reflects a "trickle up" process in which early literature is picked up and refined.
4. A mass, democratic society desires to read and to view materials dealing with oversimplification, exaggeration, strong emotion, and striking effects.
5. Violence provides a cheap way to effect a change of pace for the audience—an escape from the pedestrian day-to-day activities of the average *and* educated reader.
6. Themes in American literature move from Romance of the American Revolution to the Western hero to Indians and Negroes to Violence in the Urban Society.
7. The initial concept of change appearing in literature involved a replacement of one authority with another authority and change was justified only to remove corruption and to restore the place of the past.
8. Early American literature is characterized by agreement about the weakness of authority in American society and agreement about unregulated competition for power.
9. Early American literature reflected a fear of factionalism and anarchy and the need to place one's interests with the tradition of self-sacrificing unity.

10. The hero in 19th century literature was individualistic, isolated, and solitary; not encumbered with adult love, family relations, or set vocation; not bothered with distant goals; lived for the present; accepted a "natural" justice; and, in a simple, generous way, worked at surviving.

11. The killing of the "brute" Indian appeared in literature as a necessary step in securing the rights and privileges of what the white man's civilization promised.

12. Prior to the Civil War, American literature viewed the Negro as nonviolent—content, loyal, and satisfied. Twentieth century literature finds the Negro in the mainstream of American violence.

13. American literature reflects a worldwide complex shift in thought *away* from the rationalism as appeared in the 17th and 18th centuries. Violence appears as an antidote to the old virtues of prudence, decorum, moderation, reason, etc., by finding romatic writers supporting spontaneity of impulse as the source of truth, goodness, and beauty.

14. Violence, as reflected in American literature, became a regenerative and creative force. Traditional ideals were illusions and the irrational animal called man is moved by deep impulses which are creative because they call for self-expression.

15. The themes of violence take a number of forms: class struggle; view of reality as brutality; moments of truth; nightmarish bursts of life; unrelieved dehumanization.

16. American writers find the rebellious antirationalism supported by the native American tradition of the individualistic hero who justifies self and rebellion through acts of violence, sadism, etc.

17. The urban society supplies the setting for the hero as he uses violence as a regenerative/creative force.

18. There appears to be a dichotomy between a people professing peace and human brotherhood and the appearance of violence as a way of life as appears in contemporary literature.

QUESTIONS

The content (including the concepts) triggers a number of questions—questions which, if recorded, prompt possible relationships, need for additional data, and the realization of areas in which there is questionable understanding on the part of the reader. The questions raise one more vital factor for teaching in that they are often indices of one's *own* interest and background and suggest teaching approaches with which the teacher might feel comfortable.

1. If literature *reflects* historical conditions, how does literature contribute to historical conditions?

2. To understand literature, what *aspects* of history must one understand (i.e.: political, economic, social, intellectual)?

3. A "trickle up" process implies strata for "accepted" writers. Who determines (and how) who gets a national platform? Critics? Publishers? Advertisers? Education? Movie Producers? Television?

4. Are there any trends appearing in the "Best Sellers" list over the past ten years? Over the past fifty years?

5. What elements are involved in the label "boredom"? Are there kinds of boredom? Personality sets? Are there "boredom classes" with certain characteristics similar to "social classes"? What is the mass, democratic society?

6. Does American literature reflect an attitude toward change similar to Plato's desire to return to the Golden Age? Is this the broad canvas upon which writers paint their themes?

7. Have American social movements and reactions to such movements supported the idea of weakness of authority, unregulated competition, fear of factionalism and anarchy, and the need to self-sacrifice?

8. The hero of 19th century literature might appear as a microscopic American Nation during its isolationist period. Can a parallel be made?

9. What was the role of the individual in the era of rationalism? How does contemporary literature view the concept of "individual"? Does this jibe with the findings of the social and behavioral sciences? Against what is the rebellion, and what historical conditions are at work, now?

10. Is the present rebellion more against the social and behavioral sciences, which seem to confirm the 18th century view of man as a social being and reject him as being an autonomous individuality? Is the present rebellion conservative and perhaps reactionary? Present thinking about man does not support the old concept of American hero.

11. What criteria would one use to analyze current American

fiction? Themes? Authors? Publics? Reviews? Sales—to whom?

12. Besides American fiction, what about movies? Television? Plays? What about an analysis of humor in the New Yorker as opposed to say the comics as appearing in the local papers?

Given the list of concepts and the teacher's own questions, what questions might be raised in the students' minds? To what extent do they overlap the questions raised by the teacher? Do both sets of questions suggest possible approaches to the study? Do the questions allow for clustering? For individualizing instruction?

POSSIBLE STUDENT OBJECTIVES

The teacher's key question now becomes, What do I want the students to be able to *do*? Some of the doing may call for strict recall. Others may go beyond recall and ask for establishing relationships, reasoning, and in general seek ways of putting skills to work with data.

You will note that following the list of objectives comes a suggestion to reduce objectives to their respective components. For example, what must a student be able to do in order to do what is requested in the objective. Most objectives presuppose the student having some background in a particular area or some mastery of skill use. In deciding to use certain objectives, a teacher should explore the full ramifications of what is called for. Unless this is done, it is not unlike saying to a person, "You should be able to play bridge," and, in trying *to teach* him to play bridge, failing to recognize that playing bridge subsumes a whole host of other knowledges and skills.

1. Given a list of American authors, the student is able to place the authors in chronological periods: 1787 to 1820; 1820 to 1900; 1900 to 1950; 1950 to date.

2. The student is able to take each of the above chronological periods and identify three significant events occurring in each period which imply some concept about man and his way of life.

3. Given the categories of: (1) homicide; (2) insanity; and (3) monomania, the student is able to select from a list of

novels those that fall into one or more of the above cate
gories.

4. The novels not identified with the above categories (3) are
listed and the student is able to explain the themes used
in the novels.

5. The student is able to identify two pieces of fiction written
prior to 1830 in which the authors romanticize the Revolutionary War.

6. The student is able to identify one piece of fiction, prior
to 1830, that addresses a concept of change which sees
progress as a *return* to a former situation.

7. The student is able to select two villains from a different
piece of fiction written prior to 1830 and be able to list
three characteristics of each which contributes to making
him the villain.

8. Given a quote from Madison's Federalist papers, from
Jefferson's first inaugural address, from Jackson, from the
Compromise of 1820, the student is able to explain how
the quotes relate to fears of factionalism and anarchy.

9. The student is able to discuss Charles Dickens' attitudes
toward American literature and to list two reasons why
Dickens may have felt as he did.

10. The student is able to define the following terms: (1)
rationalism (as a philosophic position); (2) romanticism;
(3) factionalism; (4) anarchy; (5) individualistic; (6) regenerative; (7) American "isolationism."

11. Given Ishmael Bush's quote, "When the law of the land
is weak, it is right that the law of nature should be strong,"
the student is able to select two heroes in fiction (prior
to 1900) and explain how they exemplified the "law of
nature."

12. The student is able to identify and to list at least six characteristics of the Western hero.

13. Given a list of eleven characteristics of the Western hero,
the student is able to identify either an event, situation,
or stance in American history (prior to 1900) which parallels each of the items on the list.

14. Taking from Cooper (or an author of his choice) the student
is able to select a character exemplifying manliness and
is able to identify the characteristics designed to make him
manly.

15. The student is able to identify two Indians taken from
fiction who have been portrayed as "good" Indians, and
is able to list the characteristics that made them good.

16. The student is able to: (1) identify two novels in which Indians were portrayed as "savages" or "brutes"; (2) explain the white man's rationalization of his treatment of the Indians; and (3) give a *specific* political agreement made with the Indians which gives evidence of the same rationalization.

17. The student is able to explain how each of the following addressed fear of Negroes as being violent: (1) Southern slave holders; (2) Constitutional Convention; (3) legislation.

18. Selecting two pre-Civil War pro-South writers, the student is able to give specific examples of how Negroes were portrayed to be content, loyal, submissive, and nonviolent.

19. Given book reviews on Richard Wright's *Native Son* and on William Faulkner's *Light in August,* the student is able to identify how each reviewer approaches violence in terms of (a) Bigger Thomas and Joe Christmas as individuals or as Negroes; (b) the respective reports on the author's use of violence.

20. Students are able to: (1) list the human values implicit under a philosophy of rationalism; (2) give the specific historical setting; (3) contrast the items under (1) with values which current literature seems to imply; and (4) give one example of current values.

21. Taking Marx, Nietzsche, and Sorel, the student is able to give examples from the writings of each which support the view that violence is more real than is idealism.

22. The student is able to react to the concept that the novel is an instrument of aggression by supporting or denying, using two present day novels.

23. Using American literature as a source, the student is able to discuss the theory that the present rebelliousness and individualistic violence is a *conservative movement.* Students should address, in their discussion, the relationship between romanticism and social-unity.

24. Using Freud and the concept of Social Darwinism, the student is able to give three examples from each that man is considered an irrational animal whose irresistable impulses are self-expressive and thus creative.

25. Given violence in the following: class struggle; racial struggle; brutality; and truth, the student is able to select a contemporary novel in which one or more of the above

forms are in evidence and to give specific examples of how violence suggests values.

26. The student is able to contrast or compare two of the following in terms of violence and the "individualistic" hero:
    (1) Cooper's Deerslayer and Hemingway's Robert Jordan
    (2) Melville's Ahab and Faulkner's Joe Christmas
    (3) Wister's Virginian and Spillane's Mike Hammer
    (4) Ayn Rand and Martin Buber

27. The student is able to defend or attack the view that the violent individualistic hero is a "cop out" who refuses to recognize man and self as a rational as well as rationalizing being. The student should use one "individualistic hero" and one "non-individualistic hero" taken from contemporary fiction.

PROBLEM WITH B.O.'S

If the above list of student objectives is desired, there are three concerns that the teacher must address.

A. Each objective must be assessed in terms of *exactly* what is wanted, how accessible the response will be to evaluation, and what a student must be able to do in order to achieve the objectives. At this point, a *reductionist* approach is used.

For Example. *Specific Objective 13.*

The student is given a list of eleven characteristics of the Western hero.

He is asked to *identify.*

Identification takes the form of seeking *parallels* between the characteristics as listed and an *event, situation,* or *stance* in American history.

He must: (1) know what constitutes *parallelism,* (2) be relatively sophisticated about American history prior to 1900, and (3) know what is meant by event, situation, stance.

Being asked only to *identify,* is he to only list? Or, is he to explain how he sees the relationship or the parallelism of the selected event, stance, or situation.

What might be the merit of listing such things as:
    a. isolationism.
    b. no foreign alliances.
    c. the "American Adam"—the newborn who has no ties.

    d. the Declaration of Independence: goal-pursuit of happiness.
    e. Manifest Destiny.
    f. The Splendid Little War.
    g. The Monroe Doctrine.
    h. Cherokee Agreement.

One might have two lists and the student might be asked to match and to explain the matching of six out of the eleven given.

Objectives can be *reduced* and rebuilt using component parts as sub-objectives.

B. Assuming the teacher wants the student to meet the objectives, the planned experiences must be related to the objectives or random activity takes place. If one wants the student to achieve Objective 13, teaching/learning experience should include experiences allowing identification of the Western heroes' characteristics; and experiences which make parallels with various phases of American history.

C. Materials: Only after the objectives and the desired experiences have been identified are the materials selected.

Once the teacher has the concepts and has determined objectives consistent with the concepts, she uses her list of questions to help in planning student activities. In other words, for a student to be able to accomplish the desired objectives, what activities can students perform which will combine data, concepts, and skills in such a way that the student learns? Actually, if the objectives are determined first, then the activities are not hard to determine. Some would argue that it is at this point, the point when one moves from framework planning to student learning—from ends to means—that focus moves with content from teacher to teach*ing*.

Look over the objectives. Try to reduce some so that they are manageable. Then select a few objectives and try to determine specific activities which students might do to enable them to reach the objectives. Another thing that might be of value: determine materials for student use as they work with the activities you have constructed. Try to build a materials bank on violence—readings, films, case-studies, newspaper accounts, cartoons, editorials, tapes.

Do As I Do

Asked to teach something about which she was not familiar, the teacher developed her strategy by moving from one article found in an academic journal. The test of what she could do with the article was her own ability to *do* the things she expects her students to do—question, analyze, synthesize, reason inductively and deductively, generalize, transfer, etc.

THE "USUAL" SCENE

WORKING WITHIN

We have addressed what might be done when a teacher knows the concepts, skills, objectives, and activities and *then* hunts for material for support and assistance in the teaching effort. And we have seen what a teacher might do when given a topic and told to teach it when her own background in the content area was minimal. There is still another situation—perhaps the most common— in which a teacher may face some decisions about what to do. This is when a teacher is working in a system that has a fairly tight Administrative "Topic" curriculum, has the subtopics sequenced, and has rather firm expectations that the teacher move with his students *within* the framework.

Suppose, for example, one was teaching an American history class at the senior high school level. The course of study is voluminous, appearing like a chronological table of content combined with a categorized index. Just to have students memorize the given data appears to be a substantial chore. And knowing that the final examination, departmentally given, will stress recall puts the teacher in a delicate position.

If the students don't do well on the examination, their failure to compete on this basis will hurt the students gradewise as well as suggest that the teacher is not a particularly effective instructor. Such are the facts of life in many teaching situations. What does one do? What does one do when faced with textbook teaching?

It is possible to select one area *within* each topic which may act as a synthesizing study for the data covered under the topic. The selected area may allow complementary material to be used, may be explored in more depth, and may in fact provide the students with some large handles with which to move the bits of other data in the topic into some relationships.

Suppose that in the prescribed study of the colonial period one had to cover such things as the Pilgrims, Puritans, New England, and so on. Realizing that the date 1776 is known for Adam Smith's *Wealth of Nations*, a blending of economics, political thought, and social theory into an umbrella theory influential to the "American Way," and knowing that 1776 also marked another synthesis which was to influence the "American Way," the teacher may wish to work with colonial experience differently. The teacher might then correlate the conventional topics to a study of: *Economics and the Good Life*. The complementing focus area might be approached as follows:

CONCEPTS

ECONOMICS AND THE GOOD LIFE (COLONIAL AMERICA)

1. The concept of puritan individualism and laissez-faire economics had an affinity for one another.
2. The affinity allowed economic motives and activity to exist within a world-view which sanctioned it.
3. Acquisitive virtues, to the Puritan, were: industry, sobriety, frugality, reliability, temperance, simplicity of living. These serve two functions: (1) to bring profit to the possessor and (2) to gain moral approbation.
4. The acquisitive virtues included moral techniques of steadfastness, self-denial and prudence.
5. "It pays to be honest" applies *both* to a code of conscience and to a code of business success.
6. Wordly prudence has a sober regard for the future, a willingness to postpone satisfaction in order that it may be greater and more durable, a patience based upon ordering values and dispelling the illusion of proximity.
7. Wealth comes from: austerity, reliability, energy, industry, self-control, marital fidelity, frugality, sobriety, thrift, self-reliance, and foresight.
8. Poverty comes from being pleasure-loving and untrustworthy; being sluggish, idle, dissipated, irregular, extravagant, frivolous, wasteful, dependent, and careless.
9. Unequal distribution of worldly fortune is designed by God. God's will makes some rich and others poor. The pious man accepts his lot.
10. Poverty was evidence not only of a lack of virtue but of the absence of God's favor and aid' a sign of spiritual weakness, a condition to be condemned rather than pitied or relieved. Prevention stems from inculcating prudence, self-reliance, and piety.
11. Puritanism did not cause capitalism nor did capitalism cause puritanism. As common threads, both had supporting existence within their own spheres. (Note: check *Protestant Ethnic*).
12. The Puritan concept of private property: A man has a right to what he has *earned* and not just a right to what he

possesses. Property is a product of the individual's exertions, discipline, and prudent foresight—an expression of the individual's moral personality.
13. The deeper the depths of poverty from which a man has risen, the more creditable his wealth. Humble origin, low station disadvantage, material deprivation, limited education—all test his moral ascent to affluence. A model for the young.

SPECIFIC STUDENT OBJECTIVES:

1. The student is able to define what he means by the terms "individualism" and "laissez-faire capitalism." (Perhaps work with present day views).
2. The student is able to list and explain two historical reasons why the Puritan economic concepts did not cause capitalism.
3. The Puritan view transferred abstract ideas into actual behavior. The student is able to list six behaviors felt desirable for *economic* and *moral* reasons.
4. Given the contemporary problem of poverty, the student is able to write an essay describing how a Puritan would view (1) its causes and (2) its remedies and how the Puritan might view social welfare legislation on moral grounds.
5. The student is able to relate, in writing, how private property and morality were viewed by the Puritans.
6. The student is able to take the Puritan economic-moral views and construct a "model" for a young person to follow.

POSSIBLE STUDENT ACTIVITIES:

1. The students might analyze the changing concept of work as it moved from Luther to Calvin to the Puritans. Some students might check the hymns of the period and relate the wording to concepts of behavior. Some might like to do the same thing with a current "hymn" such as *Walk a Mile in My Shoes.*
2. Some students might take the current concept of poverty, identify legislation passed on the Federal and State levels within the past ten years, and compare the assumptions in the legislation to the position held by the Puritans.
3. Some students might appreciate a chance to research and address the idea of "The Protestant Ethic" within an historical context. Analyzing Willie Loman in *Death of a Salesman* or Marquand's *Point of No Return* in terms of the "ethic" can prove interesting.
4. Students interested in sociology, psychology, and social psychology could assess the changing concept of work/

leisure in the contemporary world, assess the functions of work, and assess the worker in an industrialized society.

5. The teacher might work some synthesis with the class—trying to relate myths, ideology, 17th century background, and Puritan thought and virtues—attempting to build relevance with the class. (A synthesizing effort is a periodic "must")

After establishing the framework, the teacher assumes the responsibility for bringing in additional vehicles which might help in accomplishing the study. For example:

"God helps them that help themselves." (Benjamin Franklin)

"God doth call every man and women to serve him in some peculiar employment in this world, both for their own and common good. . . The Great Governour of the world hath appointed to every man his proper post and province. . ."
(Richard Steele, 1684)

Insofar as property is the product of the Individual's exertions, disciplined will, and prudent foresight, it is the expression of his moral personality. . . a sign of moral fitness.
(Ralph Barton Perry, *The Economic Virtue*)

Poverty lives at one end of town with wife Sloth in a "ruinous cottage" which crumbles without ability to repair. Riches and his servants Pride, Oppression, Covetousness, Luxury, and Prodigality live at the other end.

Godliness with his servants Humility, Sincerity, Repentance, Experience, Faith, Hope, Charity, Temperance and Sobriety. . . tries to live by Riches who insults him; tries to live by Poverty who comes home drunk all the time. Godliness settles half way between, next to Labour and his wife Prudence. Labour has as his servants, Forecast, Diligence, Expedition, Cheerfulness, and Perseverance. Labour's estate increases and he finds himself surrounded with friends: Content, Assurance,. . . and is boundlessly happy.
(A Rich Treasure At an Easy Rate: Or, The Way to True Content. 1657)

ABSTRACT TO BE USED WITH STUDENTS

Robert S. Michaelsen, "Changes in the Puritan Concept of Vocation," *New England Quarterly:*
I. Luther: Salvation stems from God's free mercy and not from good works. "Truly good works (as those chosen by God) and comprehended within the bounds of one's partic-

ular calling. . . and. . . (they) become good only when they flow from faith."

From God comes a call to salvation; the response to this gift is through gratitude in *one's work or calling*.

II. Calvin: More systematic formulation of the doctrine of calling or vocation. Like Paul—"vocatio" refers to the call from God which constituted an indication of election, and a particular calling or station in life.

    A. "Every one ought to regard his calling as a token of his election" (Institutes)

    B. Regarded calling as the primary area of a person's reaction and response to God's call.

        a. talents in performing work came not from himself but from God and is used for God's enhancement.

        b. Calvin stressed greater emphasis on obligation and strenuousness in vocation.

III. Calling: Man responds to call by (a) religious acts and by (b) responses in his work and in his whole life— "a certain kind of life, ordained and imposed on man by God, for the common good." (Quoted from William Perkins' *Works* (1608). Particular calling is the execution of some particular office, arising of that distinction which God makes between man and man in every society.

IV. 1. Everyone must have a particular calling. Quotes John Cotton: "Faith draws the heart of a Christian to live in some warrantable calling. . . he will not rest, till he finds out some warrantable calling and *employment*."

    2. Calling on basis of public need: calling performed not for self but for the good of the whole.

    3. People encouraged to stay in a calling after it has been chosen—should *not* attempt to change "status"

    4. Avoid covetousness. Cotton: ". . . we are never more apt to forget God then when we prosper. . . ."

1. Changed concept of calling gave increased autonomy to man's natural desires.
2. Shifted idea of God's Gift to the idea that God was kind to his "good" children by bestowing wealth.
3. Poverty became a sign of God's disfavor.
4. Christian liberty: individual able to determine own destiny in economic activity.

Note: The Covenant theology emphasized individual autonomy. Later Puritans went further—concept of "calling" stressed work as a *response* to God.

Practical Considerations

This is an approach that a teacher might try when working within a tight framework. Perhaps ten or twelve such efforts might be tried throughout a school year simply as attempts to synthesize the topics and textbook coverage. And there are other possibilities. For example, one can take a chapter from the textbook, identify concepts and factual data, form student objectives — which include "testing" some of the concepts with other sources — and develop activities to tie the textbook in with other information. A textbook may be used in ways not originally intended and still give emphasis to "coverage."

We have tried to address three different teaching situations. One thing for sure: teaching involves making decisions. And the decisions must take into account the teacher's own academic background, the teacher's own ability to inquire, and the realities of the situation.

"Hell, do as I do, kid, pretend there's no one down there."

5

CONTENT MODELS

DOING IT

Prospective social studies teachers usually begin their professional preparation with a view of teaching that brings focus on an adult working with a class of students in an effort to get across subject matter. At this phase of his professional career, the prospective teacher still finds himself in the position of learner, a member of a "class," therefore it is easy to understand the initial concepts he brings to understanding teaching. To be sure, the teacher working with students in the class situation is a crucial aspect of teaching. But, this aspect is only one part of a host of necessary supporting activities.

We have tried to involve the reader in some of these activities — activities calling for different levels of decision-making that must be done *prior* to engaging students in a lesson or a learning experience. Seldom do such decision-making activities come to the direct forefront and seldom are the students aware of the full measure of the terms "preparation" and "planning". We have tried to indicate some of these aspects of preparation: Goals, objectives, concepts, inquiry, methods, materials, all as integral aspects of the teacher's content *and* all as a system for student content. If one's preplanning is effectively done, at least a teacher has a base for making decisions when on the firing line in the classroom. The number of decisions a teacher makes during one 48 minute class is surprisingly large. The plans for action imply a prediction of what can and should be done in that particular class session. But, plans don't have consequences until put into action. Plans are made separate from the actual situation. When put into action, new variables enter into and influence on-the-spot decisions by the teacher. For example, how does a teacher decide to honor one question, and delay another? How does a teacher decide to explore some unexpected question, piece of information, or experience rather than keep boring into the planned experience? In short, how does a teacher decide to alter, even discard, in the context of implementation? The preplanning at least provides a basis for making the action decisions. The preplanning does not guarantee success as a teacher. In and of itself, it is not sufficient. It is necessary, but not sufficient.

Working from Piaget, we are told that:[1]

> Every act of intelligence presumes some kind of intellectual structure, some sort of organization, within which it proceeds.

> An act of intelligence, be it crude motor movement in infancy or a complex and abstract judgment in adulthood, is always related to a system or totality of such acts of which it is a part.

We assume that teaching is an act of intelligence, that somehow it is organized, and that the parts are not disjointed and unrelated. It is fair to assume, as well, that learning is an act of intelligence, that it somehow is organized, and that the parts encountered are somehow related.

In neither case, the teaching nor the learning, is the organization of one done in complete disjunction from the other. The teacher's act of intelligence meets the student's act of intelligence and they *mutually* influence respective organization and relationships. On occasion it has been assumed that a teacher's organization can be "given" to the student and that reciprocal and reciprocating efforts at organization are not involved. Hilda Taba's work on the processes of cognition suggests that this is not so.[2] For example, she found that:

1. Cognitive processes are an *active* transaction between the individual and his environment. The teacher is part of the student's environment —this includes the teacher as a person, the teacher's plans, and the teacher's own conceptual organization. And, the student is part of the teacher's environment when in a learning situation.

2. Mental schemes or concepts are *built* from experiences people encounter and there is a state of relative flux in which conceptual organizations are modified and reorganized.

3. An individual fits new information and/or new conceptual organization into the conceptual organization he already possesses. This implies that the teacher can't "give" organization *but rather, must create opportunities to* build with students.

If, in the opportunity, there is a discrepancy between conceptual schemes, an indiviual is faced with the need to alter, modify, etc. preconceptions or find reasons for rejecting in whole or part the new experience.

---

[1]John H. Flavell. *The Development Psychology of Jean Piaget.* Princeton, N.J., D. Van Nostrand Co., Inc. 1963.

[2]See Hilda Taba, Samuel Levine and Freeman Elzey, *Thinking in Elementary School.* Cooperative Research Project No. 1574, San Francisco State College, 1966.

This makes a strong case for the view that cognitive structures are not simply wired in but evolve in forms of equilibrium resulting from the interaction between individuals and their environments.[3] *The teacher's plan forms an intentional part of a student's environment.* In the classroom situation, the teacher's organization transacts with a *number* of conceptual schemes already possessed by students — unplanned and at times unpredictable — which work at influencing what is taught and what is learned. The teacher's method is basically a means of conducting the transactions, of allowing an opportunity for the building and testing of concepts. The means used by teachers also implies a conceptual organization — a planned strategy for conducting the learning transactions.

USE OF VEHICLES

The data a teacher decides to use doesn't just exist. It usually appears in some form: an article, a film, a quotation, a chart, a map, a tape, slides, a research study, experience, or even a textbook. The form in which data appears is usually referred to as "materials". Materials are part of the means used in conducting the teaching/learning transactions. Viewed as a means, materials are not ends-in-themselves but rather are *vehicles* which allow one to address concept building and concept testing.

A number of materials or vehicles were not, in original form, designed to be used as a means in teaching. In other words, most teaching materials, in their original form, have a conceptual organization of their own and are not formulated with teaching in mind. For example, a short story may be designed to serve functions other than the teaching of social studies. Or, a political speech may be designed to pull party members together and in its existing form make no pretense at having been designed to be used in teaching.

Teachers select vehicles to use.

The selection of vehicles presupposes a number of things. For example, the selection presupposes some criteria, some idea of intended use as a means, presupposes some relationship with the teacher's conceptual organization and thus with the "whole" of the teacher's intentional plan. Selection of this vehicle instead of that vehicle, this form of data instead of that form, this level of

---

[3]Lawrence Kohlberg and Carol Gilligan, "The Adolescent as a Philosopher: The Discovery of Self in a Postconventional World," *Twelve To Sixteen: Early Adolescence*, Daedalus, Fall, 1971.

material instead of that level, all is premised upon the view that teaching is an intelligent and purposeful act and that vehicles may help in doing three things: (1) provide data related to concept building and testing; (2) provide a bridge between teacher and students in order to help in the transacting involved in inquiry; and (3) provide a means which encourages inquiry skills to be used.

As has been pointed out, raw materials may not appear in vehicle form. This necessitates the teacher to structure a strategy for the intended use of materials. Just as teachers form data banks — an open account for depositing and withdrawing data for use in teaching — so they develop materials or vehicle banks for similar use. A vehicle bank goes beyond just a collection of materials which might someday, somehow, prove useful. A vehicle bank moves from materials to their potential use, from their existing form to how the data can be used in teaching.

It should be evident that neither data banks nor vehicle banks are something that one develops only *after* having secured a position. They may be developed along the way. One encounters a barrage of potential vehicles every day. For example, one may be taking a literature course, read a novel, and see merit for its use in teaching social studies. This might be true of contemporary music or while one is working on a research assignment in a sociology or political science course. The sources may not be always in an academic setting. An article in *Sports Illustrated* may deal with the way baseball managers select and use data in making strategy decisions. Or, they may be an article in a newspaper, a picture, a cartoon or an editorial. Perhaps even an advertisement. James Barber, Director of the Antioch Graduate School at Yellow Springs, Ohio, was standing in line in an airport. He noticed a counter of credit card applications, noticed the names on the sample credit cards, took several different application forms, and banked them for use when teaching inquiry into institutionalized prejudice.

Potential vehicles surround us. Of course, to build an effective vehicle bank, one must have some generalized criteria in order to select, classify, and translate into probable teaching use.

There are problems. Granted, a prospective teacher of social studies does not know exactly what he will end up teaching nor does he know the specific students who will be at the other end of the transaction. It should be evident that materials do not have an inherent and determined way to be used. This depends on the teacher, the students, the school system, and the public. A specific form of material may not be "good" or "bad," "effective" or "non-effective," in and of itself. It depends upon what is done with the material, how it is used as a vehicle. *Mein Kampf* or *Das Kapital* or the *Declaration of Independence*, by themselves, are raw materials. It is in the ways they are used that makes a difference. If one is sensitive to a variety of uses, it is possible to at least initiate a potential vehicle bank and to start developing such a bank prior to entering a classroom. The same issue is confronted when not knowing the specific students to be involved. Again, materials translated into teaching vehicles imply a variety of possible uses and thus a variety of levels and interests.

All this suggests a need for some generalized criteria. If teaching involves the use of inquiry in building and testing concepts, then one might try to determine what concepts are implicit in the material. If teaching involves somehow predicting conceptual frameworks already held by the students, one might try to determine whether or not the data and the form might be adapted in ways that would allow students to reassess their own conceptual frameworks, construct concepts, and generally work as a bridge to help forge meaning and understanding. If teaching involves intentionally working with inquiry, what specific sub-skills might be put to work if the material were to be used in vehicle form? And there are other considerations such as is it interesting? Or can it be broken into sub parts? Can it be used with students having different levels of sophistication? Rather basic criteria are found in whether or not the material suggests possible student activities: could it be used as a springboard?

In summary, the criteria for vehicle selection and use might include:

1. Does the vehicle provide data related to concept building and testing?
2. Does it provide a potential bridge for reassessing student conceptual frameworks?
3. Does it have potential for helping a student to work with inquiry skills?
4. Does it allow subdividing and a variety of uses?
5. Can it be reworked in a way of allowing for student differences?
6. Can it be used as a springboard for other possible student experiences?

Obviously not all vehicles will meet *all* the criteria with equal intensity. At least one will be aware of the relative potential for use with students and at least there is some base for starting a vehicle bank. Of course, the test of how effective a vehicle is rests upon whether or not it does the intended job.

We are including a number of different types of possible potential vehicles. At this point, not stressing units or lesson plans or courses of study, we are interested in providing you with an opportunity to put the criteria to work. The selection and planned used of materials is a teacher responsibility. This is not to say that students can't or should not be involved. On the contrary, if a teacher uses effective vehicles and shares their intended use with students, students can and should and will bring in vehicles reflecting their own conceptual frameworks. When this happens and is encouraged, the transaction becomes a reality in that *both* the teacher's conceptual organization and the students' conceptual organization are intentional parts of the ends and means involved in inquiring. When students start to bring in their own vehicles, the question of relevance is rather moot.

Our hope is that you will start to collect your own vehicles. To make this effort more than just a move to collect materials at random, we are giving different possible kinds of vehicles and have included an application of the criteria use for each example given. The use of the criteria invites your participation. Under the Application of Criteria section for each given vehicle, we have responded to the criteria to some extent. You might wish to go beyond our response and complete the exercise.

USE OF A QUOTATION

Most of us come across quotations that "grab" and hold tight. Sometimes a quote works on us in an affective way such as Gibrahn's ". . . the pain of too much tenderness." Others push us in a cognitive manner—using and interpreting data, synthesizing a causal relationship, making conclusions. The following is just such a quotation. It is more than "just data" and might possibly be put away in a vehicle bank.

"Those who fall behind get beaten. But we do not want to get beaten. No, we refuse to be beaten!. . . Old Russia was beaten by the Mongol Khans. She was beaten by the Turkish boys. She was beaten by the Swedish feudal lords. She was beaten by the Polish and Lithuanian gentry. She was beaten by the British and French capitalists. She was beaten by the Japanese. . . All beat her—for her backwardness, for military backwardness, for cultural backwardness, for political backwardness, for industrial backwardness, for agricultural backwardness. She was beaten because it was profitable and could be done with impunity. Do you remember the words of the pre-revolution poet: 'You are poor and abundant, mighty and impotent, Mother Russia.' These words of the old poet were well learned by those gentlemen. They beat her. . . such is the law of exploiters—to beat the backward and the weak. . . That is why we must no longer lag behind. . . You must put an end to backwardness in the shortest possible time and develop genuine Bolshevik tempo in building up the socialistic system of economy. There is no other way. . . Either we do it, or they crush us."

Joseph Stalin, 1931

APPLICATION OF CRITERIA

1. Does it provide data related to concept building and testing?
    1.1 *UN* Concepts:
        (1) Russia was beaten by the Mongol Khans.
        (2) Russia was beaten by the Turks.
        (3) ——————————————————
        (4) ——————————————————
        (5) ——————————————————

    1.2 *Value Concepts:*
        (1) Those who fall behind get beaten.
        (2) ——————————————————
        (3) ——————————————————

2. Does it provide a potential bridge for reassessing student conceptual frameworks?
    2.1 *Predictions:* student conceptual frameworks:
        (1) Size and abundant natural resources make for strength.
        (2) A socialistic economic system is equated with Russian Communism.
        (3) ——————————————————

3. Does it have potential for helping a student work with inquiry skills?
    3.1 *Assumptions* to be identified:
        (1) Russia had fallen behind.
        (2) ——————————————————
        (3) ——————————————————

    3.2 *Causal* Relationships:
        (1) Russia did not have a socialistic economy. Therefore she was beaten?
        (2) The only reason for being beaten in war was Russia's backwardness?
        (3) ——————————————————

3.3 *Emotive* Appeals:
   (1) "No, we refuse to be beaten!"
   (2) _____
   (3) _____
   (4) _____

3.4 *Ambiguous terms:*
   (1) Bolshevik tempo
   (2) _____
   (3) _____

3.5 *Reasoning:*
   3.5.1 *Inductive Reasoning*
      (1) Given just the "hard data" in the quotation, what *other* possible conclusions could one have reached?
      (2) _____
   3.5.2 *Deductive Reasoning*
      (1) Old Russia lost a number of wars.
      (2) _____
      (3) _____

3.6 *Questions* (leading to the need for more data than that found in the quotation)
   (1) What standard is used in determining a "backward" country?
   (2) What was the general situation which might have prompted the numerous wars encountered by Old Russia?
   (3) Is there data to support the pre-revolutionary poet's thoughts?
   (4) Is the date of the quotation important? Why was it felt necessary to say such things in 1931?
   (5) _____
   (6) _____
   (7) _____

4. Does it allow subdividing and a variety of uses?

   4.1 Potential use in assessing nature of emotive appeals.

   4.2 Potential use in assessing Russia's role in the Cold War years.

   4.3 _____

   4.4 _____

5. Can it be reworked in a way allowing for student differences?

   5.1 The quotation can be rewritten or taped for students having reading difficulties.

   5.2 Parts of the quotation may be used to allow different types and levels of student research.

   5.3 _____

   5.4 _____

6. Can it be used as a springboard for other possible student experiences?

   6.1 The quotation from the pre-revolutionary poet might allow an assessment of pre- and post-revolutionary poetry and literature.

   6.2 The total quotation could be used to study what is meant by the term "underdeveloped" countries.

   6.3 The total quotation might be used to assess the American fear or anxiety about Russian intent.

   6.4 In American history or modern problems, the quotation might be used to assess socialistic systems of economy and socialism within the American context.

   6.5 _____

   6.6 _____

   6.7 _____

Usually a teacher is not so specific about applying the criteria in assessing the potential teaching uses of materials. But, there are reasons behind the selection and use of materials in learning situations. Initially, it seems wise to be rather specific and then, as one sees possible applications and relationships, he may wish to create his own framework for assessment. You might want to select a quotation and apply the same techniques, as used above, in analyzing its potential use.

USE OF NUMERICAL DATA

Increasingly both the teacher and the student are encountering data appearing in numerical data form. A great many pieces of data are preconceptualized and organized in table form. The preconceptualized structure, although found in most data presentation, is most evident in this form of data presentation. One need only look at surveys reported in the daily papers to understand that citizens are expected to work with and interpret some fundamental statistical ways of collecting and reporting information. This calls for some ability to understand ideas related to sampling and to understand the promise *and* limitations of statements made about a population on the basis of the sample. Most of us are not sophisticated about statistics and yet this "inquiry tool" is making a substantial difference in the kinds of data our students encounter as well as a substantial difference in the forms in which such data appear. Perhaps working with students in studying polls reported in newspapers may be a start in sharpening the tool.

On the surface, the American people pay real heed to strict moral principles, but a slight scratch below the surface reveals that substantial majorities of the public also are guided by a more elastic code of behavior on individual decisions involving questions of morality.

Recently, the Harris Survey asked a cross section of 1563 individuals across the nation:

"When you find yourself facing a moral decision, which of the following do you feel is an important or unimportant source of guidance?"

	Important	Not Important	Not Sure
Your own conscience	98%	2%	—
Golden Rule	96%	3%	1%
What your parents taught you	94%	5%	1%
Religious rules you were trained on	73%	16%	11%

If this were the only evidence available, one would have to conclude that nearly all Americans are guided in their decisions by a sense of personal conscience, the Golden Rule, parental teachings, and, to a somewhat smaller degree, religious precepts. Taken together, they would add up to an impressive roster of clearly drawn moral imperatives.

But the cross section was also asked whether or not five other possible bases for taking a particular course of action were also important to them.

SOURCE OF MORAL GUIDANCE

	Important	Not Important	Not Sure
What seems right at the time	78%	17%	5%
What you think others expect of you	75%	23%	2%
Whatever the law allows	69%	24%	7%
What comes naturally	64%	29%	7%
Whatever will work	58%	35%	7%

All of these latter five criteria for making individual decisions contain an element of interpretation, ranging from "whatever seems right at the time," which suggests a variable basis for moral behavior, to "whatever will work," which is perhaps another way of saying "what you can get away with."

Tied closely to this admittedly pragmatic basis for moral behavior is the result of still another question:

> "Let me read you this statement: if you don't watch out for yourself, nobody else will. Do you feel this is a very important part of what you believe in, somewhat important, or a not very important part of what you believe in?"

	Total Public
Very important	50%
Somewhat important	29%
Not very important	19%
Not sure	2%

While it might be argued that these last results simply reflect a healthy skepticism on the part of most people who have to live in a highly competitive world, agreement with the part of the question that states "nobody else will watch out for a person's interests" indicates considerable cynicism about the practical operation of the Golden Rule.

A breakdown of those who feel that a "very important" part of their personal philosophy is to assume the worst in others reveals some interesting differences by key groups:

VERY IMPORTANT TO BE WARY OF OTHERS

	Very Important
Nationwide	50%
By Region	
East	50%
Midwest	47%
South	59%
West	40%
By Size of Place	
Big cities	63%
Suburbs	37%
Towns	46%
Rural	51%
By Sex	
Men	55%
Women	45%
By Education	
8th grade or less	65%
High School	53%
College	46%
By Occupation	
Professional, executive	31%
Skilled labor	59%
White collar	44%

If this question can be taken as a measure of the suspicion people have for one another, it is apparent that the most wary segments of Americans can be found among the least educated, in the big cities and rural areas, in the South and the East, and among men on blue-collar jobs. Those most charitable toward their fellow citizens are the suburbanites, Westerners, the college educated, women and business executives and professionals.

The implication of the results is that large numbers of Americans feel they must substitute expediency somewhat short of the Golden Rule and the highest precepts of conscience, because they live in a society where such high standards are not shared by others. At a time when much moral self-righteousness is being generated over many issues that have polarized America, it is patently apparent that individuals might be well advised to re-examine their own moral standards.

LOUIS HARRIS, AMERICANS USE ELASTIC MORAL CODE (1969)

APPLICATION OF CRITERIA

1. Does it provide data related to concept building and testing?

   1.1 *GR* Concepts:
      (1) Stated moral principles and actual behavior may be inconsistent.
      (2) People cite the Golden Rule but are cynical about how it works.
      (3) _____
      (4) _____

   1.2 Continuum of GR Concepts or samples within the sample.
      (1) Nationwide results of the poll.
      (2) Poll results by regions.
      (3) _____
      (4) _____

2. Does it provide a potential bridge for reassessing student conceptual frameworks?

   2.1 Predictions: Student conceptual frameworks:
      (1) Students are inclined to be Absolutists in Principles or Relativism.
      (2) Students accept the Golden Rule as a "universal" moral code.
      (3) Moral codes are somehow "wired in" to the individual and are not dependent upon place, time, and past experience.
      (4) _____
      (5) _____

3. Does it have potential for helping a student work with inquiry skills?

   3.1 *Question Asking:*

      (1) Questions presuppose some purpose. Analysis of purposes implied by the Harris questions.

      (2) Does the way questions are posed have to change when dealing with each section of the "cross-section"?

      (3) _____

      (4) _____

   3.2 *Ambiguous terms:*

      (1) Moral decision.

      (2) Very important, somewhat important, etc.

      (3) _____

      (4) _____

   3.3 *Reasoning:*

      3.3.1 *Inductive Reasoning*

         (1) Given the information listed under "By Education" can one generalize that the more educated a person, the less wary he is of other human beings?

         (2) _____

         (3) _____

      3.3.2 *Deductive Reasoning*

         (1) 50% of the American people feel it important to be wary of other human beings. (Do the data support this in any way?)

         (2) _____

         (3) _____

      3.3.3 *Evidence* used in making general statements:

         (1) Carefully selected sample.

         (2) _____

      3.3.4 *Interpretation* of data:

         (1) Given Harris's findings about the sources of moral guidance, is there only *one* possible interpretation?

         (2) Interpretation goes "beyond" the data.

         (3) _____

         (4) _____

4. Does it allow subdividing and a variety of uses?

4.1 Potential use in attempting to study the idea of prediction.

4.2 Potential use in trying to determine "the" American view on anything.

4.3 _____

4.4 _____

5. Can it be reworked in a way allowing for student differences?

5.1 Each section of the poll report can be used separately.

5.2 Students fearful of or weak in mathematics can work with numbers as a communication system.

5.3 The poll can be translated into bar graphs for those having difficulty in reading.

5.4 _____

5.5 _____

6. Can it be used as a springboard for other possible student experiences?

6.1 Design, implementation, and interpretation of a poll to be conducted within the student's own school.

6.2 History and importance of census taking techniques and results.

6.3 Ways of deciding when to act when one realizes he never has all available information.

6.4 Relate problems of sampling and interpretation to ways people stereotype.

6.5 _____

6.6 _____

6.7 _____

As with the use of quotation, we have tried to be rather specific in the application of the criteria. Select some numerical information and apply the criteria with a *group* of other prospective social studies teachers. The "pooling" of the effort will open up a wide variety of alternatives, will be more efficient, and will quickly multiply the number of potential vehicles.

USE OF EXPERIENCE

A source of potential vehicles often overlooked is direct experience. Few people are denied meaningful direct experiences but few have the desire or time to *record* the experience. Consequently, a number of golden opportunities escape being used in the classroom.

Students in secondary schools are experiencing all the time. It is no longer uncommon to find students active in social protest action, in campaigning for national political candidates, in working for welfare agencies, in directly or indirectly being involved in social issues. It is rare when such experiences are used as *content* or as vehicles for teaching.

The following case study was written after a sensitive black-white situation evolved in a suburban school system. The situation found a number of social studies concepts at work in a real situation. The school system had spent considerable time, energy, and money in educating students in human relations. The case study raises some basic issues about what was learned in the classroom.

SEX OR SOMETHING

The telephone call to the office was not unusual. Four students wanted an appointment to discuss human relations. The appointment was made for the same afternoon.

Four students attending an inner city and predominantly black school came into the office. Overtly less "out-going" than the suburban students, the group seemed almost shy as they introduced themselves.

They wanted an opportunity to meet with suburban white students so that they could better understand one another. It could be worked out through the two schools but the inner city students maintained that "it would work better if the school stayed out of it." Why come to the Suburban Board of Education? Because they wanted the names of a few students they might contact and then the students would take it from there.

The inner city students presented a rough approach to what they had in mind. The students from the two communities would meet together and plan things to do. The joint group would have a slogan, decide upon "colors" and would be fined if they missed meetings. The group would be limited to senior high school students. The purpose: "To better understand each other."

A student from the suburb was called and he arranged for the first meeting. It was held on his farm. The first meeting went "as expected" —both groups were shy and everything seemed a little "forced." But, the contact had been made.

Several weeks later a group of graduates from the suburban school — college bound — called the office and asked for an appointment. It was the students meeting with the inner city group.

"Have you heard from the inner city students?" one asked.

"No — is there any reason to expect being contacted?" the school official responded.

"Well, they said that they felt they had let you down and wanted to explain what had happened."

One member of the group explained that there had been "some problems" and that they were there "just to talk things out."

Another student volunteered that "we found out that we had nothing in common — we just had completely different interests. As we got to know each other better there was nothing to talk about. . . and everything just didn't seem to work out."

It was suggested that the students "back up" and start from the beginning.

The first meeting at the farm was a start. The suburban students said that it "made them feel good" to know that at least they were doing something. The inner city group's concern with a slogan, with selecting colors, with strict rules about attending meetings, etc., seemed unnecessary and a "bit childish." "They wanted everything planned and we just figured that an informal start would be better."

Did the parents of the suburban students know of the meetings? Yes. Did the students think their parents to be fairly "open-minded" in terms of race relations? Yes. Did the parents concur in the effort the students were making? They weren't too positive about the eventual outcomes but appeared willing to have the students make the effort. Did the inner city students talk about their parents' reaction? Yes. The reaction was mixed — and so was the reaction of some of the students' friends.

After the first farm meeting, what happened? The group had an "outing" and some of the inner city girls appeared "jealous" of the suburban girls. There was some dancing. "There wasn't really too much to talk about. . . except sex."

One girl said:

"One of the inner city boys insisted that he was falling in love with me. I told him not to be silly. And, he said I did not like him because he was black. I told him that had nothing to do with it but he insisted."

The joint group planned a progressive supper — moving from houses in the suburb and inner city. Several telephone calls were made between members of the group in preparation for the supper.

The supper started off quite well but apparently some of the inner city boys had been drinking. Several "passes" were made during the evening.

"I felt as though I was a status symbol," one suburban girl said. "He wanted to go to bed with me in order to prove something and I had to keep dodging him all night."

Another student said that "Sex was all they (inner city boys) thought about — we seemed to have nothing else in common. We tried to talk about school and current topics but they didn't seem interested. And, the inner city girls were upset."

What functions might the slogan, colors, and rigid planning serve?

CONTENT MODELS / 185

What does this type of structure "need" *do* when a group is not sure of roles, role expectations, etc? Do you talk about sex with white boys? Have white boys ever made passes?

Yes. Yes, there was a recognition of how a slogan, and colors and rules might be important. . . "but, we weren't sure of our roles and expectations either." Yes, white boys talk about sex "but it was never an overriding thing. They had other interests too." Yes, white boys made passes but "we know how to handle those things. If we don't like a boy for himself, we can let him know in a number of ways but with the inner city boys, rejection was because of race. It was different."

In school did you ever discuss social class influence upon sex codes —not just black and white—but socio-economic? No. How do you think an inner city student might perceive a student from the suburbs? What might this have to do with status? Do you think that the inner city students were not interested in other things besides sex?

Do you think that the effort was worthwhile?

"No!"

"Well. . . it didn't do what it set out to do. Maybe. . . the better I got to know them and understand them, the less I liked them. And, I thought I wasn't prejudiced but I am now. And, I guess I was before. In all honesty, I don't think I want this type of 'better understanding' again. I admit that I am generalizing from this one experience but that's how I feel!"

Another student held that "the whole thing is much more complicated than I had imagined. I guess I was naive. I thought that all I had to do was make a sincere effort but there's a lot more to it."

"Maybe in a different situation. . ." one student ventured.

"What do you mean?"

"Well, we seemed to reverse things. I usually get to like someone *because* we share common interests. Here I was supposed to like someone and *then* find common interests. In the first way, I can like individuals. In the second way I am told to like a group and this doesn't seem to make sense."

"Next Fall when I get to college, I will probably have different experiences. If there is a Negro in my class and we happen to like literature, we have a base for friendship. I can accept or reject him as an individual. . . ."

"Yeah. . . you just don't put people together and say now understand each other and you will like each other. If you put people together working on something that is important to each, maybe the whole thing changes."

Did you ever get a chance to talk about these things in school? No.

"One good thing. . . we got to understand our parents a little better. My mother told me to go ahead and try it but that she didn't think it would work. I thought, 'Here it is—the modern liberal' but, you know, she had a point."

Another student said. "I feel ashamed of myself for feeling the way I do. But, I feel this way—maybe I'll change. I don't know."

If the inner city students approach us again to do the same thing—to get students together—would you try to help them make contact with our students?

No.

APPLICATION OF CRITERIA

1. Does it provide data related to concept building and testing?
    1.1 *Concepts*
        (1) Slogans, colors, and procedural rules serve functions related to identification and social organization. (*GR* Concept)
        (2) Sex involves a number of related social factors and is not simply a physical activity. (GR Concept)
        (3) "Forced" attempts to enhance human relations may prove dysfunctional unless other factors are taken into account. (*GR* Concept)
        (4) _____
        (5) _____
        (6) _____

2. Does it provide a potential bridge for reassessing student held conceptual frameworks?
    2.1 *Predictions:* Student held conceptual frameworks?
        (1) Slogans, group colors, and "club" rules are childish and are signs of immaturity.
        (2) High school students are pretty much the same regardless of experience, socio-economic background, etc.
        (3) Overcoming prejudice is a simple matter of getting people together so that they get to know and to like each other.
        (4) _____
        (5) _____

3. Does it provide a potential bridge for helping a student work with inquiry skills?
    3.1 Question Asking:
        (1) If one is not prejudiced, does it mean one doesn't react to and with individuals but rather to "positive" group stereotypes whether they be white or black, Jew or Gentile, or. . . .?
        (2) How *does* one break down preconceived views? Are all preconceived views at the awareness level?
        (3) _____
        (4) _____
        (5) _____

3.2 *Ambiguous Terms:*
   (1) Status Symbol
   (2) _____
   (3) _____

3.3 *Reasoning:*
   (1) The same "fact" (i.e., making a "pass") may be interpreted in different ways.
   (2) Given just the facts (not interpretations) involved in the effort to improve human relationships, what alternative generalizations might one make?
   (3) _____
   (4) _____
   (5) _____

4. Does it allow subdividing and a variety of uses?
   (1) Potential use in making a transfer from what is taught in social studies and what the students encounter in direct experience.

   (2) Potential use as a base in having students submit their own case studies involving themselves and social realities.

   (3) Potential use in studying change processes involving attitudes and behavior.

   (4) Potential use in allowing covert feelings and animosities to "surface" and to be addressed in a class situation.

   (5) Potential use in studying social class behavior of students regardless of the socio-economic context of the particular school situation.

   (6) _____
   (7) _____
   (8) _____

5. Can it be reworked in a way allowing for student differences?
   (1) Teacher may read the case study and have students role play.

   (2) Given the basic ingredients in the case study, students may individually plan their own "change

strategy"—what they would do and not do in the situation.

(3) There is a possibility for a group of students to study the school in terms of school colors, songs, G.O. membership costs, dress codes, etc.

(4) _____

(5) _____

(6) _____

6. Can it be used as a springboard for other possible student experiences?

(1) (See areas of numbers four and five)

(2) The issues raised in the case study may be used as a base for assessing local, state, and federal legislation.

(3) _____

(4) _____

(5) _____

Case studies may be drawn from actual situations encountered by the students in the school setting or in the community. Depending upon the timing and the degree of sensitivity, such cases may open opportunities for reflective consideration of the issues involved. This allows students to write their own case studies and to develop a criteria for writing and assessment. Such case studies may be submitted anonymously, thus allowing things to get on the table without fear of group pressure. A note of warning: such case studies are not used for personal catharsis as much as for applying inquiry to situations involving emotional and cognitive factors. Occasionally, a teacher may come across other articles that may be put into a case study framework. For example, Thomas J. Cottle's "The Wellesley Incident, A Case of Obscenity," *Saturday Review*, March 15, 1969. Cottle reported a school situation which reflected attitudes and behaviors of school personnel, students, parents, media, and others within an actual context involving a number of sensitive issues at work in varying degrees in a number of school situations. In one school, Cottle's article was made into a case study and the following suggestions were made for student use:

Teaching/Learning Guide: The Wellesley Incident (*SR*, March 15, 1969)

1. Students may be asked to establish an "Analysis Model" designed to bring structure to how one approaches a conflict situation. The model assists in: a) relating variables; b) identifying areas in which information is incomplete; and c) bringing to cognition the web of interacting issues involved. The student model might then be "tested" through application.

2. Given the complete case study, the students may be asked to read the study and to:
   2.1 List in chronological order the *facts* as they appear.
   2.2 That the author may have perceived certain things may be also a "fact" to consider. But, this does not mean that *what* he perceived is a fact. (It may be a fact that I believe something but my belief does not make what I believe necessarily a fact.) Students may be asked to give examples of this in other situations.

3. Students might be asked to identify the number of *issues* involved in the incident and be asked to cluster the issues into major categories.

4. Students may be asked to identify the "flow" of the school committee meeting in terms of: a) the sequence of who spoke; b) the nature of the comments made; and c) identification of any perceived "pattern" emerging from the flow.

5. Students might be asked to identify and give examples of the role that media played in this particular conflict situation. (local newspaper, larger urban newspaper, television...)

6. Students might be asked to identify:
   6.1 The roles played by the students.
   6.2 The roles played by the teachers.
   6.3 The roles played by the administration.
   6.4 The roles played by the school committee.
   6.5 The roles played by the community.
   6.6 The roles played by the court.

7. Students might be asked to put themselves in the other fellow's shoes and to defend such a position. For example: the chairman of the history department; the dissenting teacher who spoke at the meeting; the principal; the boy who spoke at the end of the meeting; the policeman; the lawyer; the superintendent; the president of the teachers' association; the "liberal" member of the school committee; the judge; the producer of the drama; the lady chairman of the school committee, the black lady who spoke — and the one who responded to her — etc.

8. Students may be asked to write an essay on the role emotion plays in conflict situations and compare this to behavior in classroom situations.

9. Students might be asked to go into depth regarding the role of the court and how its action and inaction proved a contributing factor.

10. The students might be asked to respond to the following ideas which appear in the case study:
    10.1 "There is a totally helpless feeling that comes over people when they become implicated in events like this."
    10.2 "This time, as the man said, they had gone too far. But who exactly were they?"
    10.3 "Equally frightening for many students during those weeks the performance of their parents. . . Many were to see their parents for the first time, and while some would be more proud than ever before, others would be wounded by their first experience with hypocrisy."
    10.4 "Some students groaned, but only a few seemed aware of the purpose of this political enterprise."
    10.5 "The boy had sought alliance with a fiery black student. He wanted in. He wanted to join the struggle. The black boy told him something to the effect that you need us, but we don't need you."

11. Students might be asked to identify *short run* consequences of the situation; i.e., families pressured to leave, breaks in friendship, faculty resignations, tightening up of school codes, custodians being deputized, etc. Students might then be asked to project *long run* consequences with an effort *to relate* the short and long run.

12. *Problem:* Students might be asked to suppose their involvement in the "incident" and to suppose an honest desire to address the problems. How would they plan and implement ways of effecting conflict resolution or modification?
    12.1 A consideration of the concept of "democracy" may be at work here. Is democracy a process of encountering different views? If so, what are the processes and are there formal procedures guaranteeing the processes? Can a majority and a minority both be guilty (at times) of tyranny? How does one check this? If a "democracy" is not this, what is it. . . how does it function?

The teacher who worked out ways to use the case study, used the criteria we have been using with other materials—not in a formal checklist way but in a manner relating concepts, attitudes, inquiry skills, activities, etc., to students. Parenthetically, it should be noted that the teacher making use of the above case study anticipated, correctly, that a similar type of conflict was brewing in her own situation. In fact, the use of the case study helped to identify issues and alternatives before the crisis descended. It came, but not without some advance preparation on the part of students and staff.

USE OF ACADEMIC FINDINGS

Prospective social studies teachers take academic course work in the various social science disciplines along with professional education courses. For a number of reasons, the pathways between the academia of the arts and sciences and the professional training appear exceedingly difficult to traverse. In many situations, there are institutionalized blocks which make obvious and necessary relationship all but impossible for the perceptive student to make. The untenable situation which separates content from teaching processes appears to place responsibility for creating such relationships solely upon the student and upon the few professionals willing to risk institutional and peer pressure.

Once one feels fairly comfortable with criteria used to assess materials as potential teaching vehicles, it is possible to use the academic course work not only for the personal background so necessary for teaching but also to use academic materials to build a vehicle bank. The two uses are complementary!

For example, suppose that one is taking a course in sociology in which he is asked to go to the *American Journal of Sociology* in order to get research findings on comparative perceptions of occupations. It is possible that academic journals may provide research findings which may prove to be of help to social studies teachers as teaching vehicles. Suppose one comes across the article by Ramsey and Smith on Japanese and American Perceptions of Occupations (*AJS*, March, 1960). And suppose, for his course work, he abstracts the research findings in the following manner.

"Japanese and American Perceptions of Occupations"
American Journal of Sociology, March, 1960. (Ramsey and Smith)

General Idea

Study compared Japanese and American students' perceptions of occupations. There seems to be a similarity regarding how occupations are viewed. The differences reflect cultural differences.

Key Ideas

(1) Both groups ranked white-collar jobs with higher prestige than blue-collar or agricultural work.
(2) Occupations requiring educational attainment were ranked higher by both groups.
(3) There were striking differences in specifics (which should be noted) but the *similarity* between the two samples is also striking.

Approach

High school seniors from rural and urban centers were selected. Students came from New York and Tokyo and centralized schools. Slightly more girls than boys were included in the samples. Questionnaires were distributed in schools.

Note

The questionnaire was first constructed in English and then translated into Japanese. . . several questions were meaningful in one culture but not in the other: some questions were impossible to translate.

Results: Occupational Ranking

JAPANESE	AMERICAN
1. College professor	1. Doctor
2. Doctor	2. Lawyer
3. Lawyer	3. Priest or minister
4. Corporation executive	4. College professor
5. Author	5. Corporation executive
6. Union Leader	6. Author
7. Primary school teacher	7. Movie performer
8. Policeman	8. Union leader
9. Small factory owner	9. Nurse
10. Private secretary	10. Primary school teacher
13. Priest or minister	13. Soldier
16. Movie performer	16. Farm owner
19. Soldier	19. Beautician
23. Farm laborer	23. Farm laborer

A. American students ranked the soldier 13th, Japanese students 19th: suggests influence of "postwar" pacifism in Japan. Urban sample and girl sample ranked the soldier higher than did the rural and the male samples.

B. The ranking of the clergy suggests "more importance. . . in the value system of American seniors." Reflection of a secular trend in Japan: "The Buddhist clergy is thought of as closer to a character in a medieval Italian farce than to Barry Fitzgerald or Bing Crosby."

Note: The roles in occupations differ within a culture: some are considered essential, others important but not essential, and some are judged to be harmful.

Examples

a. The Americans found the soldier essential and very important.
   The Japanese found the soldier of little importance.
b. The American sample found the clergy to be essential and important.
   The Japanese sample found the clergy to be of little importance.
c. The American sample found the political boss of little importance.
   The Japanese sample felt it better if the political boss did not exist.
d. The Japanese sample ranked the union leader and corporation executive as equal in importance; the American sample ranked the executive much higher.

APPLICATION OF CRITERIA

1. Does it provide data related to concept building and testing?

  1.1 *Concepts:*

    (1) Different views of occupations reflect cultural differences. (GR)

    (2) Comparative research efforts must take into account language differences. (GR)

    (3) American students and Japanese students ranked the soldier differently. (UN)

    (4) _____

    (5) _____

    (6) _____

    (7) _____

2. Does it provide a potential bridge for reassessing student held conceptual frameworks?

  2.1 *Predictions:* Student held conceptual frameworks.

    (1) Occupations assuring greatest financial return will be rated the highest in both cultures.

    (2) Both cultures will hold religious occupations in substantial respect. The Japanese perhaps even more so than the Americans.

(3) _____

(4) _____

(5) _____

3. Does it provide potential aid in helping to develop student inquiry skills?

    (1) What specific questions would be impossible to translate?

    (2) The sample of school students assumes what about geographic location and the nature of the school population?

    (3) Given the ranking listings, what conclusions can be reached? (What information would be needed to test the conclusions?)

    (4) _____

    (5) _____

    (6) _____

4. Does it provide for subdividing and a variety of possible uses?

    (1) Provides an opportunity to compare and contrast the two cultures in terms of similarities and differences; i.e., industrialized countries, economic systems, larger "value" frameworks, etc.

    (2) The study was reported in 1960. There may be an opportunity to relate the findings to what followed after the Japanese defeat in World War II.

    (3) _____

    (4) _____

    (5) _____

    (6) _____

5. Can it be reworked in a way allowing for student differences?

    (1) Some students might attempt to construct a research design on perceptions of occupations for their own school — elementary, junior high school, senior high school.

    (2) Students could be given just the listing of occupational rankings and be asked to generalize about the people so ranked. Then: plan and implement a strategy for checking out the generalizations.

    (3) Students interested in various occupations might want to check what differences there might be between what an American lawyer does and what his

counterpart in Japan does. . . or other occupations listed.

(4) _____

(5) _____

(6) _____

6. Can it be used as a springboard for other possible student experiences?

    (1) The study might be used to study different concepts of work: the traditional work ethic as opposed to emerging concepts of work. (How might this change the way students look at occupational status?)

    (2) _____

    (3) _____

    (4) _____

The Ramsey and Smith study is just one example of the types of content which one might encounter when taking academic courses. The examples are *not* restricted to the strictly social science area. Courses in American history and world history provide other materials with potential teaching use.

Suppose that you are taking a course in colonial American history. And, suppose that, as part of a reading assignment, you come across an article by Richard Merritt appearing in the *American Quarterly,* a publication by the American Studies Association. The article has a little different twist: it approaches American nationalism through a *quantitative* approach. Say that you abstract the article for your academic class and it appears as follows:

"The Emergence of American Nationalism: A Quantitative Approach," *American Quarterly,* Summer, 1965.
(Richard L. Merritt)

The designation of a group by a specific name that serves as a symbol under which members of the group can unite, as well as serving as a means of differentiating one group from another, "is indicative that a group has come of age." When did American colonists stop referring to themselves as "His Majesty's subjects" or British colonists and start calling themselves Americans?

Approach of paper: Content analysis through symbol analysis. Words a person uses in communicating are indicative of his attitude. Symbol analysis useful when a researcher has questions such as: how often? how much? how many?

Hypothesis: "The colonists' sense of group identification

shifted from the British political community to a strictly American political community gradually but steadily from 1735 to 1775.''

Method: Examination of self-referent symbols in colonial newspapers.

Implications of symbol analysis method: Trend information that results from this type of analysis can:
1. Permit us to fit single pieces of evidence into continuing patterns, rather than to focus too narrowly on single bits of evidence.
2. Cause us to focus our attention upon years or months of particular importance in the development of American community awareness. ''The recently developed tools of the social sciences can contribute as much to the study of history as the historian can — by identifying the important and interesting problems in, say, colonial history, as well as the most relevant variables — to contemporary theory in the social sciences.''

Examined were four randomly selected issues per year of newspapers from Boston, New York, Philadelphia, Williamsburg, and Charleston, S.C. Tabulated were direct references to place-name symbols (Boston, England, Americans, the colonies) from 1735 to 1775. Also tabulated were indirect symbol references (they, that place, etc.) Symbols were differentiated into five groups:
1. British identity — British North America, British colonists, etc.
2. Crown references — His Majesty's colonies, etc.
3. Implicit British identity — the colonies, or the provinces.
4. Implicit American identity — the continent or country, American colonies.
5. Explicit American identity — Americans, North Americans, etc.
   (First three above grouped together in larger category, and last two grouped together.)

General findings: Self-referent symbols increased dramatically between 1735 and 1775. ''In sum, a concept that was. . . marginal in the late 1730's was quite salient by the early 1770's.'' In the 1730's the average issue contained .66 such symbols; in the 1770's, the average issue contained 22 such symbols — an increase of over 3200 per cent.

Propensity to use American self-referent symbols also rose: from roughly 43 per cent of the collective self-referent symbols in 1735–39, to 63 per cent in 1771–75.

Use of collective self-referent symbols fluctuated, with low points in 1736, 1745, 1761, and 1772; high points in 1740, 1756, 1769, and 1775.

Only after 1764 did the distinction between ''British colonists'' and "Americans" become a real one in the colonial press. Before 1764, colonists were most commonly called "His Majesty's subjects," etc.; after 1756 the phrase "Royal Americans" was also commonly used. After 1764, six in ten of the collective self-referents identified the colonists as American rather than British.

The described approach challenges thinking of other historians—J. T. Adams, Michael Kraus, Oscar Handlin, Howard H. Peckham—who have suggested that "Americanization" was a slow and imperceptible process taking place during the whole of the colonial experience. Others have argued that the American sense of community came during the critical decade that began with the passage of the Stamp Act and ended with the creation of the First Continental Congress.

Merritt concludes: ". . . the changing processes of symbolic identification. . . seem to have been neither revolutionary nor evolutionary. Rather, like other learning situations, they were both gradual and fitfull. . . ."

Note: Article concludes with a chart describing the changes in the period of time mentioned by the author.

Now, apply the criteria to determine whether or not the material may prove to be a potential vehicle. A quick reading of the abstract suggests that it does fit a number of categories. For example:

1. It provides data related to concept building and testing.
   Example: A name may be a symbol indicating that a group is uniting under a common identification.
   What other GR and UN concepts appear in the article?
   (1) _____
   (2) _____
   (3) _____
   (4) _____

2. It does provide a bridge for students to assess their own conceptual frameworks.
   Example: The "revolution" was a sudden and abrupt change.
   What other possible student-held concepts might a teacher find?
   (1) _____
   (2) _____

3. It does provide potential assistance in developing student inquiry skills.
   Example: Analysis of author's research design.

What other possible assistance might the article give in developing inquiry skills?

(1) _____
(2) _____
(3) _____
(4) _____
(5) _____

4. It does provide a base for subdividing and a variety of uses.

   Example: Testing of the given hypothesis by locating quotations from colonial leaders during the time period under study.

   Other possible uses?

   (1) _____
   (2) _____
   (3) _____

5. It does allow ways to take into account student differences.

   Example: Students may work with charting or graphing the reported findings.

   Other possible ways?

   (1) _____
   (2) _____
   (3) _____

6. It can be used as a springboard for other possible student activities.

   Example: Current affairs. Students may assess the terminology used in regards to Red China after World War II and again just prior to Red China's admittance to the United Nations. Magazines and newspapers may be used to determine findings. (Cartoons?)

   Other possible activities:

   (1) _____
   (2) _____
   (3) _____

The following material comes from an article appearing in the February, 1966 issue of the *Bulletin of the Atomic Scientists*. The author, Roger Revelle, asks "Can Man Domesticate Himself?" The article has a substantial number of GR and UN concepts, has specific historical dimensions, and works with efforts to predict. Using the given criteria assessment base, or using a criteria base of your own, determine the potential the article has for teaching.

"Can Man Domesticate Himself?"
Bulletin of the Atomic Scientists, February, 1966. (Roger Revelle)

Population

It took hundreds of thousands of years to produce a population of one billion in 1850;
75 years to reach a world population of two billion (1925);
35 years to reach a world population of three billion (1960);
20 years to reach a world population of four billion (1980);
10 years to reach a world population of five billion (1990);
By the year 2000 the present world population will be doubled.

Population advanced through:
1. Better food production (and distribution)
2. Better sanitation
3. Better knowledge of health and health problems.

Population curtailed through:
1. War
2. Food supplies not being adequate
3. Overcrowding (biological and psychological)
4. Deliberate planning

City population will multiply 40 times in next 100 years. Example: in next 50 years Calcutta (at present growth) would reach to 60 million people.
Middle of the next century $1/5$ of land surface of the earth will be cities thus raising questions of waste, wants, and the need for new systems, new technologies.

India, Pakistan, Egypt—increase in population rate of $2\frac{1}{2}$ to 3%
Brazil and South American Countries— annual increase of more than 3%
Costa Rica and the Philippines—annual increase of more than 4%
A 3% growth means double the population within 23 years.
A 4% growth means double the population in 17 years.

"Men have to run faster in order to stand still." Total national incomes rising but the increase in production must be divided among a larger number of people.

American continents have the same number of people above the Rio Grande as below. By the year 2000 there will be twice as many people in Latin America as in Canada and the U.S.

Population rates are higher in the underdeveloped nations.

Average food production per capita for Latin America is now *less* than it was before World War II. If not for imports, diets of people in India and Pakistan more deficient than in 1935.

Egypt mostly lifeless desert: Nile is suitable for agriculture.

6 million acres—size of Mass.—supports a rural population of 30 million: highest density in the world—3000 people per square mile.

India finds the number of children under 15 years is 45% of the total population. Compare to the slower growing populations which are less than 25%.

Problems within the United States:
1. 1½% increase each year: problems of pollution, water, recreation, transportation and crime.
2. High School students number 10 million in 1960; 15 million in 1970 College students number 4 million in 1960 and 12 million in 1980.

Malthus saw population restricted through "misery and vice" but sociology and biology add a new dimension: research—when too many animals are forced to live in small geographic area, behavior changes, and they stop reproducing.

Historical dimensions:
1. Prior to fall of Roman Empire (476) there was a decline despite efforts (reward and punishment) to *increase.*
2. Tuscany (1200—1400) population decreased 75%. Factor: decline in farm products prices and increase in interest rates on farm mortgages.
3. 19th century (Europe and the United States) increase in birth rate—vaccination?
4. Several countries stable: Japan, Hungary, Sweden, Italy.

USE OF NEWSPAPERS

Not all potential teaching vehicles appear in academic settings. The daily newspaper provides a constant source of material. Teachers have used short articles to motivate, to provide data, and to involve students in inquiry. For example, one teacher found a short article on how taxes were, at one time, assessed according to window space in a house. This opened the way to study how architecture reflected economic and social values at different historical periods, opened a way to study property tax base, and opened a way to study underlying property taxes and income taxes—an issue with which school districts are now vitally concerned.

Another teacher made substantial use of cartoons appearing in the daily paper. For example, there was one depicting a king addressing the multitude about the need in the kingdom for peace and harmony. He ended his appeal by asking his people to "remember the Golden Rule. We must all live by the Golden Rule." Under the balcony, one of the peasants asks another peasant what

the Golden Rule is. A tradesman responds in the last frame: Who-
ever has the Gold makes the Rules. The teacher put the two ideas
before the class: The Golden Rule and the Gold and Rule. This
opened the way to an inquiry into values and the ways economic,
political, and social activities relate and use basic value systems.

Appearing in the New York *Times*, November 3, 1968, was an
article headlined: "City Study Shows Record Number of Homicides
in '67 Almost Matched in '31." From the article, a teacher listed
the data (see chart on page 202).

Other information appearing in the article included the comment that criminologists consider homicide rates as being the
most reliable of all crime statistics. Most of the homicides committed are known to the police. Suicides and auto deaths are excluded from the figures. Additional data reported:

1. Persons 25 years of age or older are responsible for about
   60% of New York City homicides.
2. Annual homicide rates of New York City were lowest during
   World War II and the Korean War.
3. Estimates by the Center for Social Research found Puerto
   Ricans and nonwhites making up 29.3% of the city's population in 1966. This was a 7.2% increase over the 1960
   figures.
4. Less than 2% of all homicides were comitted by a white
   person against a Negro or by a Negro against a white person.
5. During the '30's when the homicide rate was fairly high,
   the percentage of Negroes and Puerto Ricans living in the
   city was lower than present figures.

Applying the criteria in an effort to assess the article's potential
as a teaching vehicle, we find that the primary input is in numerical
data. The concepts are relatively more implicit than explicit and
suggests a little different approach in making the assessment.

APPLICATION OF CRITERIA

1. Does it provide data related to concept building and testing?
   Example: *Hypothesis:* In times of war, the homicide rate
            lowers. (?)
   Other possible hypotheses to be tested:
   (1) _____
   (2) _____
   (3) _____

Murders in New York City per 100,000

Year	Murders
1928	5.1
1929	5.2
1930	6.1
1931	7.0
1932	6.7
1933	6.1
1934	5.0
1935	5.1
1936	5.0
1937	4.5
1938	3.7
1939	3.9
1940	3.7
1941	3.6
1942	3.6
1943	2.7
1944	3.0
1945	3.8
1946	4.5
1947	4.3
1948	4.0
1949	3.8
1950	3.7
1951	3.1
1952	3.9
1953	4.4
1954	4.4
1955	3.9
1956	4.0
1957	4.0
1958	4.5
1959	5.0
1960	5.0
1961	6.2
1962	6.5
1963	7.1
1964	8.1
1965	8.0
1966	8.1
1967	9.0

(4) _____
(5) _____

2. Does it provide a bridge for students to assess their own conceptual frameworks?

    Example: Students probably hold that homicides are committed primarily by the young.

    Other predictions of student-held concepts:

    (1) _____
    (2) _____
    (3) _____
    (4) _____

3. Does it provide an opportunity to work on inquiry skills?

    Example: Given just the data on the list, students can be asked to establish (inductively) five hypotheses to be tested.

    Other possibilities for the use of inquiry skills:

    (1) _____
    (2) _____
    (3) _____
    (4) _____

4. Does the article provide a base for a variety of uses?

    Example: The data may be put in chart form.

    Other possible uses:

    (1) _____
    (2) _____
    (3) _____

5. Does the article allow ways to take into account student differences?

    Example: Students liking historical research can identify different time periods and work with comparing and contrasting such periods in terms of the homicide rates.

    Other possible uses:

    (1) _____
    (2) _____

6. Can the article be used as a springboard for other activities?

    Example: A study of national statistics or other urban statistics for the same period of time.

    Other possible student activities:

    (1) _____
    (2) _____

USE OF SLANTED MATERIAL

Most of us are constantly being bombarded with slanted material — material that may appeal more to the glands than to thinking processes, material that cloaks message in simplistic rhetoric and shabby reasoning. This material comes from all sides and positions: advertising appeals, political exhortations, ideological salvagers. Such material does have potential as teaching vehicles — especially in developing inquiry skills. There is a tendency to take for granted that teaching mass numbers to read is inherently good and that mass communication systems are of benefit in informing the many publics in a mass society. It depends. With increased access to information, there appears to be an imperative to have people become more sophisticated about how information is manipulated both through selection and form of presentation.

The following handout from the John Birch Soceity may provide a potential social studies vehicle.

MAY WE ASK YOU SOME QUESTIONS?

(1) Do you really know the score, and if not are you willing to do the conscientious reading to find out?

(2) If you know the score, what are you waiting for?

(3) In the coming showdown with the Communists, just where and what is the group you had rather have defending your country, instead of The John Birch Society?

(4) It is clear that if enough good Americans came into The John Birch Society soon enough, our concerted effort could stop the Communists. Do you know of any other way, or chance, of stopping them?

(5) Which do you value more, your present "non-controversial" status of drawing room conventionality, or the future freedom of your family?

(6) Do you want to save your country, your home, and your life itself, or to go on blindly piling up more money for the Communists to confiscate?

(7) Do you want to stand on your two feet and fight for what you believe in, or maintain your comfortable aloofness while others do all of the fighting for you?

(8) When your children are living under the same cruel tyranny that has already befallen Cuba, China, Czechoslovakia, and the Congo, how are they going to appraise what you did to prevent it?

(9) Are you willing to face facts now or, preserving your vested and protective interest in past error, remain among the willfully blind, who simply will not see?

(10) "Is life so dear, or peace so sweet, as to be purchased at the price of chains and slavery? Forbid it, Almighty God! I know not what course others may take, but as for me, give me liberty or give me death." Will you join us in that same resolve?

HAVE YOU HAD ENOUGH?

Enough of fighting Communism by helping to subjugate anti-Communists, as in Katanga?

Enough of pouring American foreign-aid money into the hands of out-and-out Communists?

Enough of having the Supreme Court destroy the safeguards of our Constitutional Republic?

Enough of the surrender of American sovereignty and independence to the Communist-controlled United Nations?

Enough of the plans now *officially* advocated by our State Department to abolish our armed forces altogether, and turn over the protection and security of the United States to the international "peace force" of the United Nations? (See State Department Document No. 7277)

Enough of a whole foreign policy run by such men as Adlai Stevenson and Dean Rusk?

Enough of Senator Fulbright's program to "muzzle" our patriotic officers and demoralize our whole armed services?

Enough of negotiations with the Kremlin butchers over how much more we are going to retreat?

Enough of inflation at home, humiliation abroad, and defeatism everywhere with regard to the future? Then you may want to join us and help to do something about it.

APPLICATION OF CRITERIA

A quick review of the written material suggests that it can be used in a number of the categories within the criteria for vehicle use. For example:

1. It does provide an avenue related to concept building and testing.

Example: There is only *one* way of stopping communism. Other implicit concepts in the material:

(1) _____

(2) _____

(3) _____

(4) _____

2. It does provide a bridge for students to assess already held concepts.

Example: People who "know the score" should take some action.

Other possible concepts held by students:

(1) _____

(2) _____

(3) _____

(4) _____

3. It does provide assistance in student development of inquiry skills.

Example: Students may be asked to determine the "emotional" components of the handout.

Other uses related to the use of inquiry skills:

(1) _____

(2) _____

(3) _____

(4) _____

(5) _____

4. It does provide a base for subdividing and for a variety of uses.

Example: A study of Supreme Court decisions in attempting to "test" how the Supreme Court could be accused of "destroying safeguards. . ."

Other examples of alternate uses:

(1) _____

(2) _____

(3) _____

5. It does allow for student differences.

Example: Students who respond to visual forms of data may be asked to compare and contrast techniques used in the handout with those used in selected advertisements.

Other possible uses:

(1) _____

(2) _____

(3) _____

6. It can be used as a springboard for other possible student activities.

Example: Students may analyze techniques of communication used by political parties, local school board elections, appeals for passage of a school levy, or. . . .?

Other possible activities:

(1) _____

(2) _____

(3) _____

Prospective teachers should be fully aware that when one attempts to use reason and rationality, it is usually looked upon as being subversive to those who Know they Know the score. Seldom do teachers accused of subversion of this sort get an opportunity to explain the criteria nor the use of vehicles to foster inquiry. In a number of communities serviced by the public schools, there are certain areas held to be immune from inquiry. An effective social studies teacher has choices to make—whether or not to take short range losses for long range gains, whether or not to stand on a particular issue, etc. Part of vehicle selection falls into the area of political sophistication. Such sophistication underscores that there are no easy decisions.

USE OF SONGS

With records and tapes and more sophisticated recording instruments, it is not uncommon to hear people speak of oral history—of ways of recording history that predated written records. This same growing sophistication suggests that music, and especially songs, may be used as potential vehicles for teaching. Several years ago the authors asked high school students to select four songs they would like to discuss in class. The four selected: Flip Wilson in his *Cowboys and Colored Folk, Harper Valley P.T.A.,* Bobby Dylan's *With God on Our Side,* and Simon and Garfunkel's *Seven O'Clock News.* It is interesting to note that the criteria for assessing potential vehicles held up.

The use of contemporary songs led to the use of classical hymns as teaching vehicles. For example, *Work for the Night Is Coming* opens opportunities to inquire into various aspects of the industrial revolution. Contemporary songs not only motivate students (if only in the sense that the teacher knows what's going on) but also can be used as effective teaching vehicles. At the time this is written, *The War, For What It's Worth, Great Mandella, My Country 'tis of the People,* and *Let's Get Together* offer possibilities.

The following will sound familiar. To be sure, it is contemporary and apparently it was also contemporary some three hundred years ago. From Old Saint Paul's Church in Baltimore and dated 1692, we find:

DESIDERATA

GO PLACIDLY AMID THE NOISE & HASTE, & REMEMBER WHAT PEACE THERE MAY BE IN SILENCE. AS FAR AS POSSIBLE WITHOUT surrender be on good terms with all persons. Speak your truth quietly & clearly; and listen to others, even the dull & ignorant; they too have their story. 🖎 Avoid loud & aggressive persons, they are vexations to the spirit. If you compare yourself with others, you may become vain & bitter; for always there will be greater & lesser persons than yourself. Enjoy your achievements as well as your plans. 🖎 Keep interested in your own career, however humble; it is a real possession in the changing fortunes of time. Exercise caution in your business affairs; for the world is full of trickery. But let this not blind you to what virtue there is; many persons strive for high ideals; and everywhere life is full of heroism. 🖎 Be yourself. Especially, do not feign affection. Neither be cynical about love; for in the face of all aridity & disenchantment it is perennial as the grass. 🖎 Take kindly the counsel of the years, gracefully surrendering the things of youth. Nurture strength of spirit to shield you in sudden misfortune. But do not distress yourself with imaginings. Many fears are born of fatigue & loneliness. Beyond a wholesome discipline, be gentle with yourself. 🖎 You are a child of the universe, no less than the trees & the stars; you have a right to be here. And whether or not it is clear to you, no doubt the universe is unfolding as it should. 🖎 Therefore be at peace with God, whatever you conceive Him to be, and whatever your labors & aspirations, in the noisy confusion of life keep peace with your soul. 🖎 With all its sham, drudgery & broken dreams, it is still a beautiful world. 🖎 🖎

(Our manuscript editor did his own *inquiry* and came up with the following piece. Seems like we were "taken".)

The author of the blank-verse *Desiderata* was Max Ehrmann, American dramatist and poet (1872–1945). He wrote the poem in 1927.

According to officials of St. Paul's Parish, home of the first church established in what is now Baltimore, in the 1950's the church rector was an ex-newspaperman who enjoyed placing small mimeographed booklets containing little sermons and other religion-oriented matter in the pews. At the bottom of each booklet appeared the line, "Old St. Paul's Church, Baltimore, Md. [Founded in ?],* 1692," the year the church was established.

Desiderata was used in one of these pamphlets and became widely reproduced. In copying the poem, somewhere, at some time, the line was changed to read, "Found in 1692."

The mistake has been reprinted, broadcast, and widely reported on television, and has caused St. Paul's Church to be deluged with requests for copies it doesn't have, and with inquiries about the origin and author.

Given "Desiderata", how might one apply the criteria?

1. Are there concepts involved in the presentation?
   1.1 What concepts are both GR *and* empirically based?
   1.2 What concepts are value concepts?
2. Do the concepts involved relate to the already held concepts of students?
3. Does the song allow any use of inquiry skills?
4. What different kinds of uses might the material be put to in working with social studies?
5. Can it be used in terms of allowing for individual student differences?
6. What possible student activities might emerge from the use of the material?

USE OF FICTION AND NON-FICTION

As the use of songs implies, not all data used in instruction need come from sources specifically designated as "social studies" material. Fiction, for example, can prove of substantial help in introducing an area of study, in synthesizing and facilitating a transfer of material studies, and even in motivating students to come to grips with social science concepts. Mario Puzo's *The Godfather* puts to work a number of political science and socio-

---

*The bracketed words are those of our manuscript editor, Charles Graham, whose research brought to our attention the true facts of the authorship of *Desiderata*.

logical concepts. Marquand's *Point of No Return* and such classics as *Othello* and *All Quiet on the Western Front* allow that the social science concepts are not isolated, fragmentary, distant, sterile findings divorced from the "real" of human life and human living. Fiction also provides a bridge between the so-called "humanities" and the "social sciences"—if you will, the difference between individualizing and generalizing the human condition.

A good example of a social studies teacher's use of fiction is the trial section of Ayn Rand's *The Fountainhead*. The students usually respond favorably to Rand's style and approach—and they usually find the trial part of the book as the epitome of the American Dream and the spirit of individualism. The main character, Howard Roark, stands before his peers "free" from being concerned about their approval or disapproval of his behavior. He tells of how discoveries in the past were made—usually by an individual "armed with nothing but his own vision", a vision unborrowed from others. As a creator, a human being owes nothing to others. It is the individual who thinks, feels, and judges. It is the individual who uses *his* own mind in the act of creating. Egotism is pitted against altruism and "Every major horror. . . was committed in the name of an altruistic motive." Roark stands as a rugged individual, apart and distinct from others, owed nothing and owing nothing to other human beings.

As a potential social studies vehicle, this portion of *The Fountainhead* poses, in a fictional context, social science concepts that can be "tested" with empirical data: concepts of the individual as a social self, influenced and influencing his surroundings, other people, and having consequences other than in terms of the distinct and separate self; concepts dealing with learning, social change, and responsibility. The testing of the concepts appearing in the books calls for the gathering and use of data, for inquiry. The issues involving values and the source of values suggest a look at the American Dream. The powerful and compelling style comes to light and is seen as an integral aspect of the message. Its use transcends itself and can be employed to raise issues about "liberalism" and "conservatism", the role of government, social legislation, and even school.

Non-fiction plays a similar function. For example, in *McCall's*, November, 1968, Robert Kennedy's "Thirteen Days: The Story of How The World Almost Ended" explained in detail the decision-making processes involved in the 1962 Cuban missile crisis. It discussed who was involved, the human factors influencing attempts at rational decision-making, the forces internal and external to the group involved, and even the influence Barbara Tuchman's book *The Guns of August* had on the President.

In Kennedy's article, the criteria were again satisfied. It provided a context for the dynamics of political processes in a manner students could grasp and with concepts that could be transferred to other situations.

APPLICATION OF THE CRITERIA TO THE USE OF TEXTBOOKS

As we have seen, most raw materials for social studies teaching were not originally intended to be used in teaching-learning transactions. In their given form, most materials have a conceptual organization of their own and are not formulated with teaching in mind. In order to become vehicles or means to teaching-learning ends, they must be worked over and assembled into viable and functional form.

We have tried to present a number of different types of potential vehicles and have attempted to apply criteria to the selection and use of materials. It is obvious that we did not include *every* kind of material. For example, movies and simulation games, slides, and even lectures are available and may prove to be effective.

But there is one kind of material that, theoretically at least, *is* designed and produced to be a teaching-learning vehicle: that is the textbook. Most teachers initially inherit the textbooks to be used by their students. In other words, most beginning teachers do not have a say in the selection of an extremely basic vehicle. This is not to say, however, that teachers cannot have a say in determining the *use* of the basic text.

It should be obvious by now that it takes a certain excitement, a desire to learn, some open-ended curiosity, and some discipline to apply the criteria to vehicle selection and use. In a sense, one must enjoy the inquiry used in the process of planning inquiry experiences for others. If the enjoyment and the learning excitement is not there, one wonders if social studies or even teaching is, in fact, a "chosen" field.

At this point we would like to suggest that you take a secondary level social studies text book, select one chapter of the text, and apply the criteria to analyzing its limitations and potential as a vehicle. Assume that the text is *not* designed to be a vehicle but rather, is simply another form of raw material upon which you go to work. Viewed this way, textbooks may have a value not originally intended.

6

BELIEVE ME. . .

Students who attempt to operationalize this book in their classrooms return and tell us that it is difficult—sometimes too difficult. Not only do they need more time to prepare but they also have to put up with flak from fellow teachers who are still caught in the straitjacket of tradition. Walking into the teachers' lounge becomes a more difficult task in survival than walking into the classroom. We include the following letter from a former colleague who eloquently expresses the difficulty he encountered in his attempt to teach his students how to inquire.

NO ONE WILL BELIEVE ME

Maybe no one wants to believe me. I know it all seems unbelievable, but I swear it's true. Let me write it like it happened.

Some weeks ago a friend of mine was asked to instruct an evening class in philosophy at the local college. At the time I was teaching a world history course to "average" high school sophomores. Now I always thought philosophy and history pretty inseparable. I guess that's why I went along with my friend on those evenings and sat in on his classes.

This friend of mine is a pretty dynamic teacher. I mean it. I sat there each Monday night for three hours, every moment enchanted. It all seemed so clear when he said it. And what interested me most was the unusual and vital way (philosophy courses I had had always seemed unusual but never vital) he approached the subject. Philosophy was to be used. Its only value was in the difference it made in our lives, now. That's exactly what I thought about history.

He placed practically everything that was meaningful in the history of philosophy into a framework of two conflicting world views. He called them the traditional and the emerging. I remember him using Huxley's quote from *The Biologist Looks At Man:*

> These two ways of approaching and thinking about the universe are irreconcilable—as irreconcilable as is magic with scientific agriculture, witch doctoring with preventive medicine, or number mysticism with higher mathematics. Because our thinking still contains elements from both, it and we are confused.

213

I was impressed. In fact, such an impression he made on me those Monday evenings that I found myself repeating what he said on Mondays throughout the week in my own classes. It just seemed to be so worthwhile, and like I say, I can't really separate philosophy and history. On that point, though, I guess a lot of people don't agree with me.

It seems that mine were the only world history classes in the school which were not using that great book, *The Record of Mankind,* or, "6000 years of nothing but drivel." Instead we were talking about ideas, and world views, and "The World Outside and the Pictures in Our Heads," and — I might as well confess openly now — just exactly what my friend was talking about every Monday evening.

Well, the principal kept asking where the history was, and everybody else was pretty worried too. These people didn't bother me much though. I just kept on thinking that what we were doing in class was so meaningful and worthwhile and important that it didn't make much difference what it was called — who cared? Anyway I don't expect my "colleagues" to agree with me as to what history is. That's quite a philosophical question in itself, and I think there's room for individual differences on this point in a pluralistic society. It's just too bad that they don't think so.

But what really made me mad was when they started saying that the "kids" couldn't do it. Now if there is one thing that really galls me it's these omniscient, omnipotent teachers who look down at the so-called "kids" and say they aren't mature enough. "The kids can't handle that kind of material," they say, "they'll never do it." Or, "Sure, that's ok for honors classes, but you can't teach it to the 'track 3's'." How did they know this, how could they be so certain? Well, they *just knew,* that's all. They worked with "kids" a long time. This was only my first year of teaching. I'd learn.

I remember one of the "colleagues" coming into my classroom one afternoon. On the blackboard was still the diagram with which I had been attempting to explain something about Dewey and Pragmatism — as you can imagine it was a rather involved diagram. Well! It was like the guy had come in with a chip on his shoulder. The first thing he says is that that isn't history. I tried to ask him what history was, but before I could even get to that — which none of the "history" teachers had been able to answer all year anyway — he said, "I'd like to see the results of the test you would give your kids on this stuff!" Now, hell, the implication was clear enough, and it seems to me that there's just so much a man can take. And I hate that word "kids." I don't even remember very clearly what I said, but one of my students, Joe, who was sitting there all the time trying to look like he was doing something, told me later that it was one of the more inspiring speeches he had heard. Joe's a good man.

Had this been the only instance of pooh-poohing the ability of the students I wouldn't have cared, but, as a matter of fact, it was not an only instance. I don't know about where you are, but where I am (I'm sorry, it's where I was) it was the prevailing view. "The kids can't do it." "The kids can't do it." "The kids can't think." "The kids can't think." Like a singsong the words kept coming at me. I heard it from administrators. I heard it from prospective department chairmen. I heard it from the "colleagues." I heard it so much, I began to wonder myself. It's strange how subtly doubts creep in and begin to undermine the most steadfast beliefs. I think I even began to think of my students as the "kids."

I came to be not altogether certain about the efficacy of my ideas. I was kinda liberal. I told my students if they found what we did in class worthwhile to come, if not, to stay away. Some days the classes seemed pretty empty. And every once in a while I'd get the "word" that somebody got caught by the school police. There for awhile, I have to admit, I got pretty discouraged.

More important, I needed feedback. I needed a sign that I was getting through to them. I started looking longingly, searchingly "into" their faces—they looked confused. I began to doubt what it was I really was doing. Give an assignment. "Go out and analyze a contemporary situation in terms of what we have been talking about in class." This would show me. Oh! The results were miserable. "God!", I thought, "what have I done?"

Over and over again, I asked myself, "What's wrong, what is it that's wrong?" The classes had been alive—some days it seemed that we really clicked. Was this merely a delusion of mine? Was this merely what I wanted to see? Was all this just going on in my head and nobody else's? I hadn't given many assignments. I hadn't given a test for a long time—I told them I didn't believe in test, test, test—was I so confident? That's it, the course has become a racket. Nobody has to do anything but come in and "shoot the bull." No wonder everyone's so happy. No wonder the classes are alive, it's social hour. "The kids won't do it." "The kids won't think." It's true. Is it true? No, it can't be true. It just can't be true because it's all so damned important.

Have them write an evaluation of the course. Why not? What's there to lose. Ask them what they've found meaningful and worthwhile. What will they say?

You rant and rave about whether or not we are getting anything out of this course—you can't put me in an indeterminate situation because all my views seem to fit. *But* you make me nervous because everywhere I go I wonder if I really follow through with my ideals. You're driving me crazy.

This class is, beyond a doubt, the most unusual course I have ever taken. It has, I believe, helped me to try to think more clearly. . . . The discussion of traditional and emerging philosophies I have found to be most worthwhile and meaningful. This is because your ideas seem to clash with the ones I was brought up to believe.

The part which has meant the most to me was the unit we have done on the scientific method of reasoning. . . . The way you presented the material, about how to solve a problem, was different than anything I have ever been told (taught) before. A problem is now a challenge not a wall that I cannot climb over.

The Traditional and Emerging points were good because it helped classify myself as to what I believed.

I never believed such a course on "man's meaning" possible. . . .Very few are able to consider "adolescents" and "green kids" like ourselves as thinking individuals; I respect this greatly.

It makes me think. . . . I've learned from this class that you've got to think for yourself because if you don't who will?. . . . The course has also taught me to think more fully. . . . I have learned nothing from it. . . . In class I might not seem interested but that is not true. . . . On the whole I have learned to *THINK*. . . .

A few weeks ago I wasn't sure if I believed in god or not. After we talked about it in class I think it helped me make up my mind.

This class to me is nothing but one big mess. . . . You have taught me one thing for the past 12 weeks and that is to think about everything I hear and question it. Maybe this is all you have been trying to get through to us and if so you have, but if there's more I for one didn't get it. . . .

It has taught me one thing. . . and that is that maybe I am taking more of an interest in school itself and becoming more of a man. Even though you have stated that if someone didn't want to come to class it would be perfectly alright with you, I have not missed a day of your classes. . . . This might not seem very important to anyone else but it shows me that I have enough self control not to let me do something I know that I shouldn't. And I have learned that when left alone I can make up my mind to do the thing I know I should.

Every Saturday morning I go to see my psychiatrist. What he is trying to have me do is precisely what you taught this week.

And I remember someone saying that you could not be all things to all men. The words were pleasing. The words were what I needed. But what all the words meant I was not quite sure. Many felt that the course helped them think. But what did they mean by think? Think about what? Could they really think—critically—I had no evidence to suggest they could.

A lot of other people by this time were wondering the same —at least so I imagined. The semester was drawing to a close. Final examinations were due to be given, made out by the classroom teacher, and handed into the department chairman after they had been graded. I figured others would be looking at them, looking for proof. "See," I could imagine them saying, "the kids can't do it. We were right. The kids can't think. We won."

The more I thought about it the madder I got. The madder

I got the more I thought the "kids" wrote in their evaluations what I wanted to read. The more I thought about it all, the more determined I was that for once and for all I should find out. It was important to find out if the "kids" could do it—it seemed the most important thing in the world.

I remembered Huxley's quote. That's what I'll do, I thought, I'll have them write a critical analysis of Huxley's quote. I wrote up the test almost in a fit of anger, turned it in to the office, and immediately regretted what I had done. Why, I thought, hadn't I played it safe? Why didn't I give them a question I knew they could answer? Why the crusade? The kids won't be able to do it. They won't be able to do it. We'll all be the laughingstock. We'll lose.

I told my friend what I had done. He's a pragmatist, which might have had something to do with his skepticism. He kept talking about consequences. Well, by this time I had had it. I don't know that I much cared about consequences, much less hoped. My friend suggested that as long as what was done was done we might as well shoot the whole bolt. We would give the same examination. He to his college sophomores, me to my "kids." There was nothing to lose.

Well, it's over now. The results are in. Here they are. Figure it out for yourself.

One of my "kids" wrote:
The two ways which he is talking about are the emerging or scientific method, and the traditional method. . . . They are irreconcilable because they operate on completely different major premises. . . . The scientific method states that truth is according to circumstances, and that it is judged by consequences. . . . The traditional states that man is a rational being composed of body and soul, and that rational men strive toward salvation while the scientific method also believes that man is a rational being, be believes that his rationality is nothing unusual, that it is a part of his biology and nothing more. . . .

College student "A" wrote:
The mind and the body are things that no one can produce desired effects from unless they agree on a point or unless they are forced. Therefore, they can not be reconciled.

One of my "kids" wrote:
The two ways of thinking, to which Huxley is referring, obviously seem to be the Empirical and the Metaphysical. The first proposes that all knowledge is obtained from experience by the use of the senses, open to a public test which will yield the same results for everyone, and therefore concludes that all hypotheses. . . must be arrived at through inductive reasoning.

College student "B" wrote:

Accordingly to Huxley, one way of thinking is by facts and the other by logic. Facts having scientific background, while logic had past experiences used in math work. Both coinside, so both are reconciled, not apart. Both need facts for a basis getting them closer together.
Our thinking and we should not be confused, but joined to help each other and not hinder them.

One of my "kids" wrote:
The metaphysical or traditional point of view makes absolute knowledge claims about the origin, purpose, and destiny of man. . . . When a person of these beliefs is asked, "How do you know?" his only reply can be simply, "Because I know.". . . . Because he believes these claims but cannot empirically prove them, the test is. . . a private one.

College student "C" wrote:
I don't especially care what Huxley thinks, but since I have to answer this question I may as well agree with him. (His complete answer?)

One of my "kids" wrote:
The other world, the scientific or empirical is completely different. It is based on the scientific method, that is, observation, classification, generalization and verification. The empirical world has no truths within it, it is endlessly searching; it not only accepts criticism, but must have it in order to function.

College student "D" wrote:
Today science seems to confuse us thoroughly by coming up with theories that seem justified in their claims. Such as one of Darwin's theories that if you had a beam of light strong enough, you could shine it entirely around eternity and it would return to the opposite side of you. . . . But science is misleading us into believing these things yet not being able to prove these theories we cannot wholeheartedly agree with science. It is thoroughly confusing as I believe we are more or less inclined to believe them.

One of my "kids" wrote:
With part of himself existing in reality and the other part in fantasy, man tends to be confused, and is not able to differentiate between what exists and what does not exist.

College student "E" wrote:
The universe is seen in many different ways by people of different ideas and beliefs and as long as we have conflicting beliefs we will not be able to deal with scientific ideas which can push man ahead and abolish old tales which confuse many and bring arguments to many. The scientific would be best met with a public test which will probably never happen.

One of my "kids" wrote:
The conflict is evident; it is inconsistent to accept both at the same time since both propagate two different manners of thinking, yet we are taught to accept both or induced into accepting both which seems logical and consistent to us for we are never permitted, or at least are made to avoid, the analysis of our own beliefs and the inconsistencies in them.

But like I say, no one will believe me. Or is it that no one wants to believe me? All sorts of reasons I suspect will be given for not believing. Some will say "insufficient evidence." But for those there will never be enough "evidence" — I have more. Some will say "no controls — not scientific." But it wasn't intended to be scientific. That wasn't the point. Some will say, "coincidence." Some may even say "act of God." No one will believe me. Is it that no one cares?

Maybe a more fundamental truth is that we want to keep the kids, "kids." Is it that we're so afraid? Are we so afraid that they might come out and speak their thoughts that we spend most of our time and effort attempting to convince them that they can't think and that, regardless, their thoughts are of no consequence? Are we so afraid that they will see us as the shams most of us are?

One of my "kids" wrote:
I have become confused by this and may never solve it completely. Before having you for a teacher I was never deeply religious, but I also never tried to wonder about the new (empirical) evidence and thoughts. I had wondered about the creation of earth and man, but it never bothered me, and, I never questioned it much. Now, however, I've given it a lot of thought. I haven't decided which method to accept, but then as society says: I'm only a confused youngster, and I'm supposed to grow out of it.

Is it true?
Well, you can believe what you want. But don't you tell me what my kids can do. And don't you call them "kids." They've grown tall. They've soared. And they'll soar as far and as high as you let them. But no one will believe me.

Shabby Arrogance

Teaching is more complex than is generally assumed. It takes a sensitivity, an intellectual "aliveness", a commitment, a willingness to work at being able to *do* what we expect our students to do, and — perhaps more important — a maturity that realizes that everything just doesn't come all at once and that a teacher is first of all a student with all the rights and responsibilities that this entails. Then he may be a teacher.

Edgar Friedenberg said in the *The Vanishing Adolescent*, that it takes a kind of "shabby arrogance" to be able to survive in the world as it is, and that it takes a "fairly romantic nature" to even want to. Friedenberg found these resources more abundant with adolescents than elsewhere. It might be hoped that those working directly with adolescents might move from the G.O.D. role to sharing what it can mean to be a student and a participant in a world struggling for survival and struggling for a reason to want to survive.

P. W. Bridgman said that "The scientist has no other method than to do his damnedest." For teachers, it might be put that the teacher's method includes his doing his darndest.

Fair enough?

No. G.O.D.s in the classroom!

INDEX

k